DACUM

The Seminal Book

ISBN: 0990714607
ISBN-13: 978-0-9907176-0-7

Printing   10   9   8   7   6   5   4   3   2   1

DACUM

The Seminal Book

Robert E. Adams

R. Lance Hogan

Luke J. Steinke

Wilmington, DE

Table of Contents

Note: Appendix A through M are available at:

www.edwinandassociates.com

Acknowledgements

We wish to acknowledge the individuals who assisted us with this book. This book wouldn't have been possible without the love and support of our families and friends. Thank you for all of your efforts in reading, discussing, and evaluating our thoughts and work even after growing weary of the term DACUM.

Special thank you to our students and colleagues for their critiques and suggestions for improving this edition of the book.

We are deeply grateful to Norma Corbett, the greatest librarian in the world, who went beyond the call of duty uniting the authors making this project possible!

Finally, we invite your comments, questions, and suggestions as we want to do our best in providing a valuable resource to enhance the development of skilled workers. Your suggestions will be very much appreciated.

Robert E. Adams
R. Lance Hogan
Luke J. Steinke

Introduction

Many trainers and instructional designers often struggle with the connection (or lack thereof) between the different phases of instructional design. We know that analysis is followed by design, which is followed by development and implementation, and that everything should culminate in an evaluation of the instruction. One of the many struggles we face is that most instructional design systems don't make the connection between these phases. While there are valid models and concepts for each individual phase, when we treat each phase as a separate entity it tends to increase the perceived amount of time and energy needed for each phase. In turn, this misunderstanding leads many of us to focus on aspects that are less valuable in creating effective training programs or skipping phases altogether.

Today's learning professionals face the unique challenges of not only designing programs that directly connect to what is done on the job and demonstrate successful transfer of skills, but also need to be done quickly. This desire for programs to be designed quickly often leads to training designers skipping important steps in developing an effective program. Many have asked if this better, more efficient way exists? The answer is the DACUM System. DACUM, standing for **D**evelop **A** Curricul**UM**, was developed in 1968 by Robert E. Adams and has been successfully implemented by organizations world-wide. The DACUM system has experienced much success over the years because unlike other instructional design systems, DACUM connects all the phases. And not only does the DACUM system connect all phases of instructional design, but it also can be done effectively in significantly less time than traditional instructional design. Since its inception however, there have been few accessible resources available on guiding someone through the DACUM system. The purpose of this book is to provide such a guide.

This book outlines Robert E. Adams' DACUM system for developing occupational training and includes specific models designed to walk readers through the development of a DACUM Learning Program, from the analysis of the occupation to the evaluation of the learning program. Also within the book are strategies and techniques for the effective administration of the DACUM systems, along with a variety of examples of prior occupational training programs that utilized the DACUM system.

About the Authors

Robert E. Adams

Born in Swan Lake, Manitoba, in Canada, Robert Edwin Adams, is the originator of DACUM. He spent a lifetime working in the field of occupational training, most recognizably as an Occupational Training Consultant for Nova Scotia NewStart Incorporated preparing individuals for work in low employment areas of Canada.

Adams also worked with Holland College during its inception to train faculty on the DACUM system so they could properly prepare Islanders for employment opportunities. Today, Holland College is recognized as one of the most successful community colleges in Canada and has roots tied directly to the DACUM system created by Adams.

Adams graduated from High School at United College Collegiate in Winnipeg, Canada. He earned Bachelors and Masters degrees in Vocational Education from Bradley University, a program pioneered by the legendary vocational educator C.A. Bennett. Adams also taught at Red River College.

Adams spent 10 years working with for-profit and not-for-profit organizations throughout North America educating and implementing DACUM, and a further 30 years designing training and job analysis.

He and his wife Colleen reside in Dartmouth, Nova Scotia, Canada.

R. Lance Hogan

R. Lance Hogan is an Associate Professor in the Lumpkin College of Business & Applied Sciences School of Technology at Eastern Illinois University.

Hogan earned a PhD from Southern Illinois University, a Masters degree in Business Administration, and a Bachelor of Science degree in Business Administration specializing in Production/Operations Management from Southeast Missouri State University, and an Associates of Arts from Mineral Area Community College.

He also has numerous professional certificates in Human Performance Improvement, Curriculum Development and Production Process Troubleshooting. Hogan has supplemented his educational development with work experience in support of companies including Federal Mogul (Production Supervisor), MOCAP, Inc. (Production Manager), DMS, Inc. (Operations Manager), and as an independent consultant.

Luke J. Steinke

Luke J. Steinke is an Associate Professor in the Lumpkin College of Business & Applied Sciences School of Technology at Eastern Illinois University and currently coordinates the Organizational and Professional Development program.

Steinke earned a PhD in Workforce Education and Development from Southern Illinois University, a Master's degree in Training, Development, and Performance Improvement and a Bachelor of Science degree in Industrial Technology from Northern Michigan University, and an Associate of Applied Science from Moraine Park Technical College.

He has over 10 years of experience as an educator, trainer, and consultant and is the author of several articles and presentations in the area of occupational training analysis and design, mentoring, learning styles, and measuring instructor and program quality.

1

WHAT IS DACUM?

DACUM was developed as a new approach for the development of curricula combined with a new evaluation process for occupational training programs. **DACUM**, standing for **D**evelop **A** Curricul**UM**, can be defined as a single-sheet profile that serves as both a curriculum plan and evaluation instrument for occupational training programs. It is graphic in nature, presenting definitions of the skills of an entire occupation on a single sheet of paper. This discourages treatment of any element of the occupation in isolation. Stated differently, it promotes treatment of any element as part of a larger whole. The DACUM System is used to develop occupational training derived through analysis, curriculum, learning, and evaluation guided by a single-sheet skill profile from a panel of experts.

The DACUM process utilizes a group of expert workers within the occupation to determine necessary skills under the direction of a co-ordinator. Expert workers are able to specifically define the skills needed to successfully perform within the occupation. The DACUM process results in a DACUM chart which is the graphical representation of the general areas of competence and skills performed within the occupation.

There are two distinct factors that make the DACUM approach unique compared to other approaches to developing curriculum. The first factor relates to the use of occupational analyses, training needs assessments, or other data collection techniques such as nominal group or Delphi. Traditional instructional design techniques tend to treat the analysis phase individually, while the DACUM system directly connects the analysis to the design of curriculum. This is because DACUM is an analysis of the occupation, rather than a curriculum evolving from an analysis. The occupation is subdivided into General Areas of Competence. Each is then analyzed to identify the skills it contains. The result is independent specification of the skills that collectively enables an individual to perform competently in the occupation. Skills are the focus of the DACUM chart (versus Knowledge, Jobs, Duties, or Tasks) because they are the behaviors that enable an individual to perform competently in an occupation. Skills, unlike tasks, specifically allow for determining the level of performance needed within the occupation. These skills are defined quite simply and are structured independently in small blocks on the chart. Each can serve as an independent goal for learning achievement.

The second factor which makes the DACUM approach unique is that the chart contains a rating scale accommodating skill levels of behavior. The DACUM Rating Scale is a 7-point descriptive scale categorizing occupational performance levels which is utilized to measure observable behavior when evaluating trainee performance. The chart also serves as a recordkeeping system, as all ratings of skills can be recorded directly on a copy of the DACUM chart maintained for each trainee. Once an adequate skill profile in the form of ratings has been developed, the DACUM chart becomes a diploma or record of skill development in the occupation. The marked-up DACUM chart also has potential application as a guidance tool prior to entry to a training program and as a placement tool upon completion.

HISTORICAL DEVELOPMENT OF DACUM

When there is a need to develop training for an occupation efficiently and effectively, traditional training development approaches tend to fall short. In particular, the occupational analysis step within the training development process is typically ignored due to the lack of understanding or time required for this step by occupational curriculum designers. The DACUM approach was designed to address issues related to occupational analysis and the efficiency and effectiveness of occupational training program development. In order to understand the rationale behind the DACUM approach, it is important to consider the foundational occupational approaches by which DACUM was derived.

Characteristics of Other Occupational Analysis Approaches

Prior to the development of the DACUM process, instructional designers typically used the *Russian and Swedish Sloyd methods* (Bennett, 1937) for organizing manual training. Both methods involved rigorous analysis and specification of skills and sub-skills, even to the point of specifying manual or manipulative movements, in order to provide clear guidelines for mass training of occupational specialists. The procedures were evolved at a time when manual skill training was of prime importance in order to improve the efficiency of workers and when work of this nature involved only the direct application of a standardized set of skills. With the beginnings of demand for more flexibility and adaptability in craftsmen, it was necessary to move beyond the skill specification of the Swedish and Russian systems. A new approach that might be called the *Course Construction Approach* (Fryckland, 1970) was developed in the United States.

Efforts in developing and improving this process were led by Fryckland (1970). A new dimension, knowledge or information, was added to the specification of skills, along with standard formats for specifying the skills in one column on analysis sheets. One feature of the Fryckland (1970) movement was that most of the work was produced by vocational instructors themselves. In other words, the definition of program goals was internalized. While this approach may have been successful in the early days of this work, as time went on it became less valuable because of the increasing complexity and diversification of the occupations involved. Whereas formerly the new instructor who was also an expert in the occupation would be expected to have all the skills in the occupation and to be able to perform in all its specialties, this was no longer possible. The newly recruited instructor, in the more complex or diversified era, generally had a good grounding in the fundamentals of the occupation and was a specialist in one or more of the occupation's specialties. As a result, curriculum became increasingly open to criticism by occupational experts with diverse points of view.

For a period of time, less emphasis was placed on the Fryckland (1970) type of analysis and more on the use of advisory or curriculum committees recruited from among industrial specialists and trainers to specify curriculum and the resulting training program. While this provided a much needed avenue for communication that was missing in the Fryckland (1970) internalized approach, the quality of analysis and specification suffered substantially because of deviation from skill specification in terms of performance required. Increasing emphasis was placed on the knowledge content of the occupation. This in turn paved the way for the opening up of the curriculum process to include several conflicting approaches or movements, e.g. the job cluster concept, the core knowledge concept, and the block building concept, all of which are built primarily on consideration of knowledge content rather than actual skill or performance behavior required in the occupations concerned. The curriculum committee approach contained a further problem in that it lacked suitable analytical or definition structures. As a result, curriculum definitions emanating from such committees were usually quite diverse and often incompatible for different programs designed to train for the same occupation.

Perhaps the most sophisticated approach at that time was that used by the Technical Vocational Training Branch, Department of Labour (later Department of Manpower and Immigration) in Ottawa during the 1960's. This approach combined the specification and procedures of the Fryckland (1970) approach with the industry-education communication needs of the curriculum committee approach. In effect, the Fryckland (1970) approach was taken out of the hands of the instructor and placed in the hands of a committee of industrial experts who were selected on the basis of their collective ability to cover the entire occupation. These industrial experts, with little prior knowledge of, or bias toward training, worked in isolation from the educational community in specifying in detail the skills and knowledge requirements of the occupation. The Fryckland (1970) techniques also were much improved. Procedures and models were established to gain a more complete coverage and level of detail in definition of skill and knowledge requirements. One unfortunate trend resulted. Because of the sophistication and increased level of detail, the analyses tended to be little used except by those training agencies and officers who were themselves sufficiently sophisticated to make direct use of the analysis. A second weakness was that, while the analysis content definition was complete and intensive, the document itself did not include any provision for either stating or integrating performance standards. Additionally, although the analysis was based on performance, the thorough listing of knowledge elements tended to lead trainers into using the analysis as a basis for developing programs with high knowledge intent.

A marked change in direction was brought about by the work of Robert Mager in the 1960s, which appeared in three publications: *Preparing Instruction Objectives (1962); Developing Attitude Toward Learning (1968); and Developing Vocational Instruction (1967)*. Methods suggested in these works appeared to overcome the two main reservations about the above analysis approaches. First, objectives were established in such a way that they were readily usable by the instructor (as well as the learner). Second, each included its own built-in standard of performance. It appeared to be a break-through in occupational training until one examined the techniques prescribed for establishing objectives. Essentially, these techniques are instructor focused. They are designed to give the instructor a better appreciation of potential terminal behaviors but there is little to prevent the instructor from establishing objectives not really related to requirements of the occupation. Of more concern is the procedure for establishing performance standards for each of the learning objectives. To follow the prescribed procedures, a certain objectiveness in stating performance criteria, which may not exist in industry, is necessary. One element in question is time. Creators of behavioral objectives for training programs tend to rely on time limits as performance criteria. In reality, when one looks at capable performers in the occupation, one finds large differences in the amount of time they require for similar assignments. A further criticism of the Mager (1962) approach is that the procedures for establishing objectives tend to force the creator(s) of the objectives to sample occupational behavior rather than describe it in total. For example, if a skill can be applied in a number of diverse applications, the creator(s) of the objectives may single out one of these, create the objective around that situation, and assume transferability.

Developing the DACUM Approach

Recognizing the value of contributions made by each of the previously discussed occupational analysis approaches as well as the weaknesses or conflicts existing within each, Robert E. Adams of Nova Scotia NewStart spent considerable time with the challenges of occupational analysis. Adams, an experienced occupational analyst in Ottawa, encountered the ineffectiveness of most conventional resources, instruments, and methodologies used in occupational training programs. Exposure to the concept of charting of occupational goals (the result of the work of General Learning Corporation for the Clinton Job Corps, Iowa) stimulated the realization that it could become a viable tool if it were made more sophisticated in the manner of the Russian-Sloyd (Bennett, 1937), Fryckland (1970), and Ottawa analysis approaches; that is according to Adams, definition would have to be much more rigorous. At the same time, it provided opportunity for involvement of the personnel one would normally have participate in curriculum committees. In short, it offered a great deal of potential and provided suitable procedures and instruments that could be devised to overcome the problems that appeared to be inherent in the Mager (1962) approach: a) it was necessary to specify the objectives as clearly as possible exactly as an employer or supervisor in the occupation would express them, and b) it was necessary to develop a suitable evaluation instrument that would facilitate observation of performance in much the same way that employers observe performance in a work environment. The DACUM approach developed by Adams satisfied the above requirements.

An experimental approach was created initially in a joint effort by the Experimental Projects Branch, Canada Department of Manpower and Immigration, and General Learning Corporation of New York, which had provided technical direction to the Women's Job Corps program at Clinton, Iowa. Early efforts at Clinton were intended to produce a curriculum guide that would enhance trainee involvement in the training program and in planning for goal attainment. The result was a graphic presentation of the curriculum similar to a time bar chart. Following these early efforts, an experimental approach in developing occupational training was developed in Canada as a model for further application.

In 1968, the concept currently known as DACUM was developed and written by Robert E. Adams (Norton, 1985) and Nova Scotia NewStart Inc. because of a number of circumstances that demanded a new approach to curriculum development. Because of the nature of the NewStart assignment, it was necessary to respond quickly to the needs of disadvantaged adults. This, in turn, created need for immediate action in planning any training program and defining it in curricular form. There was need also for immediate action in determining a method of evaluating skill in a training program, along with a need for development of realistic measures of skill change as a component of evaluation of program effectiveness.

Occupations for NewStart training programs were essentially selected from among those for which there was currently no formal training readily available for entry. Therefore, each occupation selected required a complete new development program. Time and resources were not available for developing detailed specifications of each learning element and activity, developing instrumentation for a valid comprehensive testing program to determine effectiveness, or administrating an extensive instructor training program. For example, it is difficult in most occupations to find readily established objective standards of performance, particularly in those occupations that are newly organized or in those for which there has been no formal training. These and several other resources deemed so essential for organized learning programs, particularly from a research point of view, are not available and normally must be developed at a considerable cost and effort.

Based on these needs for the development of occupational training quickly that included a method for evaluating skills, Adams began an extensive modification and refinement of the experimental DACUM approach. Adams' DACUM approach was then pilot tested in a series of programs, with each new program posing further problems or adding new dimensions. What resulted was a new approach to occupational training in general that addressed traditional problems with developing occupational training. Adams's DACUM approach was fast, efficient, connected to the workplace, and had a built in evaluation method through the development and the reliability of the DACUM rating scale (see Chapters 14 though 17).

Adams' DACUM approach was quickly accepted within the field of occupational training throughout North America. Since it represented an approach to analysis, curriculum development, and evaluation that could be developed and implemented quickly and efficiently, the DACUM approach was sought by many within both career and technical education and occupational training. Most notably, the DACUM approach was adopted by Holland College in Charlottetown, Prince Edward Island. In

1969, Holland College's, Dr. Donald Glendenning, former colleague of Adams in Ottawa heard of the DACUM approach and went to Nova Scotia to "see the DACUM model in operation" (Glendenning, 2011, pg. 42). It was at this time that Glendenning and Holland College realized the overall value of the DACUM approach. In 1970, Adams was invited to Holland College to conduct their first competency analysis and was later asked to facilitate several analyses of programs at Holland College (Glendenning, 2011). Adams' training of staff on the DACUM process at Holland College led to Lawrence Coffin and Glendenning developing the first DACUM How-to workshop at Holland College. This workshop was designed to train individuals in designing and implementing curriculum through the use of the DACUM process. From this DACUM workshop spawned numerous individuals trained in the DACUM approach. Figure 1 tracks the major developments in the DACUM process over the early years.

The DACUM approach has since been adopted and installed in numerous countries and organizations. Universities, community colleges, technical schools, and career and technical education programs worldwide have implemented the DACUM approach to develop curriculum directly connected to the workplace. The DACUM approach has also been adopted by a number of organizations to develop and enhance their occupational training. Unfortunately, the DACUM approach has also experienced a certain amount of misuse. There have been cases where individuals have deviated from the original DACUM process while still calling it DACUM. These new techniques have taken pieces of the original DACUM approach, such as only focusing on occupational analysis. While occupational analysis is an important part of the DACUM process, not completing other important phases will not arrive at an actual training program curriculum. Any derivative of the original DACUM process developed by Adams that does not arrive at an occupational curriculum goes against the very foundation of the DACUM approach and therefore, cannot be accurately called DACUM.

Therefore, the purpose of this book is to accurately present the DACUM approach as it is intended by the "originator of DACUM" Robert E. Adams (Norton, 1985, pg. viii). The true DACUM approach needs to be accessible to all career and technical education and occupational training practitioners who desire to develop curriculum that is comprehensive, affordable, learner centered, drawing on the expertise of those in the field, and has a reliable method for evaluating performance. It is therefore, this book's purpose to reinforce the original pillars of the DACUM approach in developing occupational training.

EARLY HISTORY OF DACUM

Year	Sponsor	Location	Key Contributor(s)	Result
1965	Joint Effort - U.S. Job Corps. Canadian Department of Manpower & Immigration	Clinton, IA, USA	Dr. Oliver Rice H. Clement	Time/Bar Chart Curriculum
1967 (Spring)	U.S. Job Corps. Canadian Department of Manpower & Immigration Nova Scotia NewStart	Vancouver, Canada	Dr. Rice H. Clement R. E. Adams	DACUM acronym coined
1968 (Summer)	Nova Scotia NewStart	Yarmouth, Nova Scotia, Canada	R. E. Adams	DACUM Approach Developed
1968 (Autumn)	U.S. Job Corps. Canadian Department of Manpower & Immigration Nova Scotia NewStart	Montague, Prince Edward Island, Canada	Dr. Oliver Rice H. Clement R.E. Adams V.C. LeBlanc S. Sweeney	Nova Scotia NewStart's version of DACUM emerged as the true and approved DACUM approach
1970	Nova Scotia NewStart Holland College	Charlottetown, Prince Edward Island	R. E. Adams Donald Glendenning	Adams brings DACUM to Holland College
1970	Holland College	Charlottetown, Prince Edward Island, Canada	Donald Glendenning Larry Coffin	1st How-to DACUM Training workshop
1972	Nova Scotia NewStart	Yarmouth, Nova Scotia, Canada	R.E. Adams	1st Edition of DACUM: An Approach to Curriculum, Learning, and Evaluation in Occupational Training
1972 (December)	Nova Scotia NewStart	Yarmouth, Nova Scotia, Canada	Canadian Federal Government	End of Grant Program: Nova Scotia New Start Program Shut down
1975	Canadian Department of Regional Expansion	Dartmouth, Nova Scotia, Canada	R.E. Adams	2nd Edition DACUM: An Approach to Curriculum, Learning, and Evaluation in Occupational Training

Figure 1. DACUM Historical Timeline (Sources: Glendenning, 2011; Harris, 1988; Adams, 1975)

TARGET AUDIENCE

The DACUM approach is intended for any organization or group that needs to create fast, efficient occupational training that is directly connected to the skills needed to be performed competently in an occupation. The following are specific audiences that currently find the DACUM approach useful:

Educational Programs

- *Career and Technical Education (CTE) Programs*

   At all levels of career and technical education, programs are designed to prepare students for various career options. CTE programs are designed to address skills gaps in occupations, as well as meeting the needs of high growth industries. The DACUM approach is used in CTE programs to not only make direct connections to the skills needed to perform effectively in occupations, but also to determine the overall level of performance needed by those employed within the occupation. In a CTE program focusing on the field of professional cooking, for example, the DACUM approach can be used to determine the levels of skills needed to qualify for all levels within the occupation. CTE programs can use this detailed criteria to develop learning that meets the standards of performance for specific occupations and industries.

- *Community Colleges*

   Much like CTE programs, community colleges aim to address the needs of the current workforce. Many programs at community colleges focus on occupational/trade specific training such as plumbing, electrical, automotive repair, construction/carpentry, manufacturing processes, and medical technology type careers to name a few. Within these programs, it is critical to have a direct connection to the occupations in which the programs are designed to meet the current needs. The DACUM approach in these programs is valuable in updating occupational training curriculum and evaluation measures that are up to date and creating new occupational training certifications quickly and efficiently to meet the industry needs of the community the colleges represent.

- *Applied College and Graduate Programs*

   College programs designed to address the needs of occupations requiring advanced technicians can also benefit from the DACUM approach. The DACUM approach brings with it a standard performance rating scale that is affixed to the master for printing. Four-year applied college programs and graduate programs can identify the specific need to be developed for students to go beyond the level of performance outlined in careers trained through CTE programs and community colleges. Understanding of the level of skill needed will aid in developing 4-year applied college programs and graduate programs that produce curriculum that meets higher levels of performance such as technical expertise, supervisory capacity or the ability to train others within the occupation.

Industry/Government Programs

- *Occupational Training*

The DACUM approach is valuable within occupational training for industry for several reasons. Many times, this type of occupational training needs to be developed and implemented in a short period of time. Traditional approaches, if conducted correctly, do not allow training to be developed quickly. This leads to occupational training that lacks focus on specific skills needed to perform. Additionally, the cost of developing occupational training is a concern within industry. The DACUM approach not only offers a fast and cost effective way to develop occupational training, but does this while defining the specific skills required to perform effectively in the occupation. Furthermore, the training developed through the DACUM approach is directly connected to the workplace. Traditional occupational training methods tend to focus on classroom training similar to that of a secondary school. The DACUM approach is just the opposite. It ensures that training is focused on developing skills on the job. Finally, the DACUM approach provides a valuable method for evaluating worker performance. The rating of skills provides a standard of performance to be met that is valuable not only during training, but as a performance appraisal tool as well.

- *Workforce Development Programs*

New programs to develop the workforce are constantly in demand. Questions often arise about the skills needed within these different occupations, as well as, what the skill levels are for different career paths within the occupation. Jobs and occupations can be defined to provide a foundation for new programs, redesign of existing programs, design of accurate job descriptions, and the development of career development plans.

- *Apprenticeships*

Apprenticeship programs, much like other occupational training programs, require training that focus on skills needed to perform on the job, and that can be developed in order to meet the needs of industry. One particular aspect of the DACUM approach that is relevant to apprentice training is the emphasis on mirroring the work environment during learning. Further, both the DACUM and apprenticeship approaches to occupational training evaluate demonstrated mastery of required skills. Due to productivity pressures, many apprenticeship programs are unable to conduct all training on-the-job. Therefore, the DACUM approach is an effective method for designing on-the-job training that can be taught on site as well as away from the job site.

- *Government/Military*

Governments and the Military have always been concerned with developing training quickly that is occupation/skill specific. This training also needs to be dynamic enough to meet ever-changing needs, cost effective given the obligation to be good stewards of the public funds, and it requires a focus on clear performance outcomes. The skills needed to perform within each area of these agencies, the level of skill needed for individual ranks/grades, and the direct connections to policies and practices need to be identified. The DACUM approach provides these government agencies with efficient and cost effective methods for determining the skills that are currently needed by various ranks/ grades. When developing training within the military, the DACUM approach can be used to determine not only the skills that are required, but the level of skills needed by those within the higher ranks and security clearances and those within ranks at the lower level that have limited responsibilities. This type of training focuses on the specific performance outcomes necessary and ensures that the objectives of the training are measured on the job. It also eliminates the need for time-consuming and costly classroom training.

THE POTENTIAL OF THE DACUM SYSTEM

This book will describe in some detail the DACUM approach to the development and installation of a new occupational training system. The desire for this specific occupational development approach by many in the field is evidenced by the interest that has been shown in Canada, literally from coast to coast, in the United States, and in other countries around the world. Interest arises from the fact that the system incorporates several learning principles which have long been considered desirable but, which have been found difficult to incorporate in a single system. Briefly, these principles are:

1. Immediate feedback of results to the trainee.

2. Immediate analysis of program strengths and weaknesses.

3. Positive communication between instructor and trainee.

4. Self-evaluation by the trainee.

5. Self-planning and goal-setting.

6. An interesting, efficient, and practical, yet unstructured, learning environment.

7. Responsibility for evaluation and qualification on the trainee.

8. Positive relationship between training evaluation and the type of evaluation normally made by employers.

9. Cumulative approach to achievement (the DACUM process will not allow negative or downward evaluation unless trainee and instructor agree that a previous evaluation was in error).

10. An entry measure which considers the trainee's previous training and experience allowing one to proceed from his or her own appropriate point of departure.

If these principles are important, and many consider that they are, the DACUM system would appear to have potential for most career-oriented training programs, and for academic programs as well.

Policymakers and practitioners contemplating installation of the DACUM system are cautioned again that a self-directing learning environment is essential. Present in this environment must be:

1. Replication or reasonable simulation of the job situation, in which trainees encounter "real" problems and have the tools, equipment, and materials available to solve them.

2. A curriculum that is a description of terminal behavior after completion of training.

3. A self-determining or self-directing attitude toward learning.

4. A program completely individualized to accommodate and take advantage of individual differences in learners.

5. Trainee selection of goals and sequencing of activities.

6. Trainee evaluation and promotion of confidence in the evaluation by avoiding imposition of instructor's evaluation.

7. Evaluation based on performance rather than on retention of information for test purposes.

Many of the above have long been considered to be necessary for an optimum learning environment. While the optimum may not be attainable, the DACUM system incorporates most of the components seen as being requisite for effective skill mastery.

SUMMARY

The purpose of this chapter was to give the reader a better understanding of DACUM. This chapter defined DACUM's unique approach to occupational training, described the rationale behind this approach, and explained its historical development. Furthermore, contributions from U.S. Job Corporation, Canadian Department of Manpower & Immigration, and Nova Scotia NewStart were recognized in the evolution of DACUM. Finally, target audiences and desirable learning principles were identified along with the requisite essential learning environment necessary for an optimal DACUM system.

REFERENCES

Adams, R. E. (1975). *DACUM: Approach to curriculum, learning, and evaluation in occupational training.* Ottawa: Dept. of Regional Economic Expansion.

Bennett, C.A. (1937). *History of manual and industrial education 1870 to 1917.* Peoria, IL: Bennett.

Fryckland, V.E. (1970). *Occupational analysis technique and procedures.* New York: Brise Publishing Company.

Glendenning, D. E. (2011). Holland College: Views and vignettes: As I remember. Retrieved from: https://docs.google.com/file/ d/0BwEoQ3VetLfZYmZmMTZiMzgtYzZiNi00MGZiLTg0OGUtZWI5NGM1 ODRhMjA5/edit?hl=en_US&pli=1

Harris, J. (1988). The use of the DACUM process for curriculum and training program development. Paper presented the Robots 12 and Vision '88 Conference, Detroit, MI.

Mager, R.F. (1962). *Preparing instructional objectives.* Palo Alto, CA: Fearon Publishers.

Mager, R.F. (1967). *Developing vocational instruction.* Palo Alto, CA: Fearon Publishers.

Mager, R.F. (1968). *Developing attitude toward learning.* Palo Alto, CA: Fearon Publishers.

Norton, R. E. (1985). *DACUM handbook.* Columbus, OH: The National Center for Research in Vocational Education, The Ohio State University.

2

OCCUPATIONAL TRAINING CONCERNS

Chapter 2 discusses current concerns with occupational training. Such a discussion is necessary to an understanding of the rationale for the DACUM system. However, the statements which are made should not be construed as an over-all indictment of current occupational training practices since the discussion deliberately isolates the undesirable characteristics which can be eliminated by using the DACUM system.

It is recognized that most current programs do not include all these undesirable characteristics. Some have many of the desirable features of the DACUM system and suffer from the weakness discussed only to a limited degree.

Most occupational training practitioners recognize that the problems exist, but they may not have analyzed them to the extent necessary to gain the thorough understanding that is required by the person who wished to become involved in the installation or operation of a DACUM program. Without this understanding one may be inclined to retreat to the familiar when faced with making decisions in applying the new program. Unfortunately, some of the familiar techniques contradict the principles on which the DACUM system is based and, if applied, must eventually be stripped from the new program and replaced with the DACUM system. In short, a thorough analysis of weaknesses of current programs has been found to be an essential preliminary to installation of the DACUM system and are considered here under two main headings:

1. Lack of programs for many occupations.

2. Weakness in current programs.

The observations made are subject to criticism on two counts. First, they are not the result of the exhaustive study either of current training systems or of specific problems identified. No attempt has been made to support many of the statements included, and every reader of this chapter will probably know of instances in which the statements do not apply. On the other hand, it is assumed that each reader will recognize that these problems do exist in much of the occupational training programming. Second, criticism might also be made of the fact that this is not a comprehensive treatment of problems related to occupational training. In fact, the problems described tend to be isolated. However, they were deliberately selected because they typify problems which the DACUM system is designed to overcome.

LACK OF PROGRAMS

One of the most puzzling features of occupational training is its absence. While substantial numbers of people are trained in the offerings of institutions such as vocational schools, trade schools, and institutes of technology, these offerings are quite standardized across the country and are rather meager when compared to the number of occupations that comprise the total employment opportunities. Agencies with responsibility for provision of training appear reluctant to embark on new program development. As a result, rather substantial training needs remain unmet for considerable periods of time. This inability or reluctance to respond to needs creates gaps in the offerings of our training sectors of the economy. On the other hand, we have a large number of unemployed or underemployed adults who could benefit from employment in these sectors who have no means of obtaining entry qualifications.

1. **Gaps in Programming**

   Gaps in programming are largely the result of these three factors:

   a. <u>Jurisdiction</u>. Some training needs are not met due to the problem of jurisdiction in the training field. Our training systems have, over time, developed patterns of operations and planning which discourage inclusion of occupational training programs which do not fit an accepted pattern. Vocational schools tend to select occupations for which the method and content of pre-employment training meet the requirements of the public education system of which they are a part. Trade schools have a tendency to select occupations for which training requires considerable laboratory or shop work. Apprenticeship systems normally select occupations that lend themselves to considerable learning while on the job. Institutes of technology mainly select occupations which have considerable scientific content. Adult education systems usually select occupations for which training is largely a matter of information-giving, which can be housed in existing school facilities. Each of these systems has ideal time structures for its programming based on prior experience and administrative requirements. Manpower shortages in occupations which do not readily fit at least one of the systems are seldom alleviated through the provision of training programs. The obvious result is either the importation of the skills required or the curtailment of needed services. In either case, the potential trainee remains untrained and either unemployed or underemployed.

b. <u>Limited need.</u> Most training institutions require evidence of a considerable manpower shortage before they will embark on training programs. They are reluctant to invest resources in designing a program and developing facilities, programming, and instructional staff if only a few graduates per year can be absorbed into employment. The same is true for short-term shortages that the training of a small number would alleviate for a number of years to come. At the same time, such institutions tend to continue to provide programs for occupations where the labor market is becoming saturated.

c. <u>Geography.</u> Extensive training gaps exist outside the major metropolitan areas. Training rarely occurs outside formal training institutions or in smaller communities where there may be potential employees and existing job vacancies. Institutions appear to be reluctant to become involved in programming not under close administrative observation and control.

2. **The Problem of Efficient Training**

The gaps would probably be narrower and the problems related to the gaps fewer if our training community (administrators, supervisors, instructors) were not so influenced by what might be called a "cult of efficient training" which hampers clear thinking in regard to matching the unemployed or underemployed adult with a manpower shortage or new career opportunity. Trainers are bombarded with criticism regarding the inefficiency of methods and with recommendations about how to make training programs more efficient. Frequently overlooked by both the proponents and the targets of these arguments are two important considerations:

a. There must be some relationship between cost and efficiency. Extensive attempts at efficiency in programs designed to serve several hundred learners are well worth the effort as developmental costs can be equated over the larger number. On the other hand, there is little point in looking purely at efficiency in the case of a program designed for only a handful of learners. Asking the trainer to make such a program "more efficient" is like asking the manufacturer of a small specialty off-highway vehicle to devote as many resources to design as would a major automobile manufacturer.

b. The commonly accepted indicators of efficiency in training programming, such as detailed definition of materials and procedures and tight administrative control, should be questioned. We are too ready to accept these as indicators of efficiency in lieu of actually testing programming in terms of the behavior change it produces. We also tend to reject programs in which these are absent even though they might be quite efficient in terms of results.

The initial detection of a limited training need is seldom immediately followed by positive action. It is usually followed by a lengthy series of meetings to determine if the program is feasible, which often results in a decision not to run it. Although costs and numbers of persons affected will be limited, potential developers appear to be intimidated by the perceived complexity of tasks and the fear of making mistakes.

Occupational training programs are expensive to operate, particularly those involving high skill content as opposed to information content. An administrator charged with responsibility for developing new programs who is also concerned with "efficient training" will find that development costs can easily outstrip operational costs, particularly if the program will not involve a substantial number of people or will not be of a repeating nature. Too often the administrator weighs these costs, and, while admitting that the program is badly needed, decides that there are other priorities for available resources.

3. Developmental Tasks for "Efficient Training"

It might be useful to review some of the developmental tasks required for "efficient" programming. Each involves considerable time and effort, first, in conducting the work indicated below, and, second, in organizing each activity (such as in gathering people and other resources). In the absence of a national development effort and a clearing house for developed programs, the task faced in developing an individual program is so formidable that development work sometimes does not get done and the expected training program does not evolve.

a. Occupational analysis. A prerequisite first step would normally be the definition of skills and knowledge required for performance in the occupation. This can be done in many ways, but essentially it is done by having experts in the occupation identify requirements of the occupation in detail. This is usually a very time-consuming and expensive task, although it may vary somewhat depending on the level of definition accepted.

b. Establishment of learning objectives. The next step is conversion of the behavior (skill) and knowledge requirements of the occupation into learning objectives which are considered more suitable for the learning environment. These are considered more suitable for the learning environment. These are considered to be the goals and criterion measures of each learning unit. This task is normally performed by persons who are assured, because of their educational or training background, to be capable of converting occupational requirements into learning objectives.

c. Curriculum organization. This next step involves the analysis of learning objectives and the organization of relevant subject matter or content into appropriate courses, usually subdivided by subject matter area.

d. Development of learning materials. A very extensive task is the development of learning materials. There is usually a wide range of textbooks, training manuals, programmed instruction materials, and highly developed learning aids available for programs for occupations in which programming has existed for a considerable number of years. In an occupation for which training is being developed for the first time, little of this will be available and extensive efforts will be required by textbook writers, program writers, manual writers, audio visual (A.V.) specialists, and others to provide learning resources necessary for the efficient programming.

e. Program planning. One of the requirements of "efficient training" is that the entire learning program must be planned in detail. Learning units and activities must be sequenced, theory and practice must be co-ordinated, schedules must be developed, and times must be specified. This is an onerous task in a training program where there is no precedent to indicate a reasonable rationale for establishing the best method of presentation, appropriate order of presentation, and the amount of time required for each element of presentation.

f. <u>Development of tests and evaluating procedures</u>. If done well, this task can be the most demanding in terms of time and requirement for occupational experts and other resources. Capable performance in an occupation requires the acquisition of a considerable number of somewhat unrelated skills (in terms of learning and measurement) and of units of learning focused on acquisition of knowledge. Several hundred of each may be required for a specific occupational training program. "Efficient programming" demands that a suitable test be developed for each. This is a formidable task to be faced by the developer of a new occupational training program. It is one that the developer initiates in good faith, but seldom completes. Eventually, it is decided to sample certain skills and elements of knowledge on the assumption that there is considerable transfer among them. The developmental task is even more formidable if one follows the recommended guidelines of performance testing which require specification of standards, the conditions under which the test will be administered, and specific details regarding instructions and resources available. All of this development work should logically be followed by testing for validity and reliability before conducting performance tests in the training program.

g. <u>Instructor training</u>. Another of the requirements of efficient programming is that the instructor be well trained. Efficient programming usually demands that the instructor be skilled in demonstrating and lecturing, in conducting performance tests, in constructing and administering knowledge-related achievement tests, and in analysis and evaluation of achievement. All this is fine if the program developer is initiating a program for an occupation that already has training precedents and that may even have trained instructors available. If there is no precedent, the program developer is faced with the prospect of having to select a skilled person from the occupation and arrange instructor training in a suitable institution. Otherwise, the developer must adopt the more common practice of thrusting an untrained person into a formal training situation that demands many skills that the trainer does not possess.

The preceding seven developmental tasks appear monumental to the program developer concerned with an occupation for which there is no training precedent. The cost and effort involved in these tasks tends to outweigh the value of conducting the program. Often the decision is made to ignore this program need in favor of other priorities.

<u>WEAKNESSES IN CURRENT PROGRAMS</u>

It is not difficult to pinpoint problems and attribute causes for lack of programs as in the previous section. It is more difficult to provide the same treatment for occupational training programs that are normally found in a variety of institutions. There are three main reasons for this difficulty:

1. The programs have been reasonably successful in terms of output. Except for those designed specifically to alleviate poverty, occupational training programs have produced graduates who, generally, have found reasonable employment and income in a stable occupation. Occupational training personnel can also cite cases of unmotivated young people who found their bearings in an occupational training program and became successfully employed as journeymen, foremen, administrators, or perhaps salespeople in an occupationally related position.

2. Training is usually well organized and "efficient". The special techniques of curriculum analysis commonly used and the life span of most of the programs have made possible much development work and refinement.

3. Training is usually provided only for occupations with a substantial skill and employment need. Programs that survive over a period of years are for occupations that have considerable potential for growth in time, that have high turnover due to upward mobility, and that, consequently, have a steady demand for fresh recruits at the learner or entry level.

The remarks that follow are based on certain dichotomies in on-going occupational training programs and are not intended as an over-all indictment of these programs.

Training, particularly for those occupations that do not demand high verbal skills and knowledge content, tends to be badly oriented. Occupations contain a wide range of ready-made problem-solving activities that can be readily transferred to a training situation. This feature lends itself to the establishment of distinctive training or learning systems. Nevertheless, many programs do not take full advantage of this. Consequently, the resulting training system looks quite like the learning system normally found in a general education environment.

This may be attributed to two causes. First, all the participants in occupational training programs (instructors and trainees) have formerly participated in the general education system. As a result, they have come to accept the pattern, methods, and controls found in general education. They feel somewhat uncomfortable in a different situation even though it may be more logical (as in training directly related to terminal occupational skills). Second, there is a good deal of pressure from persons not directly involved in the program to pattern the training after the system found in general education. Some like to see the same methods of achievement, evaluation, and certification, the same focus on learning from literature, the same teacher-focused posture in the learning environment, the same emphasis on "classroom" learning, the same acceptance of the learner as a receiver of information, and, finally, the same emphasis on the subject or subject-matter approach to learning.

Occupational training programs are much more susceptible to criticisms and external pressures than are other training programs. First, the costs are relatively high compared to other types of learning. Society, which has a right to be concerned, in many cases becomes overly concerned about the costs and results of training. Some efforts to improve training are merely efforts to make it more acceptable to the taxpaying citizen and the sponsoring agencies (e.g., the heavy emphasis on mathematics and science, to the detriment of more needed job skills, to make the training programs look more "solid" in terms of content). Second, occupational training is more susceptible to criticism because it is terminal and its product goes directly into a well-defined market. Any indication that the product cannot perform to expected standards results in immediate pressure on the training system to improve its performance. Overlooked in the product are such factors as lack of maturity or a need for a wider range of problem-solving activities and experiences that cannot be provided economically in the learning environment. Finally, the products of occupational training programs are absorbed into rather confined roles under the critical eye of powerful vocal employers, unions, or professional associations. Any indication of weakness in the product brings these people into action, resulting in pressures on the training institution for better performance.

Most other learning situations are not influenced by these same pressures for the following reasons:

1. Most are part of an over-all learning continuum. Program weaknesses at one stage or grade level can be corrected by applying additional resources or extra efforts in the next level.

2. Where the continuum is broken, as between high school and college, conflicts regarding the adequacy of prior training or learning are treated as internal. The college is allowed to blame high school for inadequate preparation for its program, and, in turn, the high school is allowed to blame the college for unrealistic entry programming for its graduates.

3. In most other learning programs there is little emphasis on terminal or criterion results. Most people leave learning programs at different points or at various

levels with a "general education". The programs are designed to prepare people for any specific occupational or other goal.

4. Professional training at universities (which might be classed as occupational training) is not under the same pressures as other occupational training programs. These institutions view their programs as a preparation for further development in the profession and related disciplines.

As a result of the pressures imposed upon occupational training, time has caused the appearance of a number of dichotomies in programs.

1. <u>Assumptions regarding Learning</u>

In spite of the fact that applications of learning theory such as the discovery method have shown considerable promise in occupational training, training systems have essentially been patterned after instructional models recommended by learning theorists and researchers who have developed extensive analyses and systems related to hierarchies of learning and the structure and sequencing of instruction. This is no doubt due to the fact that most occupations do have readily identified learning elements which logically build on one another in a hierarchical fashion. The content lends itself to analysis and organization to such an extent that the needs of the mature learner are very easily overlooked.

At the same time the content of occupational training lends itself to easy application of instructional theory. Occupations contain readily identified learning elements, a large number of which would be included in the lower strata of learning hierarchies. This encourages the proponent of instructional theory to plan one's program around the easily analyzed and organized content, giving little thought to the learner and their needs.

In theory, learning hierarchies are pyramidal in shape, with a large number of learning elements contained in the lower levels and fewer contained in each subsequent higher level until reaching the single problem-solving behavior at the apex of the pyramid. Thus, in occupational training, one sees a consistent pattern of progression from object identification and discrimination to psycho-motor and manipulative skills to problem-solving. Overlooked is the fact that the adult learner probably finds much of this boring and repetitious and would prefer to focus on the problem-solving ability, which is of paramount interest to them. The learner needs to acquire certain elements of the lower level subskills, but these are not meaningful to them because they are not seen in the concept of the target skill which requires them.

2. Structured Training – Organization and Sequence

Occupations are made up of a number of skills. The only feature common to all the skills is that all are required for optimum performance in the occupation. Studies have been conducted to isolate those skills that are common to large occupational areas or clusters of occupations. These have been largely unsuccessful beyond efforts at defining rather fundamental mathematics, communication, or tool-usage elements common to a number of occupations.

When looking at any one occupation, it is easy to treat unrelated skills as interrelated components on a single entity. It is then reasoned that the skills are related to each other in terms of learning. Curriculum experts and instructors needlessly strive to sequence and structure those unrelated learning elements and establish a pattern that resists change or flexibility to suit the needs of individual learners.

Occupations lend themselves too readily to detailed analysis into elements and synthesis of these elements into a variety of structures. Perhaps this should indicate that the sequencing and structure really are not that important in this kind of learning. In fact, organization and sequencing of learning are probably more closely tied to the administrative needs of the training institution and similar factors than to any need for optimum sequencing and organization or learning.

3. Emphasis on Group

The most striking dichotomy in occupational training is that program descriptions often indicate that instruction, in the form of lectures, demonstrations, and skill practice, will be provided on a group basis. Great pains are taken to break out elements of theory related to the occupation and to organize these into courses. At the same time, trainees are expected to be grouped into classes so that all may be instructed in the same content at the same time. One has only to visit a training environment such as a trade school to discover that the opposite is the case for a large portion of the training program. One might examine chef or cook training as an example. In a program designed to handle classes of as many as 20 trainees there is no evidence in the kitchen that plans were made to have on hand 20 stoves, 20 sets of pots, 20 meat blocks, or 20 sets of utensils. This would be much too expensive. Instead, trainees are cycled in the training environment, performing the various roles one might find in a commercial kitchen and making use of equipment and tools for specific learning tasks when available.

Grouping is also dichotomous in terms of the characteristics of the learners. Grouping would logically be based on the probability of finding a homogenous group of trainees. Just the opposite is usually true in occupational training programs. Unlike general education where we have groups processing from grade to grade or level to level, all with approximately the same learning backgrounds and at the same age level, occupational training programs (particularly for adults) are likely to attract quite heterogeneous groups with a wide range of age levels, prior work experiences, and prior learning experiences. One trainee may have barely a grade eight education with little relevant work experience while another may have some university training with one or more years of experience working in some capacity in the field. Beyond orientation to the training program on entry, little efficiency is gained through undue emphasis on grouping.

4. Learning – Information-Oriented

While most occupations lend themselves to establishment of learning programs that are mainly behavior- or performance –oriented, programs for many of these are highly information-oriented, particularly at the post-secondary level. This can probably be attributed to the previously mentioned pressures to make occupational training conform to patterns found in other learning systems. When faced with the development of a new training program, we often begin with a search for those elements of subject matter and theory that, if taught well, should result in increased performance by the learners. In other cases, we actually conduct an analysis of the occupation to determine skills and elements of knowledge required, but then isolate the elements of knowledge, group the knowledge elements into subject matter areas, convert the subject matter areas into courses, and then attempt to identify and develop learning-focused performance measures and standards that will predict future occupational success.

Additionally, training systems often respond to external pressure in the same way that our school systems responded to the Sputnik scare. Occupational training programs and courses are treated with little respect by persons participating in other learning programs, who criticize the lack of "meat" in training courses. Administrators and licensing bodies often react the same way. They are disconcerted when a program, in their view, has a high behavior- or skill-development base. They are pleased when the course is organized with more elements of mathematics, communication, and science, as well as theory of the occupation. These elements may be somewhat related to the program but may not be essential to development of the skills or behaviors required for performance in the occupation. Nevertheless, all concerned (with the exception of the trainees) are pleased when their institution finally offers a first-class learning program.

5. Evaluation – Information – and Concept-Oriented

Evaluation tends to be developed in much the same way as learning programming described in **4** (*Learning – Information-Oriented*). In most learning programs, achievement evaluation is usually based on what has been taught. If specific skills are taught, these can be evaluated to determine achievement; if complex concepts are taught, the learner's grasp of these must be evaluated to determine achievement. Undue emphasis on the acquisition of information in occupational training programs causes a companion emphasis on the evaluation of information retention and information application in the same program.

One would expect that both the criterion measures and the internal achievement measures for occupational training programs would be the behaviors required for competent performance in the occupation. Unfortunately, this is not always the case. The traditional curriculum development process involves a series of transfers or translations (from occupational analysis to knowledge element extraction to grouping of elements by subject or discipline-focused courses). Much of the relationship between the original skill objectives and the new course is lost during the process. We find that achievement in the original skills identified in an occupational analysis does not represent achievement in a specific subject-matter-focused course.

Even though the evaluation system is information-oriented, the trainer must also respond to pressures to measure behavior change attributed to their instruction. The poor trainer must spend considerable time exploring and developing simulated performance testing situations related directly to one's courses while overlooking the most realistic measure, the occupational performance required. It is apparent to most people concerned that these are not adequate or relevant measures, and this phase (measurement of behavior change) is usually given less than the information-oriented achievement evaluation.

6. Escalation of Entry Requirements

The foregoing weaknesses all contribute to a need for increased entry requirements for trainees or learners. Basing instruction on group activities demands that entrants to the training program be rather homogenous in terms of the prior learning (knowledge and skills) that they bring to the program. Because it is difficult to rationalize the elimination of the more highly qualified applicants to a training program, the usual procedure is to raise entry levels achieved in public schooling because this is the only common, already measured, prior experience available for consideration.

The fact that learning is information-oriented also tends to increase the need for trainees with higher verbal skills, particularly reading skills. Most information-oriented learning programs place a high priority on reading ability because there is emphasis on reading assignments prior to lectures and in review following presentation. Because the evaluation system leans heavily on testing related to information and concepts, the individual trainee must have adequate reading ability for interpreting test questions and adequate writing ability for presenting his answers.

A further problem relates to the length of the training program. The process of grouping permits the establishment of standardized completion times or course durations for the group. It is subsequently found that those who have less skill or knowledge on entry usually cannot complete the prescribed work in the prescribed time. Conclusions are drawn that persons of this caliber should be eliminated from the program. Little thought is given to the possibility that the course may be too short for these persons and needs to be lengthened, or that the course can be modified, allowing high achievers to exit early and others exit late (after the prescribed completion time and after they have had the benefit of additional learning experience and instructor attention).

Often needs for increased entry level arise out of administrative decision to alter program duration. A program of ten months' duration might be quite successful in preparing trainees who entered with only a grade eight level in, for example, mathematics and communication skills. A decision to shorten the program to six months in the interest of economy could result in a requirement for an increase in entry level to perhaps grade ten or eleven as a prerequisite.

7. <u>Lack of Measures of Behavior Change</u>

As noted in (6), measures developed to test the trainee's ability to apply knowledge, principles, and problem-solving skills to performance situation are often not closely related to the kind of performance required in the occupation. While the creation of performance measures is a standard procedure in most learning programs that are related to behavior change, there is little point in applying the same approach to occupational training. Performance required in occupations is easily identified and readily observed and need not be simulated.

Historically, however, there have been no instruments developed that adequately evaluate occupational performance as well as trainee achievement in the learning environment. Instructors, evaluation specialists, and certification bodies have been unable to draw on this resource in developing in-process and terminal evaluation instruments. They have been forced to take two different approaches to evaluation.

First, they have been forced to rely on information- or subject-matter-focused evaluation instruments. Not surprisingly, the trainee with higher ability in reading and writing tends to perform better. Unfortunately, the occupation itself may require little in the way of reading and writing. On one hand, we are faced with a group of the most highly qualified who may later be frustrated by lack of need for their already developed communication skills. On the other hand, we may have a group of the least qualified made up of those with low communication skills, but who most want to prepare themselves for employment that really does not require extensive facility in reading, writing, and verbal skills.

Second, efforts to place more emphasis on evaluation of behavior have been frustrating. Some efforts have been made to quantify production, but this is suitable only for those occupations in which a definite output must be produced at an acceptable rate (e.g., assembly line jobs or work such as typing). Other efforts have been directed at developing independent performance measures for each skill required in the occupation. This becomes an unmanageable task considering the number of independent skills that may be found in any one occupation. Such efforts have usually resulted in selection of only samples of behavior and use of these samples to predict future occupational success. Not only are they merely samples, but they also tend to be based more on course requirements than on occupational requirements. Further efforts have been devoted to developing job performance checklists and to soliciting testimonials from employers. The latter are obtained after the formal institutional training program is completed or in the course of on-the-job activities during apprenticeship. Because they lack both detail and range as instruments, they really do not measure behavior change. They are more concerned with recording factors such as time spent.

8. The Inhibiting of Self-Direction

Graduates of an occupational training program have probably reached the end of their formal education and must enter industry as an employee quickly demonstrating ability to perform competently in the occupation. Unless the graduate is entering a highly structured or operative work situation, modern employment demands a self-directing individual, that they take charge of the job, that they adapt their skills very quickly to the unique requirements of specific jobs, that they learn to respond to the unique problems in the workplace, and that they continue to learn in order to keep abreast of new technology related to the occupation. Graduates are seldom adequately prepared in occupational training, which does not offer experiences that would allow them to develop the desired behavior.

In occupational training the assumption is made (much like the assumption in general education) that there is a certain set of general skills and knowledge the individual needs and that somehow the graduate will transfer these to actual industrial or employment requirements when faced with unique situations. This is true only for some persons. We are constantly reminded of others who have completed prescribed occupational training and who experience difficulty in transferring the skills and knowledge acquired to job situations.

The successful employee in modern industry does not acquire new skills in the conventional training way. They do not approach each new problem at work with a previously developed set of skills and elements of knowledge that enable them to solve it. The graduate does, however, have the ability to identify the problems, isolate the components, and seek out the resources to develop the elements (or skills) required for successful solution. Occupations are too diverse and changes occur too rapidly to hope to provide all prerequisite learning necessary for solution of all or even most problems that will be encountered.

A further assumption in occupational training is rationalization: "Let's continue to do what we can to prepare the individual with all the prerequisite skills and knowledge, and let's make the assumption that the learner will somehow pick up others. The learner may be provided with detailed training by his employer or through some other training program."

The structure, organization, and evaluation methods of occupational training do not encourage the trainee to gain experiences in self-direction. Because the program is well prescribed, there is little opportunity for the graduate to decide what problem to tackle, what skill must be developed, how problems will be tackled, and what resources they might bring to bear on it. More important, the graduate is discouraged from gaining skill in self-evaluation, a key to the success of a self-directed person.

As a result, the trainee too often leaves the learning environment and enters an employment situation much bewildered by what is expected of them. The graduate is asked to assemble a group of components for some machine never seen before without the usual training-program set of instruction sheets or list of detailed operational procedures.

HOW DACUM OVERCOMES CONCERNS

The first part of this chapter outlined a number of fairly universal problems in occupational training. The following deals with the potential of the DACUM for resolving these problems.

l. The DACUM and New Programs

The DACUM process, particularly as it is used in developing training programs for occupations where there is no training precedent to draw upon, is a particularly effective device for short-circuiting much of the extensive developmental work and costs normally required for "efficient" training. Consequently, its application should contribute to a reduction in the number of gaps in training offerings.

DACUM chart development typically takes, on the average, three days. This three-day activity effectively replaces the first three extensive development activities: occupational analysis, establishing of learning objectives, and curriculum organization.

The expensive and time-consuming preparation of learning materials is not required. Available materials are gathered and packaged for each learning objective. Although there may be few well-developed sources such as textbooks available for occupations with no training precedent, there is usually a wealth of material that can be acquired from a variety of different sources. If little or no material can be located for some skills, nonprofessional in-house materials are adequate to satisfy the needs of this kind of training program.

Because the emphasis is placed on individualized learning and self-programming by the trainee, little effort is expended in program planning other than provision of the resources required.

The heart of the DACUM training system (what makes it work successfully) is the rating scale which is a part of each DACUM chart. It is used to evaluate each trainee's performance as an employer or supervisor would evaluate an employee's performance. It is applied equally well to each skill on the chart. Consequently, tests and evaluation procedures do not have to be developed.

Formalized instructor training is virtually eliminated. Essentially, instructor training is reduced to orientation and some practice in the few procedures essential to successful use of the DACUM system. Any extensive instructor skill development would and must take place while the instructor is operating their program and gaining meaningful learning experiences.

In summary, the DACUM process lends itself quite ideally to the development of new training programs. Too often curriculum specialists and program planners devote extensive energies to detailed planning and definition of a system which they are not even sure will operate entirely or in part. The DACUM quickly provides a more than acceptable level of definition and a system that lends itself to evaluation of effectiveness of procedures and materials as well as to rapid program change as soon as need is detected.

2. The DACUM and Existing Programs

The DACUM system was specifically designed to overcome the weaknesses of on-going occupational training programs previously described. The DACUM chart, the rating system, and the over-all training program that encourages while it controls learning could all contribute to the reduction of these weaknesses or problems in many programs.

The DACUM system avoids structuring adult learning in ways that might be suggested by studies of learning conditions and resulting instructional models for children. The findings of studies are not ignored. They are merely organized into a new learning model rather than an instructional model. This model provides enough flexibility to ensure that each adult learner has an opportunity to learn in the way that best suits that learner's individual characteristics and background.

The DACUM system directly avoids the usual move to structure, sequence, and integrate the many unrelated skills required for completion of a training program and entry to an occupation. Each skill or behavior is treated as an independent terminal goal and an independent learning activity. Developed for each individual learning activity is a set of materials and other learning resources selected specifically to facilitate reaching the specified learning goal. Although circumstances may vary and different degrees of assistance may be required for initiation of a learning activity, it is assumed that the trainee can select these learning activities in the order that best suits their developmental program and in the order of their immediate interests.

The planning and organization of the DACUM system are based entirely on individual learning. In this system, it is assumed that individual trainees begin the program at different times, progress at their own rate depending on their own ability and aptitudes, and select learning goals on the basis of personal interests. The only time they receive group instruction is when two or more feel they could best learn some aspect of their work as a group.

With a direct focus on observable behavior in defining the learning goals on the DACUM chart, much of the pressure to make learning information-oriented is removed. Each learning activity becomes a problem-solving situation in which the learner brings to bear whatever resources the learner can obtain in the form of information, instructional assistance, or meaningful experiences.

Because of the approach to learning and the provision of a universal skill rating scale, evaluation also ceases to be information-oriented. The system is not geared to teach specific information; therefore, there is no need to evaluate the degree to which it has been absorbed by the trainee. The system is geared to achievement of behavioral goals, and the evaluation focus is on the degree of success in achieving these goals.

Prescribed entry level requirements (prerequisites) become relatively unimportant using the DACUM process. With the emphasis on individual learning, there is no need to set entry level requirements based on groups and group learning. At the same time, the focus on achievement of skill objectives removes much of the need for bringing an extensive educational background to the training program. There is, for example, less need to be expert at reading learning materials. As long as the individual can read at a level normally required for performance in the occupation itself, the DACUM system can accommodate them.

One of the features of the DACUM system is that it has an evaluation process that not only measures behavior change but measures it in the way in which it would be measured in a work environment. In fact, it is as suitable for evaluation in the work environment as for evaluation during training. It has enough intervals to make it a useful tool for distinguishing between levels of ability as they are observed in and by the learner.

The DACUM system recognizes the need for self-direction when trainees leave the training program and enter employment. The process demands that this self-direction begin as soon as the training program starts. The trainees make their own decisions regarding the nature of their learning experiences, the ways in which they will learn, the evaluation they will place on their progress, and the areas in which they must overcome skill deficits. The learner also gains extensive experience in a method of learning that is quite similar to the method by which successful people in industry continue to learn and develop, namely the skill-oriented approach.

SUMMARY

Chapter two explored the lack of, and overall weakness in current programs. Specifically it outlined the concerns with traditional occupational training that ultimately lead to the need and development of training using the DACUM system. Finally, the DACUM systems ability to overcome concerns with traditional occupational training was addressed.

REFERENCES

Adams, R. E. (1975). *DACUM: Approach to curriculum, learning, and evaluation in occupational training*. Ottawa: Dept. of Regional Economic Expansion.

3

THE DACUM DEVELOPMENT MODEL

To apply the DACUM system effectively, the overall development process must first be understood. The Development Model for DACUM Learning Program (see Figure 3 -1 below) serves as a guide in understanding this process by identifying categories that should be considered and the sequence in which they should be treated. Following will be a discussion of each major element of the model.

DEVELOPMENT MODEL FOR DACUM LEARNING PROGRAM

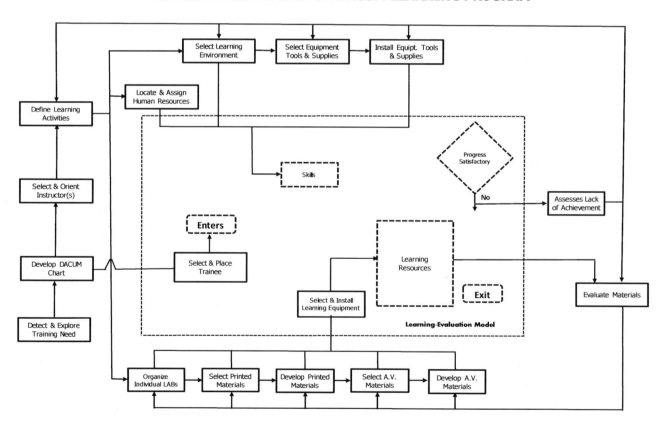

Figure 3-1. Development Model for DACUM Learning Program

I.   Detect and Explore Need

The first category in the model is "Detecting and Exploring the Need" for training. This phase consists of establishing the need for a training program or for extensive modification of an existing program. Assuming this results in a decision to use the DACUM process, the following must be identified: the employing community, the decision makers, potential instructor(s), and potential resource persons for specific components of the program.

II.   Develop DACUM Chart

The second category to be discussed is "Develop DACUM Chart" which is comprised of several sub-categories ranging from Preparation for DACUM Charting to the Application of the Rating Scale.

a. Preparation for DACUM

Abraham Lincoln stated, "If I had eight hours to cut down a tree, I would spend six hours sharpening my saw." Like President Lincoln, proper preparation is critical for development of a successful DACUM Chart. Ensuring success begins first and foremost with the successful selection of DACUM committee members and a DACUM co-ordinator who is responsible for guiding the charting process.

i. Selection of the Co-ordinator

A co-ordinator is an individual who directs the facilitation of the DACUM chart. This is done by navigating DACUM committee members through the identification, defining, and sequencing of general areas of competence and skills for an occupation. The co-ordinator serves as a catalyst and avoids influencing committee members who state the requirements of the occupation. Further, this individual should confirm the accuracy and validity of committee members' contributions by stimulating discussion and occasionally suggesting re-evaluation of the problem at hand. Ideally, the co-ordinator should not have extensive experience in the occupation since this might make it difficult to be objective.

DACUM chart development is dependent upon the selection of a skilled co-ordinator who has the ability to: resist the influence of committee members technical judgment, resolve issues, provide guidance, write clearly, relate to a large variety of occupations, resolve "the skill-knowledge debate", be extremely patient, be unyielding in applying the basic principles of DACUM, orient committee members to DACUM, keep committee attention on the charting wall, and assist in defining skills. Finally, the co-ordinator must be an individual who can take corrective action to maintain committee focus to assure the quality of the DACUM chart.

ii. Committee Selection

A DACUM committee is a group of experts in a given occupation assembled to construct a DACUM chart. Committee members should be individuals who have been nominated by an employer and persons skilled in the selected occupation, many of whom have progressed to a supervisory role. In some cases there may be specialists in the occupation who are able to contribute a more global view of what is required. The group of experts will work together in developing the DACUM chart under the direction of the co-ordinator. All the development work of the DACUM committee is done as a group. Time required is approximately 3 days, depending on the complexity of the occupation.

iii.   Charting Supplies & Environment

Once the committee members and co-ordinator are selected, the environment and supplies must be taken care of. First, the environment must be comfortable; providing adequate space, lighting, room temperature, appropriate levels of ventilation, walls that reduce visual and auditory distractions, and comfortable tables and chairs. In addition to the environment, there will be necessary supplies needed for charting. Cards and felt-tipped pens are used by the co-ordinator to develop hand-lettered file cards which are used to record committee identified skills (3x5 cards) and general areas of competence (4x6 cards).

These cards are adhered to the wall by the co-ordinator, giving the group a graphical representation of the entire occupation. Finally, previously developed DACUM charts are supplied which can be utilized by committee members to reflect upon as a part of the charting process.

b. Charting

Once the preparatory activities have been fulfilled, it is time to begin the next phase of developing the DACUM chart. This phase begins with orienting the committee and ends with the application of the rating scale to the DACUM chart.

i. Committee Orientation

To begin, the co-ordinator orients the committee to DACUM. This takes place during the first one and one-half hours of the first morning of the workshop. The purpose of the orientation is to provide an overview of DACUM and explain how the committee will operate for the remainder of the workshop.

ii. Review the Occupation

After committee orientation, a review of the occupation begins. Although this is not always a necessary step, it could be helpful by providing committee members with a visual representation of the occupation and related functions. The review usually includes the identification of occupational related items such as: the range of the occupation, its specialties, job overlap, levels above and below, and the jobs surrounding it. It is carried out by the co-ordinator depicting relationships between the items by drawing on flip chart paper or a whiteboard. Finally, the committee is asked to comment on the future of the occupation.

iii. Defining General Areas of Competence

The first major stage following the occupation review is the development of the DACUM Chart by defining General Areas of Competence in the occupation. This is not a complex activity, as these are usually quite readily identified by experts in the occupation. As they are defined, they are lettered on file cards and affixed to a suitable wall surface with putty that makes it easy for the co-ordinator to remove or shift them. General Areas of Competence are of three types: (examples are from Appendix A) :

1. Those obvious divisions of skill in an occupation related to specific divisions in work assignments or to specific components of the object worked on in the occupation. For example, in auto mechanics, General Areas of Competence readily identified in this way were SERVICE & REPAIR FUEL SYSTEMS, SERVICE & REPAIR ELECTRICAL SYSTEMS, etc. (see Appendix A).

2. Those divisions of skill that can be identified as being extensively used as part of one or more of the types of activities identified in (1) above. These are usually discovered and organized later in the definition of General Areas of Competence and may evolve because of problems in handling undue repetition in skill definition. An example from auto mechanics might be USE REPAIR TOOLS & EQUIPMENT or USE MEASURING &

TESTING DEVICES (see Appendix A), which are also involved in each of the examples used in (1).

3. Those divisions of skill that may become obvious later in development from an occupational or learning point of view. It may be found that certain obvious divisions as in (1) can be grouped for convenience. For example, SERVICE & REPAIR COOLING & EXHAUST SYSTEMS. On the other hand, certain extensive areas of competence may be found too unwieldy to handle and there may be obvious subdivision, as SERVICE & REPAIR ENGINES and REPAIR & OVERHAUL ENGINES (see Appendix A).

iv. Individual Skills

The second major activity in developing a DACUM chart is to identify, isolate, and define Individual Skills (behaviors) for each General Area of Competence. Skills are hand-written on file cards and affixed to the wall in horizontal bands adjacent to the General Areas of Competence. They are destined to become learning units in the proposed training program. The level of definition of these skills is kept quite simple. In oral definition, each is prefaced by "The individual must be able to...". This is omitted in transferring the definition to the card, leaving a simple action definition, always introduced by a verb. Verbs such as "understand" and "know" are not used. This makes the definition of "concrete" skills such as OPERATE CHASSIS LUBRICATE EQUIPMENT quite easy. The definition of abstract or reasoning skills is more difficult but can be done. For example, DETECT & DISGNOSE ENGINE FAULTS.

A definition is adopted when it is felt that most persons with an adequate background in the occupation would understand what is meant.

The skill definition exercise is judged to be complete when the co-ordinator detects that the committee has exhausted its collective knowledge of the needs of the occupation and has begun to repeat definitions or make trivial modifications to those already specified and accepted. At this point the co-ordinator asks, "Have we completed our activity?" and solicits the agreement of the committee.

v. Sequencing & Structuring

After agreeing upon a set of General Areas of Competence and Individual Skill (behavior) definitions, the committee, under the direction of the co-ordinator, proceeds to structure the skills into a desired learning sequence. This is done, not as it would be done in traditional educational programming, but from the point of view of an individual learning to acquire those skills in a work setting. Traditional methods of handling subject matter are ignored. They are, in fact, suppressed. Assuming that the trainee would begin at the left side of the chart and work toward General Competence on the right, those skills most needed and most readily applied early in an actual work situation are shifted to the left. Those skills that are little used or that the supervisor might wish to have left until the learner has developed some competence are shifted to the right. For example, REMOVE, INSPECT, REPAIR & INSTALL WHEELS, TIRES, TUBES VALVES would precede TEST, ADJUST & REPLACE TORSION BARS.

Once each band is sequenced in this fashion, the committee brings the skills into a final structure by vertically aligning skills in different bands that would be first applied at approximately the same time.

When the committee's work is completed, the definitions are typed, producing a DACUM chart. Any changes the committee desires to make can be readily made by revising the chart. Instances of change are rare however, and generally include basic title revisions.

III.   Select and Orient Instructor(s)

Once the DACUM chart is finalized and prepared, the selection and orientation of instructors for training takes place. The chart indicates the scope of skills that must be handled in the program, and from this the skill requirements of prospective instructors can be assessed. Demands in terms of instructor capability in the DACUM system are somewhat different from demands in more conventional training programs. These capabilities include, but are not limited to expertise and responsibility in the occupation, the ability to direct others, and the ability to assess performance on the job. Introductory orientation should take place before placing heavy development responsibility on the instructor. However, orientation will continue informally well into the actual operation of the program. Instructor orientation includes the review and rationale of the DACUM system and review of the DACUM chart.

IV.   Define Learning Activities

Once the selected instructors are oriented to the DACUM system and charts, learning activities are defined to enable learners to apply and develop skills and demonstrate competence. This critical component of program development is the process of assessing each identified skill on the DACUM chart and visualizing appropriate work-oriented activities through which the student can gain experience and through which achievement can be evaluated. Learning activities can be directly applied or transferred work activities, directly applied or transferred components of work activities, simulated activities, created projects, LAB projects, programmed learning, or information learning alone.

V. Select and Place Trainee

This is done in two stages. First, the trainee is screened on the basis of their predicted ability to succeed in acquiring each of the skills on the chart, as opposed to assessing their ability on the basis of past learning performance. Second, the trainee can be placed directly in an on-the-job training environment if adequate resources are available or they can be detained until all the resources are available for an in-center training program.

VI. Select Learning Environment

Each skill and its associated learning activities are assessed to determine the availability of learning resources and realistic learning experiences in a number of environments. It may be decided to locate training for the skill in a work environment because the experiences will be more meaningful or the training less expensive. On the other hand, it may be safer and more convenient to locate training for the skill in a more specifically created learning environment.

The selection of the learning environment is particularly important because some occupations do not lend themselves to extensive training in either the work environment or in a controlled specifically created learning environment. In most cases, however it is found feasible to conduct part of the training for the skill in each environment.

VII.   Select and Order Equipment, Tools, and Supplies

Program developers analyze each of the skills on the DACUM chart in order to select the occupational tools, equipment, supplies, or parts required to provide the learner with the opportunity to successfully perform on the job. These may be available in an on-the-job-training site or must be obtained for a centralized training program.

VIII. Install Equipment, Tools, and Supplies

Once the nature and quantity of equipment, tools, and supplies required are established, it is necessary to plan how they will be installed in the learning environment. This involves the process of organizing or modifying the selected learning environment(s) in preparation for the trainee's first skill-oriented experience and ensuring that all resources are organized and accessible for their convenience.

IX. Locate and Assign Human Resources

In order to ensure that available human resources staff adequately cover all components or skills of the chart, it is necessary to assess each staff member's ability, interest, and willingness to perform in each skill and learning activity. This involves assignment of instructors to skills and arrangements to bring in resource persons to handle any skills that cannot be handled by the instructional team. Trainees can also seek individual specialized assistance and advice through visits to employment sites.

X. Organize Individual Learning Activity Batteries (LAB)

The organization and development of Learning Activity Batteries (LAB)s involves two steps. First, an individual package or container is prepared for learning materials for each skill on the DACUM chart. Only one LAB is developed per skill, but it is possible for multiple learners to work on a LAB at one time. Second, an assessment is made of each skill and its associated learning activities to determine what supporting knowledge will likely be required. It is important that this is done after the learning activities are developed in order to reduce the amount of superfluous information or resources that can delay the trainee's skill achievement.

XI. Select Printed Materials

Readily available printed materials are the primary resources for LABs and selection is the first step normally taken in their development. Materials are selected on the basis of their projected value in terms of facilitating learning. No materials are included which are not directly related to the skill identified. Printed materials can include textbooks, journal articles, pamphlets and brochures, industrial training manuals and equipment-manufacturer-supplied service, repair, and operational manuals, and catalogues and equipment specification sheets.

XII. Develop Printed Materials

When necessary, printed materials can be developed to supplement those that are already available. While printed materials are generally the most commonly available and used as resources for LAB, learners can benefit from instructor developed printed materials such as a listing or description of applications of skills, job sheets, or from instructors redesigning or modifying existing printed materials.

XIII. Select A.V. Materials

The use of A.V. materials is desirable because it provides an alternative media for presenting information and allows the learner to observe and model desired performance. Effectively selecting A.V. materials involves two separate assessments of requirement. One, there may be a need to have audio-visual materials available for those learners who may have reading deficits or may not be attracted to reading as a method of acquiring information. Two, specific skills that require extensive procedures, intricate motions, or the acquisition of complex concepts may best be learned from audio-visual materials. The materials in this category are usually commercially available.

XIV. Develop Audio-Visual Materials

When there is a lack of suitable A.V. materials, the development of these materials needs to be created by instructional staff. In particular, occupations where physical performance or movement of the skilled performer is critical, A.V. materials allow for capturing the techniques in the form of formal demonstrations. These may be digital video recorded demonstrations and presentations, or audio recording accompanied by workbooks or other printed materials.

XV. Select and Install Learning Equipment

Once optimal learning resources and processes are established, assessment of the learning equipment can take place. This involves analyzing what equipment and furniture are required, space requirements, and overall learner access to equipment. After analyzing the learning equipment in relationship to the Learning Activity Battery resources, installation of equipment can begin.

XVI. Assess Lack of Achievement

The preceding activities are all part of establishing the initial program. The following activities take place after the first trainees have had an opportunity to cycle through the steps in the *Learning Evaluation Model*. Assessment of achievement is based on observation of performance, which is measured by utilizing the DACUM rating scale. It is important to note that, with ratings recorded continuously, it is possible to extract planning and progress review data at any point in time. If through this review of data lack of achievement is identified, the learning program should be refined and redesigned to address any issues. Lack of achievement might be attributed to the ineffectiveness of learning resources or even a lack of motivation or specific learning difficulties on the part of individual trainees. A lack of motivation or individual learning difficulties would not necessarily indicate a need for program revision.

XVII. Evaluate Resources and Materials

If it is observed that the learners lack achievement, the obvious starting point is to look at refining the learning program. Lack of achievement might be attributed to ineffective resources. Resources might be ineffective for a number of reasons:

1. Learning activities may be inappropriate or insufficient.

2. Learning activities are not related to realistic work problems or conditions.

3. Learners having inadequate access to equipment, tools, supplies, and human resources. Necessary equipment or supplies may not have been made available or may not be appropriately located to facilitate skill achievement.

4. Inadequate or limited access to printed materials, A.V. materials, or learning equipment.

5. The learning environment may not be adequate.

6. LABs that are clear for ease in information retrieval, not located properly, or not in the suitable environment.

7. Materials in a LAB may be inadequate or insufficient. This will be indicated by learner difficulty or frustration while working with materials. Materials may need to be added, or removed because they are confusing or inappropriate.

SUMMARY

This chapter set the initial framework for developing occupational training using the DACUM system. The Development Model for DACUM Learning Program introduced is at the heart of the DACUM system and provides a theoretical road map for creating fast, efficient occupational training. This chapter was dedicated to reviewing each category of the model with intent to increase practitioners' holistic understanding of the DACUM system.

REFERENCES

Adams, R. E. (1975). *DACUM: Approach to curriculum, learning, and evaluation in occupational training.* Ottawa: Dept. of Regional Economic Expansion.

4

EXPLORATION OF TRAINING NEED

The DACUM system was developed to design fast and effective occupational training. To develop training that is fast and effective, it is first critical to determine the overall need for training. Some professionals call this investigative process cause analysis. This phase in the development of a DACUM Learning Program is referred to as *Detect and Explore Training Need* (see Figure 4-1).

DEVELOPMENT MODEL FOR DACUM LEARNING PROGRAM

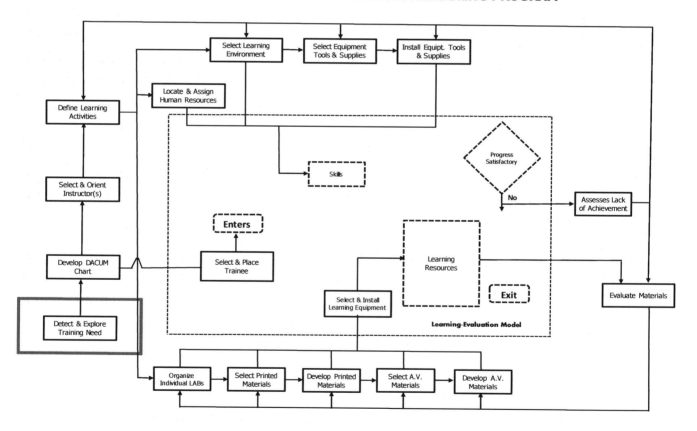

Figure 4-1. Development Model for DACUM Learning Program

Much like any training program, it is important to determine whether or not a training need exists before identifying the necessary skills for the program. It is important to note here that this chapter isn't to discourage the use of the DACUM system, but to ensure that DACUM is used properly. While DACUM is an ideal system for developing occupational training to close performance gaps related to a lack of skills, it isn't appropriate for closing all performance gaps. Therefore, this chapter will explore the importance of detecting training needs , explore the reasons and rationale for training, and identify when utilizing the DACUM process for developing occupational training is appropriate.

WHY DETECT TRAINING NEEDS

The DACUM system is designed to develop fast and efficient occupational training. Occupational training is the process of providing employees with skills to perform effectively within a given occupation; however the rationale for developing and conducting training can vary. Most often occupational training is developed based on needs stemming from new knowledge and skills in an occupation as the result of new processes, products, or technology. Further, needs stem from occupational changes resulting from emerging occupations, new laws and regulations, changes to industry requirements, and updates within the occupation. Training can also be developed when employees are not performing at a desired level. There are times when a lack of performance can be the result of a lack of occupational knowledge or skills. It is important to note here that on average, less than 17% of all performance problems are the result of a lack of knowledge and skills (ASTD, 2009).When developing occupational training that results from one of these reasons, the results as explored in Chapter 2 are often unsuccessful. In fact, while over $170 billion was estimated to be spent on training activities, less than 10% of all training is "transferred" onto the job (Aik & Tway, 2005; Brown, 2008, Lim & Morris, 2006).

This lack of success is often the direct result of either a lack of cause analysis resulting in a misdiagnosed performance gap or poorly designed/delivered training. While the DACUM system is specifically designed to develop fast and efficient occupational training, it is important for practitioners to understand the process and need for properly detecting and exploring a training need.

TRAINING NEEDS BASED ON NEW PROGRAMS

Who or what determines the need for a new occupational training program? The DACUM approach originally was developed out of a need to develop occupational training quickly addressing the needs of disadvantaged adults. Therefore the DACUM system of designing occupational training can be used when new skill needs based on emerging trends, critical changes, or technological updates are desired by the occupation. These needs should be identified by those that have close connections to the workplace and are currently experiencing skill deficiencies. For example, the need for an occupational training program at a community college, CTE, or university may be identified by an industry advisory board, or the need for a new program within an organization may be identified by a production manager and employees needing to implement a new system or technology.

The detection of training needs does not end with determining an overall need for a new training program. When many new occupational training programs are developed they miss the mark as far as developing skills within the given occupation. This is because the skills needed within the training program are often identified by individuals not doing or performing the skills within the occupation. This results in training that fails to develop employees in the skills that are necessary, and often provides training in skills that are irrelevant or less important to optimum performance. The DACUM system utilizes a built-in *Training Needs Assessment* (occupational analysis) that focuses on expert workers within the occupation to determine necessary skills through the development of a DACUM Chart. This *Training Needs Assessment,* or process of determining what goes into and what is not part of a training program, determines the skills that need to be trained, the level of skill needed, and ensures that no unnecessary skills are developed (Rossett, 1999).

TRAINING NEEDS BASED ON PERFORMANCE PROBLEMS

When an employee has performed inadequately on the job or has observed others performing to a level that is less than acceptable within the occupation, it is critical to pinpoint why the performance was unsatisfactory. The following questions should be asked:

- Did the performer not know what they were expected to do?

- Did the performer not have the appropriate tools to do their job?

- Was the performer not rewarded for doing a good job?

- Did the performer not have enough knowledge to do their job?

- Was the performer not capable or ready to do the job?

- Was the performer not motivated to do the job?

What was the solution to the identified problem? Many professionals believe that training is the solution for all performance problems. As stated by Fuller and Farrington (1999), performance is a real problem and training is a potential solution. However, training is not always a correct or sufficient solution to address performance problems. In fact, it has been determined that training is an appropriate intervention in less than 20% of all performance problems (ASTD, 2009; Dean & Ripley, 1997). Training is a solution that can be used to address a lack of skills and knowledge within the occupation, but is it an effective solution to address issues of motivation or lack of rewards for performing effectively? The answer is no. Training is commonly suggested as a solution to performance problems because organizations do not adequately determine the root cause of performance problems. Organizations have training departments and employees and managers understand training; therefore, training tends to be the easy answer to performance problems.

If training is not a typical solution to performance problems, when would it be appropriate to apply the DACUM system to address a performance problem? In order to determine the appropriateness of utilizing the DACUM system to address performance problems, we must first determine whether or not the performance problem is training related. Performance problems within an organization do stem from a lack of knowledge and skills on the job and training is an appropriate performance intervention. The performance problem is training related if it is determined that individuals are failing to adequately perform based on a lack of knowledge or skill.

ADDRESSING PERFORMANCE PROBLEMS

If training isn't the solution to all performance problems, we must determine what is causing the specific performance problems before we can select the appropriate intervention. In order to address performance problems, we must understand that everyone within the organization is performing within a system. This system includes factors within the work environment itself, as well as factors related to individual workers. Deficiencies with any of these factors within the system can cause performance problems.

Cell 1: Environment Information	Cell 2: Environment Resources	Cell 3: Environment Incentives
• Relevant and frequent feedback about the adequacy of performance • Descriptions of what is expected of performance • Clear and relevant guides to adequate performance	Instruments: • Tools and materials of work designed scientifically to match human factors • Work processes	• Adequate financial incentives made contingent upon performance • Nonmonetary incentives made available • Career-development opportunities
Cell 4: Individual Knowledge	**Cell 5: Individual Capacity**	**Cell 6: Individual Motives**
• Scientifically designed training that matches the requirements of exemplary performance. • Placement	• Flexible scheduling to match peak capacity • Selection • Match people and position	• Assessment of people's motives to work • Recruitment of workers to match realities of work conditions

Figure 4-2. **Behavior Engineering Model.** Gilbert, T. F. (2007). *Human Competence: Engineering Worthy Performance* (Tribute Edition).

In order to diagnose the cause of the performance problems and to determine appropriate solutions, Gilbert's Behavior Engineering Model (2007) is commonly applied as a diagnostic tool. The Behavior Engineering Model (BEM) is used to address factors, barriers, or drivers that impede performance within both the organizational environment and with individuals.

Work Environment Factors

Gilbert (2007) states that when support factors within the work environment are provided, employees are able to perform effectively. When these support factors are not in place however, even specialized training will not address performance issues. The top row of the BEM (figure 4-2) represents factors within the work environment. The factors within the work environment that influence performance fall under three basic categories: Information, Resources, and Incentives.

Information

This factor within the work environment explores the question of whether or not a performer knows what is expected of them. If performers are unclear of what is expected of them to meet the desired level of performance or received no feedback on their performance, they are unlikely to produce at an exemplary level. When we are asked to produce within this inconsistent environment, we typically produce unreliable results. If we were to ask four chefs to cook a meal, but didn't specify what a good meal looked like, would we get consistently good meals? What is more likely to happen is that each chef will interpret success differently. Additionally, if chefs are producing substandard meals and we fail to provide adequate feedback, they are likely to continue producing substandard meals until they are corrected. Gilbert (2007) stated that "improper guidance and feedback are the single largest contributors to incompetence in the world of work" (p. 91). If performance problems are identified as information related, solutions are relatively easy to fix. Organizations can establish job standards and descriptions, accurate feedback and data can be provided, and guides can be created on how to perform.

Resources

This factor looks at performance problems related to the tools and materials on the job. Let's explore our previous example of the occupation of a chef. If chefs know what is expected of their performance and receive timely feedback, but are asked to cook with substandard equipment, can an employer still expect consistent performance? In this case, performance can be expected to suffer. We will most likely see the chefs, while following all guides and standards properly, not meeting the expected outcomes because meals were cooked improperly in a broken oven, an unreliable burner, or other faulty equipment. We also could not expect a chef to produce a high quality meal consistently with low quality ingredients. The solutions to performance problems related to resources can be expensive, but are necessary if ideal performance is desired. While purchasing working technology or materials may be a short term expense, these resources are necessary for performers to produce the outcomes of their jobs.

Incentives

Incentives can relate to a variety of factors within the work environment. Most often it is thought of as the salary or wage someone receives in order to perform. While rewarding good performance is important, it is not the only part of incentives that needs to be explored. One aspect of incentives that happens often, but is overlooked, is the rewarding of poor performance. Let's look at an example of 3 car salespeople. If the salespeople are expected to sell 15 cars per month and the first salesperson sells 30 cars in a month, the second salesperson sells 15 cars in a month, and the third salesperson sells 7 cars in a month, would we expect each of them to be rewarded the same way? We would probably say that the first salesperson deserves to be rewarded because they far exceeded the standard. But what happens if each salesperson received the same bonus or raise? Is there an incentive for the first salesperson to far exceed the standard? Is there an incentive for the third salesperson to meet the standard? Solutions related to incentives generally revolve around ensuring that all rewards are made contingent upon performance. Rewards are based on superior performance, while those not performing to the level expected are provided with the necessary feedback to perform more effectively and not simply rewarded for showing up.

Individual Factors

The bottom row of the BEM (Figure 4-2) represents factors within the individual. Factors with the individual that influence performance fall under three basic categories: Knowledge, Capacity, and Motives.

If performance problems within the environment are explored but still haven't been addressed, then we can begin to explore those factors, barriers, or drivers that impact individuals. Individual factors that influence performance are addressed after those within the work environment because, as stated by Gilbert (2007), issues related to individuals, particularly related to defects with an individual's capacity or motives, are the exception, not the rule. Whatever defects might appear with an individual, generally can be addressed by other variables within the BEM. If fact, Gilbert orders the cells of the BEM based on the likelihood of where the performance problem will exist. Therefore, performance problems are much more likely to exist with information factors within the work environment then with an individual's motivation. This doesn't mean that an individual's motivation is less important than information within the work environment. It simply means that issues within the work environment are much more likely to be the cause of performance problems than individual factors.

The following will explore each of the individual factors that impact performance. Unlike the BEM, we are going to address the issues in reverse order (motives, capacity, and knowledge). This will be done first because the two most common suggested causes of poor performance within organizations is that "employees are too lazy" (motives) and "employees are too dumb" (capacity) (Gilbert, 2007). As stated earlier these causes are the exception, not the rule. Therefore we will address these factors before discussing training as a potential solution to performance problems.

Second, the DACUM system's primary use would be in addressing knowledge and skill gaps with performance. Therefore we will explore this performance factor last.

Motives

This is typically the last place to look for performance problems simply because it is rarely a substantial problem (Gilbert, 2007). Individuals generally care a great deal about how they perform on the job. There are instances however where the motives of an individual can lead to poor performance. If the system in place is inherently dull or unrewarding, this may impact individual motives. Again, while these instances are rare, motives of an individual can be addressed by ensuring career development opportunities are available, providing positive reinforcement, and creating a work environment that ensures job satisfaction (clean, organized, etc.).

Capacity

Much like motives, an individual's capacity to perform is often suggested as a cause of poor performance. However like motivation, it is very rare that an individual is "too dumb" to perform adequately on the job. While some individuals may be better prepared or quick-witted than others, if proper standards, incentives, and training are in place even the slowest witted individual can perform at least adequately (Gilbert, 2007). Issues with capacity however can arise if job scheduling isn't in place to maximize performance or individuals are improperly placed or selected for jobs. Issues with individual capacity are dealt with by ensuring that employee skills match the requirements for the job. This can be done through proper selection and placement procedures during the hiring process.

Knowledge

The factor most likely to lead to training as an appropriate intervention to a performance problem is represented within the fourth cell of the BEM, individual knowledge. The knowledge cell addresses performance issues that specifically relate to addressing gaps in knowledge and skill. This gap in knowledge and skill can be the result of new technologies, not knowing as much as exemplary performers or the training doesn't match the requirements of the job. Because training is often very expensive, it is important here to note that some lack of knowledge wouldn't require training. If the lack of knowledge is related to not knowing performance standards or it is knowledge that doesn't need to be memorized, solutions other than training, such as job aid, can be used.

In exploring individual knowledge, we are looking at situations where the performer has performance standards in place, the proper tools and incentive to perform, but still cannot produce the desired outcomes. Knowledge and skill deficiencies in these cases might include a lack of skills with tools/technology needed or even a lack of specific advanced knowledge needed to perform effectively. Often in the cases of knowledge and skill deficiencies, the knowledge and skills of the exemplary performers is different than that of other performers. These exemplary performers apply different knowledge and skills, resources, tools, and abilities to produce outcomes at a higher level.

If the identified performance problem is due to a lack of knowledge or skill, we would then move to conduct a Training Needs Assessment to determine what specific knowledge and skills are needed to include in an effective training program. As discussed earlier, the DACUM system utilizes a built-in Training Needs Assessment (occupational analysis) that focuses on a group of expert workers (exemplary performers) within the occupation to determine necessary skills through the development of the DACUM Chart. When developing a training program, this DACUM Chart and rating scale serve as an outline of the skills of exemplary performers and provide the level of performance needed. The remaining chapters of this book will discuss how effective training is developed through the DACUM system.

TRAINING NEEDS AND DACUM

Whether a training need is determined because of a gap in performance or the need for a new program, the DACUM system can be effective. The DACUM system is a fast and effective means of developing training. It not only focuses on the skills of expert workers that can address any performance problems of existing performers related to a lack of knowledge and skills. It is also effective in developing training programs to develop new trainees.

While addressing non-training related performance issues is not an intended purpose of the DACUM system, one of the unexpected benefits of adopting the DACUM approach (at least in the eyes of program designers and installers) is how DACUM skills could potentially be used to address other performance gaps related to issues other than a lack of skill. The DACUM chart identifies what workers do within the occupation and the rating scale determines the level of performance needed to be successful. Organizations have found these data to be useful in the development of new job descriptions and standards, therefore addressing some unanticipated gaps within the work environment.

Another unexpected benefit was the increased input from employers and experts in the occupation. This is particularly important in designing programs which attempt to match a limited number of prospective trainees with a limited number of job openings in a local community.

As soon as a training need has been tentatively detected, employers are called together to explore the nature and extent of the need.

A key step is to expose employers to a sample DACUM chart, stating that this is the model that will be used to develop the training program. Also described briefly is a combined training program and on-job-training (O.J.T.) model that illustrates to the employers that (a) a solution is possible, (b) they must become committed to participate, and (c) financial assistance can be made available to ensure they do not have to accept an undue financial burden.

The presentation of the sample DACUM chart makes employer observations and contributions more realistic. They discuss the skills needed by their workers and the extent of skill development required for various jobs. Without the chart before them they are likely to discuss what knowledge should be taught, how much of it, and how long it would take. Therefore the DACUM chart focuses the discussion on the specific skills needed to perform on the job.

The presentation of a tentative training model eliminates much discussion concerning doubts about the program materializing. It frees the group to discuss the real issues at hand, namely the nature and extent of the need.

Additionally, the prospect of having to serve on a chart development committee and participate in a program through provision of O.J.T. generates commitment from the employers which, in turn, improves the quality of information provided. Some are restrained in their enthusiasm for placing demands on "someone else" to provide training service to them. Others are motivated by the prospect of achieving what they formerly believed to be an impossible goal.

If a DACUM chart for the occupation already exists, the information-gathering task should be even easier. Prospective participants are able to see a clear definition of the components of the occupation on which to base decisions and contributions. They are able to specify which skills need more emphasis locally and the skill composition of particular jobs in the occupation which most need attention.

SUMMARY

This chapter explored the importance of training needs , identified when utilizing the DACUM system is appropriate and showed the reasons and rationale for training. There are times when a lack of work performance can be the result of an employee's knowledge or skill deficiency. Other times poor work performance is a result from the work environment or individual factors. Work environment factors include the lack of information, resources, or incentives. Individual factors include motives, capacity, or knowledge. Gilbert's Behavior Engineering Model was used to explain each factor and to identify causes of poor work performance. Further, it was asserted that training is the only performance intervention that can improve work performance when causes are directly related to a deficiency in an employee's knowledge or skill. The DACUM system is used to develop fast and effective occupational training to close performance gaps caused by the lack of knowledge or skill or to develop new trainees. A DACUM chart is developed by expert workers to identify what workers do within an occupation. The DACUM rating scale helps determine the level of performance needed to be successful. This is done after successfully detecting the need for training.

REFERENCES

Adams, R. E. (1975). *DACUM: Approach to curriculum, learning, and evaluation in occupational training.* Ottawa: Dept. of Regional Economic Expansion.

Aik, C.T. & Tway, D.C. (2005, January). On the job training: An overview and an appraisal. Proceedings of the International Conference of Applied Management and Decision Sciences (AMDS 2005), Athens, GA.

American Society for Training and Development. (2009). *Analyzing Human Performance.* Alexandria, VA: Author.

Brown, T.C. (2005). Effectiveness of distal and proximal goals as transfer-of-training interventions: A field experiment. *Human Resource Development Quarterly, 16,* 369-387.

Dean, P. & Ripley, D. (Eds.) (1997). *Performance Improvement Pathfinders: Models for Organizational Learning Systems.* Washington, DC: The International Society for Performance Improvement.

Fuller, J. & Farrington, J. (1999). *From training to performance improvement: Navigating the transition.* San Francisco: Pfeiffer.

Gilbert, T. (2007). *Human Competence: Engineering worthy performance.* San Francisco: Pfeiffer.

Lim, D.H. & Morris, M. (2006). Influence of trainee characteristics, instructional satisfaction, and organizational climate on perceived learning and training transfer. *Human Resource Development Quarterly, 17,* 85-115.

Rossett, A. (1999). *First Things Fast: A handbook for performance analysis.* San Francisco: Pfeiffer.

THE CO-ORDINATOR

The next four chapters are focused on the Chart Development element within the Development Model for DACUM Learning Program (see Figure 5-1). A successful DACUM is dependent upon a skilled co-ordinator who directs the facilitation of the DACUM chart. This is done by navigating DACUM committee members through identifying, defining, and sequencing skills for an occupation. This chapter covers skills and abilities needed by a co-ordinator and potential challenges when dealing with a committee.

DEVELOPMENT MODEL FOR DACUM LEARNING PROGRAM

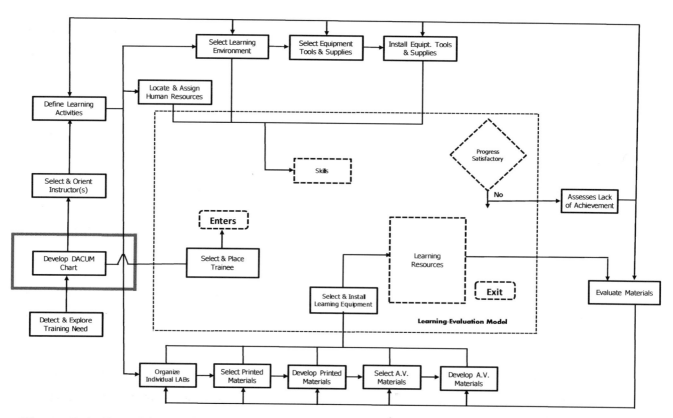

Figure 5-1. Development Model for DACUM Learning Program

Because DACUM chart development is a relatively new activity for most and because committee personnel will not be familiar with its requirements, it is necessary that the co-ordinator be able to provide the committee with a solid framework within which to operate. In time one would expect that, if DACUM is applied on a wider scale, committee members will not come into the sessions unfamiliar with the process or what it demands of them. They may have opportunities to read about it or to see charts for other occupations. They may also meet with colleagues who have served on another committee and who will have mentioned some of the principles and some of the experiences they encountered.

The co-ordinator is cast in a difficult role. A co-ordinator cannot influence the technical judgments or contributions of the committee. If members of the committee agree that a specific skill or behavior is required for performance in their occupation, the co-ordinator must include it in the chart. If there is a specific arrangement of skills, a way of subdividing the skills, a level of breakdown of the skills that is satisfactory to the committee, the co-ordinator must agree with it. If there is a terminology that may not be acceptable in educational or dictionary terms yet is widely used and is readily understandable in the field and the committee insists that it must be used, the co-ordinator must agree. Nevertheless, the co-ordinator must insist that the committee work within a specific framework. The co-ordinator must provide them with criteria, direction, sets of guidelines, and analogies that will help them accomplish their task.

Primarily, this must be done on the spot because the work demands continuity and a certain momentum. The co-ordinator must resolve all issues, provide all guidance, etc., within the time limitation of the three days that have been assigned. The co-ordinator is not able to solve problems in isolation or by getting another expert's interpretation or by talking to other curriculum personnel. The co-ordinator must develop skills sharply in advance to be able to respond to situations as they occur in the workshop.

The following is a list of skills or abilities that the successful co-ordinator must possess. In some cases, the brief description of the skill is followed by a description of a situation or situations in which a co-ordinator will likely have to apply it.

1. The co-ordinator must be able to hand letter clearly in a size that will permit accurate definition of a skill on a 3x5 file card. The lettering must be clear enough to enable all committee members to read the card reasonably well from their positions in the room. Illegible or sloppy lettering frequently results in a

loss of interest in the wall, the issues being discussed, and even the total assignment. The co-ordinator should check and, where necessary, re-letter the cards at every opportunity (lunch times, evenings after committee work has been completed).

Since there is not time to painstakingly letter each one clearly when a committee begins specifying skills in quick sequence the co-ordinator should practice lettering rapidly until he or she can prepare cards almost as quickly as skills are specified.

2. The co-ordinator must be thoroughly familiar in a curriculum sense with a large variety of occupations and should be able to make curriculum decisions about a number of applications. This ability may only come from being involved in a number of DACUM workshops or other curriculum work and will not be as easily acquired as many of the other abilities or skills listed. There are a number of compatible or similar characteristics of occupations in relation to their training and curriculum needs which the co-ordinator must be able to relate to the committee. The co-ordinator must be able to make rapid, in-process decisions about the way the chart is developing, the quality of definitions, and the accuracy of analysis in terms of its cohesiveness and structure. These decisions may be made without the awareness of the committee, but they must be made if the co-ordinator is to maintain control of the situation. Of persons who have been trained or partially trained in co-ordination work, the most successful and those who have learned most rapidly have been those with a curriculum construction background; for example, persons working in a career technical education school, vocational school or technical institute who have had to assist in developing curriculum and training programs for a variety of occupations. The person with curriculum training who has only worked in a single field does not seem to adapt as readily. This type of individual typically lacks the broader experience which would lead to sensing the commonality of application of these principles.

3. The co-ordinator must be able to resolve what might be called "the skill-knowledge debate". DACUM work relies heavily on the principle that the skills or types of competence required for performance in an occupation can be defined and that the definitions can be usefully applied as the goals of a learning program and in installing the trained learner in the subsequent work environment. If the co-ordinator is not committed to this principle, the committee will detect the co-ordinator's doubts and lead him or her into specifying knowledge in vague terms rather than undertaking the painstaking

work of specifying the skills that are actually required. The co-ordinator can only be sure of committee member commitment when able to handle arguments, provide responses to questions, and handle severe criticism in relation to themselves and the DACUM approach.

4. The co-ordinator must be extremely patient. Observers of curriculum sessions have commented that this appears to be the outstanding characteristic of the co-ordinator. The committee must be free to identify the skill or competence requirements of their of occupation. Extreme or persistent interference on the part of the co-ordinator in attempting to lead it in this task, in resolving the debates with regard to it, and in trying to determine whether or not specific skills are needed will only cause the committee to become subservient and allow the co-ordinator to take command. By being patient, the co-ordinator allows the committee to realize that it has to make the decisions, it has to resolve the debates, and it has to exhibit responsibility. This is sometimes difficult for the co-ordinator. Frequently, because of unfamiliarity with the nature of the work, the committee will search for a solution to an immediate problem to which the co-ordinator may suspect that they already has the answer. The co-ordinator must not provide the answer but must let the committee find it. If the co-ordinator provides a few such answers, the committee is likely to give him or her the responsibility of finding others. The chart then becomes the co-ordinator's work rather than the work of the committee. Finally, the co-ordinator must be patient in allowing the committee to explore in some detail issues which appear to be insignificant or irrelevant but which are real and important. If unsure, the co-ordinator must be patient and allow the committee to explore in order to resolve issues. Finally, the co-ordinator can capitalize on the member's enthusiasm over resolving the issue themselves and seeing the results of their efforts in the form of words on cards on the wall.

5. The co-ordinator must be unyielding in applying the basic principles of DACUM. This is sometimes difficult. The person to whom it is important to be liked or to be the leader is not likely to succeed in this kind of work. The basic principles of DACUM are simple and direct. They are so direct, in fact, that committee members often try to challenge them by making alternate suggestions or refusing to follow the principles to see if the co-ordinator will stick by their guns. It is necessary to be unyielding even to the extent of being resented by the committee. Application of some of the principles demands a good deal of hard work, and at times the committee will begin to wonder about the value of the assignment.

When a committee member first realizes the quality of analysis demanded, he or she may overestimate the amount of time and effort required to complete the chart. At this point, the committee member will challenge the principles and will want to avoid establishing behavioral objectives by specifying skills each of which can be prefaced with the words "The individual must be able to and each of which must be detailed and clear enough to be a usable product".

It is important that the co-ordinator refuse to compromise these and other principles when it is apparent the committee (or a member or two) is attempting to avoid the task. The co-ordinator can hold them to the task by pausing frequently for review of rationale, review of successful portions of the work already completed, and reference to success in developing charts for more complex occupations. The co-ordinator may have to insist that the committee follow his or her direction for a time until enough work is completed to convince skeptics of the benefits of the approach.

At the end of most DACUM workshops to date, committee members have commended the co-ordinator on his or her ability to keep the committee on the track, making it possible to bring to fruition a task which, but for the co-ordinator's strong leadership, would not have been completed.

6. The co-ordinator must be able to provide an on-the-spot orientation to the DACUM process. The co-ordinator must describe the general principles under which the committee must operate and models that will allow them to make decisions, and must also give them enough insight into the rationale and values of the DACUM system to make them feel that their effort will be worthwhile.

This orientation must be oral. The experience is too new and different to expect committee members to become oriented through prior reading. Because each occupation has a different structure and characteristics, it has been difficult to arrive at a formalized presentation, such as a PowerPoint presentation, that would serve to orient all committees. The co-ordinator must make this presentation extremely flexible and must note the reaction of each person. Further, the co-ordinator should use varied techniques to involve individuals in thinking about their occupation so that the co-ordinator can be sure that each explores the issues at hand. Attempts at exposing committee members to a rather inflexible presentation have resulted in the loss of committee members at the orientation stage, with subsequent difficulty in getting them on the track. During the orientation the alert co-ordinator can pick out those committee members with whom he or she is going to have difficulty; there is the person who does not smile or react in any way to suggestions made about training and training programs and how they develop, and there is the person who during the question period does not ask any questions at all, seems to ignore the questions of others, or asks questions that indicate a bias. If the co-ordinator encounters such reactions, it is often best to expand the orientation with further analogies, descriptions of training programs, and exploration of the DACUM principles until the co-ordinator is sure each individual is beginning to identify with the process. In other cases, an orientation period as short as one hour may be enough to assure the co-ordinator that each committee member is satisfactorily oriented.

7. The co-ordinator must be able to tell when the committee or individuals within the committee have begun to drift away from the framework provided during orientation. This will happen frequently through the three day workshop, and action should be taken immediately once it is certain that some other model or framework is being used for arriving at decisions. It may be necessary to call a halt to the proceedings and review some of the basic principles. It may be necessary to open up a discussion about the principles and give other committee members an opportunity to try to get the lost individual back on track. Often this is the best technique as the committee member may have some reluctance to follow the co-ordinator and be influenced more directly by their peers in the occupation.

   At the same time, the co-ordinator must not overdo this sort of activity, but rather   should note indications that individuals are losing sight of the concepts or principles, and select an appropriate time for action. There is not time during the three-day workshop for review of this sort each time an individual begins to stray.

8. The co-ordinator must be able to keep the attention of the committee on the wall. This is an extremely difficult task because at times members become tired of this activity. The co-ordinator must visualize the group as a single individual writing or diagramming the DACUM chart as well as ensuring that each person in the group focuses attention on appropriate parts of the developing document.

   Some committee members resist because they dislike participating as part of a group and giving up their more usual leadership role. Others like to sort out their ideas and contributions in some detail before offering them to the others in the group. Use of the wall prevents them from doing this and demands that all look at each issue at the same time.

The co-ordinator can use a number of techniques to help committee members focus attention on the wall. *First,* the co-ordinator can walk along the wall or to a specific location and point out specific skills or cards for review of a question at hand. *Second,* from his or her seat the co-ordinator can refer to specific skills and request clarification from the committee. This will necessitate that members first locate the skill and then attempt to clarify it. *Third,* the co-ordinator can ask committee members to reinforce points by reference to specific cards. For example, they may be having difficulty identifying with the process of specifying only skills. This will force them to take a look at specific cards to point out exactly what they mean. *Finally,* it is sometimes necessary to halt proceedings to point out to the committee that it is avoiding its responsibility to focus attention on the wall and allowing a few members to lead the rest away from the objective.

The co-ordinator must control the tendency for the focus of the workshop to shift away from the wall to the co-ordinator or to one of the committee members. Once attention has focused on the co-ordinator, perhaps because he or she has had too much to say or taken too strong a lead in helping the committee to identify skills, it is extremely difficult to shift it away.

9. The co-ordinator must be able to assist the committee in defining skills. Specifically, the co-ordinator frequently has to assist in the selection of the action verbs that introduce each of the skills. Because this is a new activity for members of the committee, they may not be adept at finding the right words. The co-ordinator, on the basis of personal knowledge and ability in occupational analysis and familiarity with acceptable definitions on a variety of DACUM charts, should be able to help out when the committee experiences difficulty. The co-ordinator can frequently describe a method used for arriving at a skill definition for another occupation. Standard applications, with examples of action words, are described in Chapter 8 – Skill Definition of this book.

The co-ordinator often must help select verbs that introduce skills which are difficult to identify and which have in the past been treated as knowledge that is merely applied. In some cases, the committee may even have difficulty in isolating just what it is that people have to do and consequently has difficulty in phrasing definitions. The co-ordinator's input at this time is most valuable to focus attention on the action desired by suggesting a variety of alternative action words that might be suitable or even, in the early part of the workshop, by actually stating the skill as the co-ordinator sees it. Without this assistance the committee work is likely to bog down. For example, a committee might suggest that there is a body of knowledge that the person in the occupation must have and be able to apply. The co-ordinator must help them to describe the actual skill that must be applied, and the co-ordinator may have to suggest verbs such as "analyze", "determine", extract", "organize", which will help the committee to pinpoint the real activity.

The most difficult skills to identify and the skills which probably need the most assistance on the part of the co-ordinator are those relating to the analytical, problem-solving activities that are at the heart of the occupation. Skills that are mental-problem-solving in nature may only be visible to the person expert in their application. For example, an architect does more than apply their knowledge of ideal room arrangements. An architect accommodates traffic flow, balances room size to available space, etc. These skills may not be physically observable or visible in the resulting work and hence are difficult for committees to specify without assistance.

The co-ordinator, however, should confine their own contribution to providing words for the committee members. Once a co-ordinator has established a pattern for the committee members to use in defining skills for a band, no additional assistance should be offered until a new class of problem appears. The co-ordinator may later criticize some of his or her own contributions to ensure that the committee members feel they are appropriate and did not accept them merely to avoid a difficult specification problem.

A useful reference source is a variety of other DACUM charts, particularly those for similar fields. However, if these are used, the co-ordinator must constantly question subsequent contributions to be sure the committee is not adopting words from other charts which are not appropriate for the occupation being analyzed. Committee members may do this to avoid the rather painstaking process of establishing their own more appropriate definitions.

In some cases, the co-ordinator must construct an entire skill definition. The co-ordinator will notice individuals struggling to identify a particular skill, or may overhear a subgroup discussing a problem area that they cannot identify. The co-ordinator may have to suggest a number of ways in which the skill may be stated to try to stimulate them to examine it. Again, the co-ordinator must make sure the committee have not adopted the co-ordinator's idea to avoid a difficult decision.

An additional responsibility is to assist the committee in qualifying the skills. Too often the committee will insist that the person in the occupation must be able to "weld" when all a worker has to do is be able to "tack weld parts prior to assembly using portable equipment". While the committee member may not be technically competent to qualify skills, the co-ordinator may overhear discussions and detect possible divisions that may apply. The co-ordinator can take these opportunities to suggest a more qualified definition to see if there is in fact a need for further clarification in order to set a pattern for more precise skill specification.

While the co-ordinator must be alert to any opportunity to make the definitions clearer, they must control their own input. The co-ordinator can do this by drawing only on what has been heard in the room. They may sense that a skill is being overlooked, but should not suggest it unless hearing one of the committee members mention it as part of discussion. This will give the co-ordinator the opportunity to raise questions about the skill. However, if the subject is not raised by a member, the co-ordinator has no right to suggest it, except during final review when a number of avenues are pursued and questions raised to confirm completeness of the coverage.

10. The co-ordinator must be able to maintain a schedule of progress and activities to ensure that the work will be completed within the allotted period. It has been found that extension beyond the recommended two or three days results in less efficient work in the later stages as committee members seem to be able to work well for not more than three or, at most, four days. One thing the co-ordinator can do is establish interim goals. Once an activity is falling behind schedule, the co-ordinator must make some adjustment decisions. For example, if the committee cannot establish the General Areas of Competence within an hour and one-half or two hours, the co-ordinator may have to set this task aside temporarily and begin the process of establishing the skills for one of the more obviously accurate General Areas of Competence, trusting that the committee will begin to get a better understanding of the task and be able to return later to consolidate the General Areas of Competence in a much shorter time. The co-ordinator can readily apportion this time once the General Areas of Competence are established by dividing the available time equally among the bands that are established for the chart. If difficulty arises and a band requires additional time, it may be best to drop that one temporarily and proceed with those that are obviously easier to work with. It has been found that the committee members,

who are learning while this process is on-going, become more proficient at identifying skills in the more difficult bands at a later point in the workshop.

11. The co-ordinator must be able to maintain a steady work pace. Although the work is exhausting, one cannot afford to reduce the pace if the chart is to be completed in the allotted time. The co-ordinator can stimulate a good work pace by example such as responding immediately to contributions and quickly writing and placing the card on the wall. Committee members tend to provide skill definitions more rapidly if working at this pace. The co-ordinator can also stimulate a steady work pace by soliciting skill definition contributions from members who may have some suggestions but are withholding these until there is an appropriate opportunity. If the co-ordinator sees that a member has become fatigued, restless, or uncomfortable, they may suggest to that individual to get up and stretch, have a cup of coffee, and even stand and watch the proceedings for a while to get a better perspective. Sometimes one talkative member can slow the pace. The co-ordinator must be concerned that the rest of the committee are not taking an opportunity to relax while one of their number does all the talking. The co-ordinator may have to be directive to draw the committee back to its assignment.

12. The co-ordinator must maintain momentum when it is present. Achievement by the committee essentially occurs in spurts. Frequently, the committee will be stymied for a while by the difficulty of finding the appropriate breakdown of skills or action words to specify skills. This will usually occur on encountering a new band, during a period of disagreement, or during the initial attempt at identifying General Areas of Competence. Once they do break through, however, after a period of struggling with the problem, one or more of the members may suddenly suggest a series of skills in fairly accurate form. The co-ordinator would slow this process if attempting to write and locate each skill on the wall individually. In such circumstances, it is useful to list quickly all the skills as they are mentioned and then take time to letter all the cards and place a series of skills on the wall at one time. It is important, however, to pause for a review of these skills to confirm that the committee as a whole agrees that the skills belong and are reasonably well stated.

13. The co-ordinator must encourage and promote brainstorming. The work of the first three-quarters of the workshop (i.e., all the activities prior to consolidation of the chart and the final structuring) is accomplished through a brainstorming approach. The co-ordinator encourages this process by writing cards and

placing them on the wall as quickly as possible after a definition is stated. This tends to keep contributions flowing, which is not the case if the committee is allowed to debate the worth of each definition before proceeding to another. This is not to say that the co-ordinator accepts and inserts all suggested definitions. Ill-stated skills do not get written up.

The co-ordinator must promote a free flow of ideas by encouraging contributions from each member. They have to be aware if individuals are not contributing and seek ways of getting them to make their initial contributions to the work. In some cases, the co-ordinator might provide the action words to get a less vocal member of the committee to start to contribute. That individual may feel that their competence is not equal to that of others on the committee and that their contribution is not needed. The act of extracting one or two skills from such persons and locating them on the wall will do much to promote a brainstorming approach for the entire committee.

14. The co-ordinator must maintain a positive approach to skill definition and the task at hand. Because of the newness of the assignment, there is a tendency on the part of individual members of DACUM committees to doubt the value of the work and to begin to treat details, even those that are obviously acceptable, rather negatively. When contributions are being questioned because there is doubt about the way in which the skill is stated or whether it is needed, the co-ordinator can encourage a positive approach by asking for consensus from the committee member. When faced with the consensus, in most cases the person who has not maintained a positive approach has to agree with what is being said.

15. The co-ordinator must be able to control and perhaps inhibit tendencies on the part of committee members to be overcritical. To encourage brainstorming, it is necessary to keep criticism to a minimum, particularly during the earlier stages of the exercise. Three kinds of criticism are damaging and must be controlled: First, consistent criticism of the contributions of other members. This tends to slow down the pace and instill a negative attitude on the part of the entire committee. *Second*, criticism of the value or the feasibility of the assignment. This tends to happen when there is difficulty in isolating a particular set of skills or selecting appropriate terminology. *Finally*, resistance to dealing with issues being discussed. There may be some aspect of the work in which individuals have not had training or an opportunity to develop skills. Some individuals

resist even having the others discuss these skills because they feel they may be discredited if they cannot contribute.

16. The co-ordinator must be able to control and assist in final clarification of skills. In early stages of the committee work (particularly the first band) it is possible to persevere in having the committee provide clear, complete definitions. If this is successful, it reduces pressure in later stages because committee members will have developed skills that will enable them to specify the remainder of the chart much more clearly and easily. However, in later stages time becomes more important and it is often necessary to postpone clarification of the skills until the latter part of the workshop. This enables the committee to get on with the job of isolating and beginning to define skills.

    Clarification is essential as one of the final tasks of the workshop. The co-ordinator must be able to encourage the committee to re-examine all the skill definitions with particular attention to those suspected to not be clearly stated. Committee members may resist this activity as they may feel they have done a good job in their original attempts at specifying the skills. It is, however, useful for the co-ordinator to review each skill on the chart, asking for clarification. The co-ordinator may be able to begin with some obviously weak definitions in order to convince the committee that clarification is required.

17. The co-ordinator must be able to allow (and encourage) the committee to talk out issues on its own. Issues are raised that the co-ordinator cannot resolve because the committee has not yet put its trust in them or because it rejects one or more of the DACUM principles. A useful activity is for the co-ordinator to stop talking and cease functioning as leader of the group. The co-ordinator can let conversation ramble for a time, observing what is happening, perhaps even asking questions, but offering no direction. Frequently a committee, at the insistence of one or two of its members, will come to grips with the problem and suggest that they are not going to complete their assignment if they do not drop personal issues and begin to work under co-ordinator direction.

    Most committees need this sort of leeway at some point during the workshop. If sensing a loss of control of the committee, or that the committee is not working within the specified framework, it is important for the coordinator to risk turning control over to the committee members to make them realize that they do have to work on this assignment under the co-ordinator's direction and that they have to operate within the framework in order to complete the task..

A second circumstance in which this is useful is where one or more individuals reject some of the basic concepts or guidelines or even the co-ordinator's role of directing the process. Frequently an opportunity for the group to talk out the problem (or a related problem) will enable the committee to control those individuals, thus shifting the onus from the co-ordinator.

18. The co-ordinator must display commonsense. This would appear to be a rather nebulous skill definition, but nevertheless it is a necessary skill. The entire procedure is a relatively simple commonsense approach to the problem of specifying training requirements. It is not commonsense to allow the simplicity of the approach to be complicated by the airing of committee members' views on learning, education systems, training programs, and a variety of similar concerns such as unionism, socialism, and motivation to work. The co-ordinator should permit some satisfaction of this need on the part of committee members but should avoid becoming personally involved in the discussions unless they are leading to disorientation of the committee. In such cases, the co-ordinator may have to make authoritative statements to clarify the issue in terms of the DACUM principles and then direct the committee back to its immediate assignment. Normally, however, these issues are quickly resolved by one of the committee members who will take much the same action. This frees the co-ordinator from the necessity of involvement and makes it easier to maintain the role of leader in a simple direct process with which most committees can readily identify. On the other hand, the co-ordinator who gets involved in rather peripheral arguments, philosophic debates, and in proving how much they know about the subject will tend to lead away from the very direct approach which they insist is required of the committee. This will discredit the co-ordinator in the eyes of the committee, and may result in loss the leadership role.

19. The co-ordinator must be able to encourage acceptance procedures. Because the activity is so new to committee members, they are sometimes puzzled by, or unaware of, the procedures in some of the chart development steps. Lack of knowledge of the details and value of the procedures will cause certain members to question specific activities heatedly and to resist applying suggested procedures as in:

    (a) Resistance to specifying certain kinds of skills or functions as prescribed by DACUM guidelines.

    (b) Resistance to completing a single band which "probably contains several hundred skills".

(c) Resistance to the practice of completing one band at a time.

(d) Resistance to relegation of structuring to the last step of analysis.

When it is apparent the issue will not be resolved quickly or easily, the co-ordinator will have to solicit acceptance of his or her suggested approach. The co-ordinator may advise the committee that they will, perhaps, react differently to the approach bonce they can see results of the sort the co-ordinator visualizes emerging. The co -ordinator may also refer them to results achieved in other DACUM charts where similar conditions and similar committee reactions existed.

In extreme cases, the co-ordinator might have to become directive with the committee and insist that they follow the co-ordinator's lead for a while so they can start to see how the chart will develop or how the specific skills break out. Sometimes this action is required when one or two extremely vocal members begin emphasizing their concern for the lack of knowledge in the program (or a similar issue) and try to lead the rest away from the DACUM focus.

20. The co-ordinator must be able to resolve disagreement among committee members about structure, skills, or skill definitions. Consensus is encouraged through the use of the wall, the cards, and the group procedures. Nevertheless, there are times when members do not agree.

Frequently disagreement relates to terminology. One member may prefer a word or phrase commonly used in their specialty while another will disagree and insist that the terminology of that specialty be used.

The co-ordinator can resolve such disputes in two ways, first by writing a definition including the alternative word(s) in parentheses, and second, by writing the two definitions and placing them adjacent to each other on the wall. This temporarily satisfies both members and allows the work to proceed. Eventually, another committee member may suggest an alternative that satisfies both. Or the co-ordinator may have to resolve the disagreement by getting the rest of the committee to let a definition stand until it is time for it to be further processed. In such a case, the card should be marked with a question mark or check mark to indicate that the definition must receive further attention.

It is interesting for the prospective co-ordinator to note that few of the disagreements really revolve around the issue at hand – whether the individual does or does not need a skill and whether it is accurately specified. Many of the disagreements revolve instead around such issues as an individual's wanting to see their particular school of thought in the occupation emphasized through specific use of its unique terminology. They do not want as much emphasis placed on one portion of the chart as on another in which their application of the occupation is more prominently described.

21. The co-ordinator must be able to determine when all skills are covered. This is a difficult decision for the co-ordinator because of their lack of knowledge of the occupation. Nevertheless, there are a number of useful strategies that can be applied to help in reaching a decision.

    (a) The co-ordinator can ask the committee if the job of specification is now complete. Consensus should be treated with caution, however, as the committee may not have the same need for completeness, or may be exhausted and want to finalize the chart quickly.

    (b) The co-ordinator can note the frequency with which the committee begins identifying skills which are really only subskills of those already identified. This is an indication that the committee is drying up in terms of identifying new skills or suggesting areas that have not been covered.

    (c) The co-ordinator may notice that the conversation of the committee has tended to shift to matters other than the specification of skills.

    (d) The co-ordinator may note while working on one band that the committee has begun to mention skills that are already included in another. This is an indication that they are only seeing the same skills from a different perspective and that all that is required is to review the over-all structure of the chart to bring this into focus.

    (e) Finally, the co-ordinator can test completeness by beginning a skill-by-skill review of each of the bands on the chart, beginning with those attempted first in the assignment. This may be done for clarification of the skill definitions or for some other purpose, but it does confirm to the co-ordinator that the committee has few, if any, additional skills to offer, and they know that the job is essentially complete.

    It is important that the co-ordinator apply these skills quickly when it is suspected the job is complete. Prolonging analysis could break down the committee's positive reaction to the assignment and influence it to query legitimate decisions made earlier. On seeing this begin to occur, the co-ordinator should terminate the skill specification activity and initiate the structuring of the chart.

22. The co-ordinator must be able to terminate sessions with committee members in a manner that leaves them with a favorable reaction to the process. This applies to both daily termination and to termination at the end of the workshop. Daily termination should follow a brief review of progress and an indication of achievement expected the next day. Sometimes committee members are discouraged by progress made to that time. The co-ordinator can alleviate this by describing progress made in a similar time span by other committees who successfully developed charts for occupations of similar size and complexity. It is also useful to describe how work progresses more rapidly as committee members become more expert in isolating and specifying skills without time-consuming discussion. Final termination should include a recap of the workshop and of the use to which the chart will be put. Some committees like an explanation of what is going to happen to the definitions on the wall, how they are going to be reproduced on paper and subsequently produced in quantity for distribution, and how they will be used in a training program. Ten or 15 minutes spent in explaining this process appears valuable in assuring that committee members will leave the workshop in a positive frame of mind. Most are mentally and physically exhausted when the workshop is over, and it is important to pick them up so that they do not leave the assignment with a negative feeling which they may relay to others.

23. The co-ordinator must be able to disband a committee if they find it is unable to handle the assignment. This is an essential skill that the co-ordinator is going to need at some point in time, particularly if other persons are responsible for planning program development, selection of committee participants, scheduling of sessions, etc. It is possible for quite inappropriate committee members to be selected; such persons may even constitute a majority. If this happens, there is no point in prolonging the agony. It can only hamper further curriculum development participation by the associated firms. It is best to bring the committee proceedings to a halt and disband the committee in as pleasant a way as possible.

One way of accomplishing the above is to suggest that, because of a number of difficulties and for a number of reasons, the assignment will not be completed in the time available. It is useful to suggest that the project may have been undertaken without adequate preview of the occupation and its specialties, that a larger and more diverse committee should be selected, and that the present work will be a starting point for the new committee, thus reducing its time and efforts. After such explanation, the committee members will likely agree to disband – they no doubt will welcome the opportunity to be rid of a distasteful assignment they are unable to complete and to be relieved of it in a way that saves face.

At a less critical level, it may be necessary for the co-ordinator to remove a single committee member after it has become apparent that they do not have either the insight or the skill to specify the requirements of the occupation and is only disrupting the activities of the committee as a whole. Or the co-ordinator may decide to proceed, relying on the other members of the group to ignore the objections of the disruptive person. This person may voluntarily withdraw. In severe cases, it may be necessary for the co-ordinator to meet them in private to point out in what ways they are disrupting the workshop and ask or insist that they withdraw.

These circumstances, however, are rare and seldom involve persons who are highly competent in their occupation. Usually disruptive members are persons who do not work directly in the occupation or who have entered the workshop with biases or misconceptions about the project because they are misinformed about its intent and procedures.

POTENTIAL COMMITTEE CHALLENGES

The foregoing suggested techniques for organizing committees and conducting committee workshops to develop DACUM charts are stated in terms of the functions of the co-ordinator and the demands that must place on the committee in order to achieve quality. Nevertheless, there are a number of situations that can and will interfere with chart development. The following are problems that have been encountered. The co-ordinator should be aware of these, and take the suggested corrective action to maintain committee focus and better assure the quality of the analysis task.

1. **<u>Committee Too Small</u>**

   A committee of three or four persons presents special problems. Normally members serve as a sounding board for the co-ordinator, helping to determine if contributions are accurate and applicable in the wide range of activities in the occupation. If the committee is too small, the co-ordinator has less opportunity to verify accuracy. First, there is a tendency for one person to dominate. It is easier for one person to make most of the contributions and cast the others in a supporting, confirming role. Second, small committees selected on a regional or local basis tend to focus their contributions on immediate needs even though the task calls for wider coverage. Finally, small committees tend to focus on a particular area or specialty and may be reluctant to explore diverse activities or specialties in the occupation.

   The co-ordinator must consistently steer discussion away from the single person, the local community, or the single specialty in the occupation. The co-ordinator may have to ignore the dominant person at times and solicit contributions from the others, casting the dominant person in the role of confirming other contributions. When a small committee becomes too localized or begins to focus on a familiar specialty, the co-ordinator should periodically halt proceedings for a review, pointing out the previously established boundaries and range of application of the occupation. It is also useful to solicit confirmation from committee members that they have adequate knowledge of or prior experiences in the applications they are tending to de-emphasize. In other words, it may be necessary to reconfirm for them that they are indeed capable of handling the entire scope of the analysis. The co-ordinator can directly broaden the coverage of the analysis by consistently asking the committee if each definition would apply in and is adequately stated for specific regions or firms he might designate.

2. **<u>Committee Too Large</u>**

   In cases where committees are very large (15 or more) problems of a different sort appear. A number of committee members make relatively few contributions unless a definite plan is made to stimulate the contribution of each member. Overt efforts to do this, however, might dampen the enthusiasm of more vocal committee members who obviously are ready to specify skill definitions they know must appear on the chart.

In some cases the large committees will consist of a number of members who are content to sit back and allow a more vocal group to provide most of the contributions. In the interest of the assignment, the co-ordinator may allow this to continue throughout the workshop. However, steps must be taken to ensure that it does not become a problem. The co-ordinator can periodically ask specific members who are less vocal to describe applications of skills in their own firms or specialties. This gets them participating and gives them an opportunity to describe differences and to help in specifying the skills more accurately. In reality, they are beginning to contribute skill definitions of their own which in turn generates enthusiasm for becoming a part of the skill specification process.

The co-ordinator can also involve the less vocal committee members when the prime contributors run into difficulty over wording and, more importantly, during the final stages of chart development in order to ensure the skill definition is suitable for their own and other environments.

3. **Disadvantageous Seating Arrangements**

Seating must be arranged so all persons can see the wall surface and read the definitions. In large committees, the more vocal participants often cluster in the front row and block the view of those who sit behind. Through some simple techniques, the co-ordinator can begin by arranging the chairs close together in two rows so there is not need for a third row. Second, the co-ordinator can place the front row four or five feet from the wall. This brings those in front into close contact with the wall and allows the back rows to move closer. It also tends to balance contributions, as those in front may have to rely on those behind to read the extremities of the chart. Third, the co-ordinator must take steps to place persons with audio or visual difficulties to best advantage. Those having difficulty in reading the cards from a distance should be moved to the front (which also provides an opportunity to request that a more vocal member move to the back). Similarly, persons with hearing problems should be situated near the co-ordinator and the center of discussion. If such arrangements are not made, these persons will miss points and later make inappropriate contributions.

4. **Late Arrivals for Orientation**

Orientation provides the framework for the workshop, and it is important that all persons be present when it begins. Some persons attend meetings only to present a point of view. They do not intend to participate full-time. Others arrive late due to unavoidable circumstances.

It has been found useful to orient these persons immediately and in private. This may be done by stopping for a coffee break. In some committee work, the presence of a second co-ordinator has enabled one to leave the workshop, orient the new arrival, and return with him or her to observe for a time and review work completed.

A late arrival will disrupt committee proceedings if not provided with orientation prior to making contributions. If there is no opportunity to do this immediately on entry, it is best to ask the late arriver privately to refrain from contributing until the individual has been provided with appropriate orientation. The late arriver will learn a lot by observing and will not feel compelled to debate issues at once.

5. **Persons Who Treat the Workshop as Just Another Meeting**

Occasionally, one encounters persons, particularly those who are in peripheral positions in the occupation, who attend a large number of meetings. They view curriculum and similar meetings as opportunities to renew old acquaintances, to discuss a variety of issues, and to raise special issues of their own.

It is difficult to convince such a person that the workshop is an activity which demands a lot of hard work be done in a short period of time and that he or she must quickly learn to work within the required framework if the job is to be done. It is best to take the individual aside at the first opportunity such as a coffee break to discuss the issues and to encourage taking a more objective view in working as part of the team.

6. **Persons Concerned with the Prestige of the Occupation**

One sometimes encounters an individual who is convinced that the prestige of their occupation will be enhanced by the prestige of the training program. This individual is unwilling to allow an activity of this sort to clarify exactly what the occupation is about lest this expose its simplicity. That individual will talk around issues and attempt to inflate them rather than share in the process of specifying a number of easy-to-define skills. A committee can work quite rapidly in specifying the more manipulative, procedural skills of the occupation, but this individual will try to involve the committee in discussing related issues such as philosophy of the occupation, the long-range future, and the effects of changing technology.

There are several techniques which the co-ordinator can apply to overcome this kind of resistance.

a. The co-ordinator can ignore the individual and use others in the committee for contributions to the specific area or band in the chart that is being analyzed. While this person will resist and attempt to make some contributions, the co-ordinator should ignore these and allow the rest of the committee to contribute their specifications. The member may react by falling silent and may subsequently begin to participate as part of a committee. If the resistant committee member reacts by becoming even more vocal, the other members can usually be relied on to take action to reduce his or her interference.

b. The co-ordinator can take the individual aside to re-explain the nature of the exercise and even to suggest that the resistant committee member consider leaving the workshop if the co-ordinator thinks this individual cannot participate.

c. Occasionally such a person will insist that there are really only one or two skills in an area being analyzed or that the area is not significant or worthy of this kind of analysis. A useful technique is to proceed over their objections and assist the others in defining a number of skills in that area. This will expose the resistant committee member's unreasonable attitude and arguments to the rest of the committee as well as to himself-or-herself. In short, this is a definite move to turn the rest of the committee on the resistant committee members so that they, with their occupational expertise, can control a situation the co-ordinator cannot control.

7. **Persons Concerned with Training for Purposes of Prestige**

Some persons feel that if the chart reflects sophisticated theories and principles from a variety of fields it will make the graduate appear more sophisticated and thus enhance the prestige of the occupation. These persons are sometimes difficult to detect and subsequently handle because one is never sure whether specific information and skills are required until the co-ordinator can generate enough debate. Sometimes a person so concerned will influence the remainder of the committee to specify unnecessary content. The co-ordinator must be alert to the fact that they may be being influenced by someone or something other than their professional judgment. In addition to the techniques recommended in (6), the co-ordinator can refer the committee to other workshops where this tendency was present, describe the subsequent difficulties it caused, and suggest that this committee would not wish to dissipate effort in this way. Most members will jump at the opportunity to reject the influence of the person who initiated the problem.

8. **Persons Concerned with Knowledge for the Sake of Knowledge**

Persons who feel strongly about the dominant place of knowledge in training systems tend to emanate from three sources:

a. There are persons in evolving occupations which have been ill-specified in terms of skill requirements. This is particularly noticeable in occupations that are evolving from several other occupations. There is a tendency to guess at what knowledge is required for application in several areas of expertise and assume this will enable the graduate to function at once in a new occupational role.

b. There are persons in occupations which have traditionally provided on-the-job training with knowledge being provided on a release basis as an external activity at a technical institute or trade school. They see training as that portion of the individual's development that occurs in the external institution. They have difficulty in specifying what the individual does on the job and what competence he must acquire there.

c. There are persons in nonprofessional occupations which operate under strong professional direction or control. The professional, because his or her own training was highly knowledge-oriented, is usually not accustomed to specifying skills in the way that is required and may tend to resist doing this, feeling that knowledge in itself is more important.

Sometimes there is a strong feeling that a wide background of information and theory is essential to enable the employee to speak intelligently about their own field, as well as to perform capably, in order to be a credit to the occupation. In such cases it is useful for the co-ordinator to draw on examples which detract from this feeling. It is easy to point to occupations such as nursing or teaching in which increasing emphasis was placed on knowledge to the exclusion of useful occupational skills. This is one place in which it may be necessary to stop and debate some of the issues before proceeding. Persons who feel strongly about this issue will resist committee activities until such debate takes place.

9. **People Who Believe that Knowledge Leads Directly to Performance**

Self-trained persons who read extensively in order to keep informed in their field sometimes have difficulty in isolating and specifying skills. They attribute their own success primarily to the fact that they accumulated a good deal of knowledge, which, to them, is important. Consequently they prefer to specify competence by defining the elements of knowledge which they feel contribute to the competence.

Such persons are generally more difficult to work with than formally trained committee members, whose contributions are typically more precise. The co-ordinator must apply extra effort in assisting such persons to convert their ideas and contributions into skill definitions. Their input is, nevertheless, important for they generally have a wide background that can be capitalized on to improve the coverage of the chart.

10. **Persons Concerned with Problem-Solving, Analytical Thinking as the Prime Requisite**

There are those who believe that the analytical problem-solving thought process is the most critical component of any training program. They refuse to participate in direct specification of activities and functions in which the individual must apply knowledge, and they discourage the attempts of others to do this. The co-ordinator frequently must counteract this by ignoring such persons and focusing attention on those who are contributing skill definitions.

11. **Persons Concerned with Attitudes as Opposed to Skills**

Some committee members express more concern for desirable employee attitudes than for skill specification. Such a person will argue that the problem in an organization is attitudes and not skill weakness, and will attempt to divert discussion away from skill definition and toward attitudes. This may be due to inability to specify skills because of lack of detailed knowledge of the occupation. Or it may be due to emphasis in a current work role that is related to employee relations or over-all productivity and, consequently, to concern for workforce attitudes.

The co-ordinator can apply three techniques to encourage such a person to function as a member of the committee. First, the co-ordinator can redescribe and expand on the rationale for first obtaining a comprehensive description of skills required. It is impossible to develop appropriate attitudes if there is not a suitable skill or competency base on which to build. Second, the co-ordinator can ask what is meant by the attitude being discussed, and how it would be manifest in the work environment. Often members will, in spite of themselves, begin to specify a number of skills which can be recorded on the wall. Where this has been successful, it has been apparent that the member was specifying attitudes because neither the attitude focused committee member nor the other members had been able to define the related skills. As a final resort, the co-ordinator may have to allow such a person to talk out their concern, depending on other members to control this person when repeated reference to attitudes interferes too much with their work.

12. <u>Persons Concerned with the Technicalities of Correct Terminology</u>

Occasionally one encounters an individual who is concerned with the status of the occupation and will insist that "correct" terminology be used in all application. This individual will slow the pace of committee achievement by wanting to debate the adequacy of each skill as it is specified. This inhibits the brainstorming process. This happens most frequently in workshops for occupations in which there is current debate between schools of thought.

The co-ordinator can readily resolve this problem by agreeing to use both of two suggested definitions. Frequently, all that is involved is a choice between two descriptive words. This can be settled by placing one of the words in parentheses behind the other to satisfy both proponents.

Another technique is for the co-ordinator to keep insisting that all editorial review be reserved for the latter portion of the workshop. The co-ordinator must emphasize that brainstorming must continue and that final editing will be done at an appropriate time in the development of the chart.

13. <u>Persons with Narrow Learning Experiences</u>

Some occupations have a history of standardized training to which most who have achieved occupational competence have been subjected. This might be a block release information theory training program, a process of indentureship, or employment in a series of sub-jobs until the learner has adequately performed in each and is allowed finally to perform the real skills of the occupation. In such cases, committee members will frequently question the wisdom of changing this pattern. They come up with such arguments as "There are intrinsic benefits for persons who have to learn in this way", "It's good discipline", "It will make a better man out of him".

Such situations demand frequent review of the DACUM principles. The co-ordinator must go beyond the initial brief orientation and draw on rationale that supports the use of this procedure. It is also necessary for the co-ordinator to assure committee members that the DACUM system contains similar learning experiences and that the learner is soon going to have to demonstrate perseverance in achieving, ability in completing skills, and interest in furthering in the occupation.

Another person of this sort is the professional who believes all learning takes place through books and lectures. This type of person can frequently be encountered in looking at an occupation directly supporting a professional field. Books and lectures are mandatory for most professionals, and they feel that others should learn in the same way in order to be as adaptive and creative as they have been in their occupation.

14. Persons Who Believe There is Only One Way of Training for Their Field

One may occasionally encounter difficulty with an individual in an occupation with a long history of reasonably successful training. It is assumed that this is the optimum method of training for the occupation and that nothing should be allowed to change it. This sometimes becomes apparent during the restructuring of the chart in terms of establishing sequencing. If a particular sequence of skill acquisition has been the accepted mode in the field for many years, the individual will want to see this pattern repeated, feeling that someone at some point in time did a careful analysis and discovered an optimum way for providing training. This individual sometimes fails to see that it may have been established by accident or through hasty decision-making which resulted in a standard pattern because the training institutions in that field wanted standardization and merely adopted the initial pattern. In such cases, the co-ordinator should halt proceedings, explore these issues, try to determine the origin of the pattern, and determine its suitability for application in the DACUM system.

15. The Person Who Rejects the DACUM Approach

Occasionally one runs into a committee member who dislikes the DACUM approach because of its permissiveness, feeling it is too liberal in allowing people to determine what they are going to learn and how they are going to learn it. This individual suspects this may cause a breakdown of discipline considered necessary in the occupation.

This individual is typical of persons who function in an authoritative or autocratic fashion in relation to the people they employ. They fear the development of a new breed of workers who are self-starting and self-thinking and who may take views quite opposed to conventional practice. They can frequently be detected by such remarks as, "There is nothing much wrong with our system right now. We just need to tighten up entry requirements so that a lot of people who have been getting in won't be getting in any more. Then we'll only take the cream of the crop for our occupation."

A most useful technique for dealing with such cases is for the co-ordinator to involve other members of the committee in discussing these issues. Normally the co-ordinator can rely on one or more committee members to be adequately alert to the potential of the DACUM process (even with limited exposure) to counterbalance the contributions of the dissenting committee member.

16. The Committee that Talks for the Sake of Talk

Some committees are heavily weighted with persons who like to attend meetings, are quite articulate, and enjoy discussion. They prefer to avoid the painstaking work at hand and treat the committee work as an opportunity to air views.

If this attitude dominates and committee work begins to suffer, there is little the co-ordinator can do. Efforts have been made in the past to apply techniques such as attempting to get the committee to focus more clearly on objectives or attempting to get it to pace itself toward completion of a set of goals. These have seldom been effective. In extreme cases it has been found necessary to disband the committee and resume DACUM charting with a new committee.

17. The Negative Critic

There are persons who excel at criticizing the contributions of others: "That skill isn't specified correctly", "That skill really doesn't apply", "That is a rather insignificant skill to be placing in an occupation like ours", "It's really much more complex than we have suggested". At the same time they will avoid making positive contributions.

Such persons may normally function in negative controlling or monitoring roles and not be comfortable in the positive brainstorming process.

One useful technique is to listen alertly to their conversation and promptly write and place a card on the wall when they begin to discuss what could be an identifiable skill. Specification of a series of skills in this way has been effective in converting some to a positive approach.

The only other useful technique has been to encourage the committee to deal with the problem. The co-ordinator should avoid personally debating the issues raised. This rarely succeeds because it is the negative approach, rather than the issues, that is the problem.

18. <u>The Person Who is Afraid to Contribute for Fear of Exposing Ignorance</u>

Occasionally one encounters a well-qualified recognized expert who has always worked in a situation in which they did not have to describe the characteristics or requirements of their occupation. Such an individual avoids contributing even though they appear to know what is transpiring in the workshop and be capable of contributing. This individual may fear that their lack of verbal skill will indicate technical incompetence to their colleagues in the committee. It is important for the co-ordinator to detect such an individual almost as soon as the committee's work begins and encourage them to make contributions. This is easily done by discussing poorly worded contributions of others, and having the fearful individual help refine the definitions. The co-ordinator should also take every opportunity to solicit a contribution from the fearful individual so that theye may begin to feel like a contributing member of the group. Frequently, when such a person emerges from silence, they becomes the most valuable participant in the workshop because they are direct and do not over-verbalize.

19. <u>The Person Who Rejects Co-ordinator Leadership</u>

At times an individual will resist the leadership of the co-ordinator who is not an expert in the occupation, and distrust their ability to lead a committee in specifying requirements for a field about which they know little.

It is important in such cased to maintain leadership and to apply techniques that will overcome such misgivings. One way to provide examples of charts that have been developed by diverse committees and in which the co-ordinator had no more ability that they have in this particular occupation. Another technique is to describe the rationale of having an independent person perform in this role.

20. The Authority Figure Who Typically Controls

Some persons typically want to control a group and expect to lead any activity in which they become involved. If not controlled, they will focus discussion, issues, debates, and final decisions around themselves. It is interesting to note that this frequently occurs when most of the committee members have been selected from one firm or one specialty in the occupation. They may have become accustomed to allowing a dominant individual among them to chair meetings and lead activities, and, as a consequence, they allow the authority figure to assume leadership in the DACUM workshop. Such persons are difficult to control, and at times it is necessary to apply environmental techniques to overcome this difficulty. It may be necessary, for example, to change the seating arrangements to place the dominant individual either on the periphery of the group or next to the co-ordinator where they may be more easily controlled. In extreme cases, the co-ordinator may have to assert responsibility and challenge the member, demanding that they cease trying to control the group.

21. Instructors Concerned about the Teaching Role

The inclusion of instructors on committees has not worked out well either from the point of view of having the chart developed within a reasonable period of time or from the point of view of focusing as directly as possible on the requirements of the occupation. While there are benefits for the instructor in terms of opportunity to learn more about the occupation and the views of its experts, the instructor's participation tends to hamper the committee process. In cases where instructors must participate, it is frequently necessary to remind them that the issue is not what to teach or how to teach but the requirements of the occupation. Maintaining this perspective for instructors places a good deal of pressure on the co-ordinator, and it has been found that committees function more effectively if no instructors are present. If there are facilities available, it is useful to have instructors and other observers stationed in an adjacent room from which they can view the proceedings through closed circuit T.V.

22. Persons Who Will Not Address the Co-ordinator

Sometimes committee members appear to misread the co-ordinator's role and consistently disregard the co-ordinator. Contributions must go through the co-ordinator if he or she is to maintain control of the process.

The co-ordinator may insist that all contributions be directed to the co-ordinator and refuse to write and put up any definitions that are not so directed. Arrangements may be made to have the offenders located near the co-ordinator so they will have to address the co-ordinator while studying or commenting on the wall.

23. The Person Who Keeps Attention Away from the Wall

An occasional committee member will resent the idea of working with a wall. Few persons are used to working with this kind of format or with the brainstorming approach. An occasional member may ignore the wall when fearing the chart is developing in the wrong way, or on losing sight of objectives. This individual will turn to discuss issues with other members, will make notes, will write out statements rather than view the statements on the wall, and, in effect, will do everything but use the wall as a focus.

It is possible to overcome this by changing the environment. If the offender is located in the back of the group, he or she may be relocated in the front near the co-ordinator. If the individual is already at the front and tends to turn around to face the group while working with the wall, it may be necessary to shift that person to the back of the room so that they have to face the wall while talking to others. At times it may be necessary to point out to the offender exactly what he or she is doing and how it is affecting the process. The individual can be warned that others may want to do the same thing and that the committee may lose its focus. Frequently, this will change the person's attitude, although it may be necessary at times to remind the individual that he or she is a part of a group using the wall as a medium.

24. The DACUM Learning Enthusiast

Some persons have had an opportunity to learn about DACUM beforehand and have become over-enthused about its potential for occupational definition and learning. These might be persons who have been previously exposed to DACUM to solicit their assistance in selecting committee members. Or they might be instructors (or prospective instructors) who expect to work with the system and are recruited as part of a committee.

These individuals at times tend to lose sight of the specific purpose of the committee. They may begin to think too far ahead and worry about structuring or sequencing when the skill definition process is not yet complete. They may not grasp the implications of each analysis step because they are too influenced by what they expect to see in the finished chart.

It is necessary to play down the contributions of such persons and recognize only those which are directly based on performance. If such a person is rather vocal and persistently disrupts proceedings with concerns about the training program, it is best to take directive action and explain to him or her in front of the group that this committee's concern is not with training, it is with accurate definition of the skills of the occupation. The training program will be the concern of another committee made up of persons more qualified for the task of specifying training.

SUMMARY

Chapter 5 discussed the importance of the co-ordinator. Successful DACUM projects are dependent upon a skilled co-ordinator, whose main function is to provide criteria, direction, guidelines, and analogies to help the learners accomplish tasks. Successful co-ordinators must possess many skills including: clear handwriting, familiarity with curriculums, ability to resolve "skill-knowledge" debates, patience, unyielding in applying DACUM principles, ability to conduct on-the-spot orientation of general principles, ability to determine when members are drifting from basic framework, able to keep attention on the DACUM wall, and assistance with composing skills definition statements. These abilities are characteristics of an experienced facilitator and leader in the context of a DACUM project: understanding that the learning method may be new to the committee members and encouraging them to stay focused on this new technique.

The co-ordinator is sure to face many challenges. This chapter provided a list of the most common challenges and possible solutions. Examples of these challenges include uncooperative individuals, large and small committees, persons who reject the DACUM approach, and those who reject the co-ordinator's leadership. Solutions typically involve keeping the project focused on the DACUM approach in order to eventually convince the committee to adopt this new method and by using fellow committee members to influence other members to join them in embracing a new model.

REFERENCES

Adams, R. E. (1975). *DACUM: Approach to curriculum, learning, and evaluation in occupational training*. Ottawa: Dept. of Regional Economic Expansion.

COMMITTEE SELECTION & CHARTING PREPARATION

Chapter 6 is a continuation of the Chart Development element within the Development Model for DACUM Learning Program (see Figure 6-1).

DEVELOPMENT MODEL FOR DACUM LEARNING PROGRAM

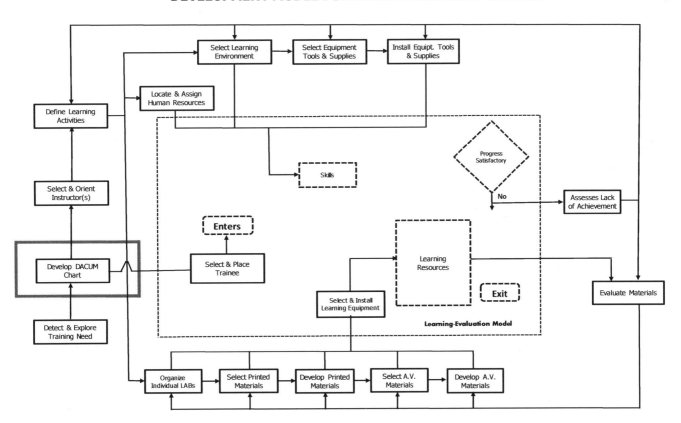

Figure 6-1. Development Model for DACUM Learning Program

The purpose of this chapter is to help practitioners understand the guidelines for selecting committee members and ensuring the charting environment is conducive as well as the necessary supplies for successful charting. The chapter first explores the committee selection by specifically describing guidelines to be used in identifying workers who are capable of contributing and positively influencing the work of the charting committee. The chapter then presents the necessary resources and physical arrangement for the charting room.

COMMITTEE SELECTION

Before beginning to select committee members, it is useful to take a brief look at the occupation to determine the range of its organizational applications, the nature of the firms employing its skills (for instance, large or small firms), and jobs contained within the occupation.

For most occupations the analysis can and should be conducted on a national basis. The skills of an occupation tend to be somewhat the same regardless of the locality in which they are applied, and the definition of the skill structure can be assumed to be relatively standardized. Once a comprehensive national analysis is completed, local or regional committees can use the model developed by the national group. This would clarify the extent to which each skill is needed by local practitioners and to isolate those skills that should not be considered or stressed in a training program designed to provide manpower for a specific locality.

In selecting a committee one should try to ensure that it is representative of the entire region that is being considered for application. In Canada for example, there might be representation from each province, or from each major region when differences between provincial applications are minimal. Considerations in ensuring coverage of the occupation are:

1. **Adequacy of coverage of the major defined categories of a specialty or occupation.** In an occupation such as Automotive Mechanics, one need only select an adequate number of persons qualified to perform in the occupation. This is because the skills required in the wide range of work environments and in large and small firms are much the same and would be defined in much the same way. On the other hand, in an occupation such as Electronics Technology, it is necessary to involve as committee members specialists from each of the specialties of the occupation, such as repair, troubleshooting, design, development, supervision.

2. **The size of the typical firms that utilize the occupation.** If the firm is large, the occupation may be broken down into specialties within the firm. Consequently, representatives of the large firm would see the occupation as having several specialties, each with a narrow range of highly developed skills. On the other hand, representatives of the small firm employing only one or two persons who are expected to perform the entire range of duties of the occupation would specify more skills, including some that might not properly be part of the occupation even though job incumbents might be applying them. If all representatives are selected from either large or small firms, the resulting document is unlikely to serve as a universal description of the occupation.

3. **Adequacy of coverage of concentrations of specialization in the field.** In a field such as welding, one might find the application of specialized equipment and techniques and a subsequent demand for relatively sophisticated skills in a metropolitan area surrounding, for example, an aircraft or aerospace industrial complex. It cannot be assumed that the skills required in this concentration are those required in another kind of concentration such as one might find around a fabrication industry in a smaller, less central location.

4. **Minimal committee size.** Frequently the above requirements can be met in a rather small committee. It is possible to locate capable people who are able to relate the analysis work to several of the specialties or locations. For example, it may be possible to recruit as a committee member an experienced welder who has worked in large firms, on large rough welding jobs, in specialized organizations utilizing sophisticated techniques, and in a small firm which demanded diversity of skills. This individual is quite capable of relating the requirements of each of these specialties to the analysis committee. In fact, the sort of person who has performed in more than one specialty or situation is often a more valuable committee member. This individual is less likely to over-emphasize one specialty or to be unaware of the relationship between the various specialties and the degree of compatibility of functions within his or her occupation.

In addition to the requirement that the committee include representation of the major categories and specialties in the occupation, individual members should have the following qualifications:

1. **Competence in the occupation.** The individual chosen to work on a DACUM development committee must have worked, or be working, in the occupation, have developed a high degree of skill, and be aware of current developments and needs in the field. Sometimes persons prominent in a field are not

competent in the occupation. For example, one might be a personnel manager with an electronics firm and be considered quite an expert in electronics personnel selection and training and yet not be able to contribute to an analysis of Electronics Technology or Electronics Service and Repair.

If possible, the person must also be competent in terms of training. In newly evolved occupations there may be a tendency to select persons who are not fully skilled in all aspects of the occupation. In a new technology, for example, jobs may be occupied by persons who were formerly trained at a craft level and gradually acquired on the job many of the skills required of a more technical occupation. On the other hand, some jobs within occupations may be occupied by persons trained at a higher level. It has been found necessary in some industries to install professionally trained personnel such as engineers in what might normally be considered technician level jobs.

Another type of person who may not currently be technically competent in the field is the individual who has formerly performed to a satisfactory level in the field but has since become a union official, an instructor in a training program, a manager, etc.

2. **Full employment in the field**. It is important to select persons with full-time involvement in the occupation. They may be supervisory personnel, although in this case they should be directly supervising persons performing the functions that are to be analyzed. The committee can function with persons who have been somewhat removed from the occupation but the DACUM charting process becomes much harder because they have more difficulty in accurately specifying contributions to the chart and in organizing and integrating the details that must be part of the occupation. They may have an excellent overview of the occupation but lack the facility to present organized detail due to the lack of current detailed knowledge of the occupation.

3. **Forward thinking and considered by associates to be alert**. It is important that the analysis be somewhat predictive. Due to the lead time necessary to develop and operate training programs, it is necessary to predict the set of skills trainees will require. The ideal committee member is a person who keeps abreast of the field by reading trade magazines or journals and explores the potential of new inventions and who can apply relevant knowledge to the analysis. The member who is not able or refuses to consider anything beyond what people actually do now will not be able to contribute effectively.

4. **Capability of verbalizing the needs or skills of the occupation**. It is important to select persons who are not only skilled but have demonstrated an ability to describe skills and needs orally. Some of the most highly skilled people may be incapable of verbalizing exactly what they do and the requirements of their occupation even though they are extremely capable of performing the work.

5. **Capability of functioning as a member of a group**. Past performance in groups would indicate whether or not an individual has the ability to function in a group without dominating or being dominated, whether they are likely to be a contributing member, and whether the individual is likely to react well to criticism or having their contributions analyzed and re-organized.

6. **Freedom from bias**. The committee member must be open-minded and free of biases related to training methods, training time, training costs, qualifications, status of the occupation, etc., which might prevent functioning effectively as part of the team or make it difficult for the individual to take a fresh look at his or her occupation. Some who might otherwise be selected might be excluded on this basis. A person filling an auxiliary role such as union leader might have a great deal of information about the field but be influenced by his or her auxiliary role more than by the real requirements.

> *For this reason instructors do not perform well and are not recommended for inclusion on DACUM chart committees. It has been found, through a number of experiences, that the committee work tends to slow down and that the organizational representatives' work is hampered by the inclusion of an instructor (particularly one who is going to install the chart in their course). While some instructors are capable of functioning well for the entire duration of a committee session, it is seldom worth the risk of selecting someone with strong biases.*

> *Part of the problem is that the instructor spends time visualizing what this chart, when completed, is going to mean when they later have to apply it in the development and operation of a training program. The instructor will resist (and will also encourage the other members of the committee to resist) stating some skills for which it is likely to be extremely difficult to provide instruction. Further, the instructor will visualize difficulties due to cost, or problems in providing realistic learning experiences, or lack of space.*

> *The instructor will also resist including in the chart those skills which they themselves do not possess. These may be skills that the instructor had little opportunity to learn or apply in former work experience and, therefore, has not attempted to include in their training programs. The instructor may feel incapable*

of providing training in these skills, does not know what resources would be required, and will tend to delimit the committee's work to avoid dealing with anticipated problems.

Finally, the instructor tends to hamper analysis and specification of difficult-to-define skills such as analytical or problem-solving skills. Instructors for some current training programs are selected from among a number of occupationally skilled applicants on the basis of their superior theoretical knowledge and their ability to verbalize this knowledge. Through experience in a program in which information, concepts, and theories have priority and actual skill development is left to the organizational environment, the instructor may have developed the posture that information and theory are all that is required in training. The instructor will resist specification of theory-based analytical or problem-solving skills and encourage specification of the theory or knowledge itself; disrupting the committee's momentum during the process.

7. **Confidence.** The committee member must be competent and capable of self-direction. The committee member who functions best is aware of his or her abilities and can speak with confidence about the nature of the skills and the relative weight to be placed on each.

8. **Freedom to devote full-time for the required period.** If in selecting a committee it is found that one or two desirable members will be unable to attend all the sessions, it is best to eliminate these persons. Because the concept is new, it is particularly difficult for someone to step into the activity once it has begun. While a late arrival may be capable of mastering the concept and begin to function within two hours or so, these two hours often become lost time for the committee as a whole and little is gained by bringing in a person who is unable to attend the first and, indeed, all subsequent sessions. It must be clear to all participants that they must be free to attend and must attend all sessions.

A number of organizational people, particularly those who typically serve as volunteers on committees, have developed a habit of making a brief appearance and voicing their views quite strongly during the time they are present. Such contributions tend to disrupt the controlled developmental process that is taking place.

Integration of new or part-time committee members has only been accomplished by having more than one person with co-ordinator skills on hand during the sessions. In these circumstances the co-ordinator can take aside any new arrival and attempt to provide a short orientation before allowing the newcomer to participate with the group.

One way to ensure full-time participation is to provide daily reimbursement for the committee members and to make such reimbursement conditional on attendance over the entire period specified. This arrangement is somewhat new to educational or training curriculum work. Traditionally, training agencies have relied on voluntary participation by organizational personnel. It was felt that organization(s) should provide this resource since they are going to receive the benefits of this work in the form of trained personnel. However, there is a difference in the DACUM work in that the DACUM committee cannot effectively use the volunteer who normally sits on advisory or curriculum committees; the person, for instance, in a public relations role, part of whose job is to participate on panels and committees.

Experience has provided some additional clues for the avoidance of selection of committee members who are not really capable of contributing and who, in fact, can negatively influence the work of the committee.

It is important to make direct contact with prospective committee members. The person making the contacts should be familiar with the DACUM system, able to describe the nature of the assignment, and able to provide rationale for the DACUM approach.

Awkward and unfruitful experiences can result from selection and recruitment by letter:

1. Written requests to companies may be referred to and handled by a public relations officer. Because of the lack of knowledge about the assignment the public relations officer may nominate themselves or some other person who is not technically or personally suitable for the work.

2. Good prospective committee members may turn down the assignment because of a misunderstanding of what is expected of them. The type of person who normally avoids meetings or curriculum-development work might well be drawn to the DACUM approach to analysis, but because of incomplete information the prospective member rejects it.

In gathering leads on who might be appropriate resource persons, the co-ordinator or selector of the committee will sometimes be directed to a wrong choice. It is obviously best to reserve judgment and avoid committing a place on the committee until an individual has been personally contacted and assessed. One way to approach this is to suggest to the prospective member either by correspondence or telephone that there is a job to be done and you would like to discuss persons who might be suitable for this activity. The first step in the meeting is to describe the nature of the assignment, emphasizing some of the personal characteristics discussed above, and soliciting their views. *During the ensuing discussion you can form an opinion as to whether the selector possesses the desired characteristics. If you are convinced of this, then you can suggest that they appear to possess the necessary qualifications. If not, the individual need never know that they were being considered and rejected. .*

It is important to avoid encouraging someone to become a committee member if they are not really interested in this type of activity. The presence of such a person can be destructive to the chart development process.

Some persons who are very competent dislike being involved in external activities like DACUM work. Once it is apparent that a person feels this way, it is best to drop the matter and take advantage of the contact to obtain names of more suitable people.

It is important to avoid concession to political pressures in the occupation in selecting committee members. There may be pressures to include persons prominent in the field but not otherwise suitable, and it takes skill sometimes to avoid including these persons. There may be pressure, for example, to select a union official in order to gain greater acceptability for the final product. In such a case, it is best to contact the official and solicit his or her help in selecting the most capable person from the membership. Similarly, there may be pressure to involve persons who have spent a good deal of volunteer time working as members of vocational or career & technical education curriculum committees. It has been found in work to date that insistence on rejecting such persons is necessary. Again, they can be used as referral sources because of their knowledge of people in the field.

SUPPLIES & PHYSICAL ARRANGEMENTS

Once the co-ordinator and committee members have been selected, it is time to prepare the supplies and physical location for charting. While physical arrangements are relatively flexible, this section provides guidelines based on testing in the development of a number of charts. Over a period of time, a variety of techniques were tried. Many were rejected because they resulted in an incomplete assignment or an inferior chart. The techniques outlined here are recommended because they achieved the desired results.

The materials used are simple. All definitions are hand-lettered on either 3x5 or 4x6 file cards. The 4x6 file cards are used for the General Areas of Competence and are lettered somewhat larger than the 3x5 file cards which are used for each of the skills or behaviors identified. One package of 4x6 file cards is sufficient, but there should be 10 packages of 3x5 file cards on hand.

The cards are lettered with large felt-tipped pens. It is important that the tips be large enough to produce lettering that can be read from any position in the room. Thin-tipped pens result in difficulty in keeping the committee focused on the wall and specific cards. Approximately six pens should be on hand as they dry out and have to be interchanged frequently.

The cards are affixed to the wall surface with a plastic putty. The putty that has been found most useful for this purpose is "UHU tac" Scotch 3M adhesive putty which can be purchased at your local office supplies store (e.g. Staples). Approximately 10 sticks of this putty will be required for a single workshop.

The ideal space for DACUM chart development is a long, narrow room with an unbroken wall surface of at least 30 feet. The wall surface should be pleasant to the eyes and should be such that it will hold the plastic putty so that cards do not fall off during the workshop.

The most useful wall surface has been found to be prefinished plywood or simulated plywood paneling. The putty adheres well to this surface and it provides a good background for the cards.

Painted concrete block walls are adequate as long as the paint is not dull dry paint (which will not hold putty) and as long as the block material itself is not too rough.

A fully painted plaster wall is excellent provided that the paint is smooth enough and of a type to hold the putty. A flat dull paint will not hold the cards in place. High gloss paint is hard on committee members' eyes.

It is important that the wall surface be unbroken to prevent any artificial breaks in the chart. The longer the wall surface the better, because the committee, in working with General Areas of Competence that contain a great number of skills, will tend to be limited by the space and feel that they are finished when they have reached the end of the wall. It is crucial that they should not feel constrained by the lack of space.

A row of tables should be placed four to six feet from the wall, and the committee members seated behind the tables, facing the wall. The co-ordinator takes a position near the right edge of the wall and has a separate table for cards and lettering materials and to provide working space.

Chairs should be comfortable because committee members will have to sit continuously through the three- or four-day workshop. Most convenient are small swivel chairs that allow the individual to turn and address another member or the co-ordinator without moving in his or her chair and without straining. For small committees (four to eight members) it is best to place the chairs in a single row behind the small tables. For larger groups (10 or more) it is best to place the chairs in two rows or more. It is important that all chairs be close enough to the wall so that all committee members can read the definitions as they are placed on the wall.

The row of tables is not intended for paperwork, but to prevent the committee members from approaching the wall and tampering with the definitions. All additions or changes must be made by the co-ordinator who gets consensus from the committee for each move or change that is made. Without the tables certain committee members will get up and change something without obtaining consensus from the rest of the group, who may be unaware that a change is made until a later problem is encountered.

Lighting for a DACUM chart development workshop is extremely important. Few rooms contain adequate lighting to illuminate fully the critical working surface, and frequently it is necessary to provide additional lighting for the workshop. It is sometimes necessary to control natural light which may interfere with the reading of the definitions.

It is important to consider comfort of the committee members. The most useful rooms have good ventilation and temperature control. It is easy for committee members to lose interest and become drowsy if they have to work in a room that is too warm or that has poor ventilation. In fact, it is better to have a room that is slightly chilly and that has good fresh air. Sound also can be a problem. As an example, in one session in DACUM chart development it was necessary to work in a room directly over a workshop from which ensued pounding, sawing, and motor noises. At times these became too intense to talk over.

Some equipment is helpful in orienting the committee to the work. For example, it is helpful to develop audiovisual presentations that are used to acquaint committee members with the concept, a resulting training model, and a framework for completing the DACUM chart. A whiteboard is also useful for some aspects of the work. Also necessary is a battery of sample DACUM charts that have been completed for other occupations, not for detailed analysis to show members how to construct charts but simply to let them see how the process has been applied in other occupations.

It is also desirable to have on hand written material on DACUM for those who wish to supplement the information received during orientation. It has been found useful to place a brochure (see Appendix D) in the hands of committee members and lead them quickly through the brief illustrated text which describes the steps in DACUM chart development and the way in which the DACUM chart is used in the learning and subsequently in the work environment.

No additional resources should be allowed in the room. Textbooks and other resource materials can hinder the work of the committee. If available, they will be referred to quite extensively by some committee members (particularly those who are less skilled) who will try to lead the committee into using subdivisions and organization typically found in textbook tables of contents, chapter breakdowns, and listings of topics prepared in another context. They will be distracting to others, who may be tempted to retreat to them when under attack or when the group is developing an area of the chart with which they are not familiar.

DACUM development workshops are often best located in some independent location. It is frequently best to locate the workshop in a town or city that is away from the normal residence of the committee members. In this way they will all be away from office distractions and can devote the three days to the work.

The room itself is best located outside a training environment for three reasons. First, there is often a need on the part of the training institution to get its input into the DACUM development work. Instructors or other personnel like to sit-in and offer opinions and raise issues. Institutions like to make DACUM development workshops an opportunity for in-service training for instructional staff. While this might be useful, it tends to distract committee members. Second, some committee members tend to view DACUM development work as curriculum development rather than as occupational analysis. Location in a training institution tends to reinforce this view. Guided tours through training departments and other activities stimulate concern for curriculum matters rather than occupational analysis. Third, training institutions often see the DACUM development process as a useful public relations exercise. This it might be; but it cannot be allowed to interfere with the task of getting the analysis done within the reasonable time period that is suitable for the committee.

If it is felt necessary that instructors and others observe the committee's work, it is best to set up video recording service or closed circuit transmission to another room. This has not hampered the DACUM committee in its work and has tended to remove the pressure of having observers sit in the back of the room. If this is done, it is necessary to use video recorders that are capable of reading the cards as they are placed on the wall and also capable of scanning the entire wall to note the relative location and permit viewers to see structure as it begins to evolve. Some equipment that has been tried has not been capable of reading cards unless it was placed so close to the wall that it was incapable of scanning the remainder of the chart or of focusing in on committee members during their deliberations. Sound is extremely important. A good conference microphone, with hookups that will transmit the sound to the adjacent room, is necessary.

Scheduling of DACUM committee work is quite important when one considers the amount that is expected to be achieved during the course of the workshop. The committee should plan to put in a good long working day, each day, and have a specific target or set of targets for each day. A frequent problem when sessions were conducted in training institutions was that committee members were informed they would be expected to be on hand during normal working hours in a training institution (9 a.m. to 4 p.m.). The committee members normally were used to longer working days and would not have resisted working from 8 a.m. to 5, 6, or 7 p.m., thus adding a number of valuable hours to the workshop.

It is best to get an early start each day and have a flexible time schedule. The work progresses in spurts, with lengthy periods of discussion, review, and analysis followed by brief periods of rapid specification of a large number of skills. Such momentum should be maintained when it occurs and not broken off to accommodate a precise 12:00 o'clock lunch or 4:30 termination of the day's work.

Normally, committee sessions continue over a three-day period. This depends a great deal on the skills of the co-ordinator, the pace that can be maintained, the complexity of the occupation, and the ability of the committee members to analyze the occupation and verbalize the skills contained in it. Regardless of the nature of the occupation; however, there appears to be a relatively standardized pattern that does not vary a great deal in terms of time. The first one or two hours are spent in orientation, followed by a question period. Before the first morning is completed, the committee generally has agreed on the General Areas of Competence.

Sample 3-Day DACUM Charting Workshop Itinerary		
Date	**Activity**	**Duration**
Tuesday, January 6	Orientation	1-2 hours
	Question & Answers	30 minutes
	Review the Occupation	30 minutes
	Establishing General Areas of Competence	1-2 hours
	Lunch	1 hour
	First Skill Band	1-2 hours
	Skill Band Development	1-2 hours
Wednesday, January 7	Continuation of Skill Band Development	3-4 hours
	Lunch	1 hour
	Continuation of Skill Band Development	3-4 hours
Thursday, January 8	Completion of Unfinished Skill Bands	2-3 hours
	Review & Refine Terminology	1 hour
	Lunch	1 hour
	Skill Sequencing & Structuring	1-2 hours
	Final Agreement	1 hour

Figure 6-2. Sample 3-Day DACUM Charting Workshop Itinerary

Sometimes they will have also identified a few skills in one of the General Areas of Competence. By the end of the first day, at-least one and hopefully more of the bands will be completed. The second day is a continuation of this process until all the bands have been attempted and almost all have been completed. The third day is spent in completing any bands that are unfinished, in reviewing the work to ensure that no skills were overlooked, and in identifying areas that may have been avoided because of difficulty in specifying the skills contained therein. The last afternoon is spent in a quick review of all the skills to refine terminology, to broaden the scope of some skills, or to limit the scope of others now that the committee is more familiar with the method of writing the skill definitions. The last one and one-half to two hours will be spent in structuring the chart and in obtaining final agreement that the chart is a reasonably satisfactory identification of the skills of the occupation. Above is Figure 6 -2 which shows how a co-ordinator used time in a 3-Day DACUM Charting Workshop.

It is a good practice to have beverages and snacks on hand and to encourage individual members to stand up and stretch, get a beverage and/or snack, and then come back into the discussion, rather than having the group take a break simultaneously. It is difficult to get a committee functioning well again after taking a complete break. Except for a lunch break, it is best to keep the committee working.

SUMMARY

This chapter provided preparatory guidelines for DACUM chart development. First, the guidelines for selecting committee members were discussed. Committee members should be competent individuals fully engaged in the occupation having respective specialization in the field. Further, each expert should be forward thinking with the ability to verbally express skills, free of bias, and capable of functioning as a member of the group for the full duration of the workshop. Next, guidelines for selecting charting supplies and physical room arrangement were presented. Necessary supplies include cards (3x5; 4x6), large felt-tipped pens, and "UHU tac" Scotch 3M adhesive putty. The room selected for charting should provide adequate space, lighting, room temperature, appropriate levels of ventilation, walls which eliminate distractions, and comfortable tables and chairs.

REFERENCES

Adams, R. E. (1975). *DACUM: Approach to curriculum, learning, and evaluation in occupational training*. Ottawa: Dept. of Regional Economic Expansion.

7

DACUM CHART DEVELOPMENT

The accurate preparation of a DACUM chart is the most important aspect of the Development Model for a DACUM Learning Program (see Figure 7-1).

DEVELOPMENT MODEL FOR DACUM LEARNING PROGRAM

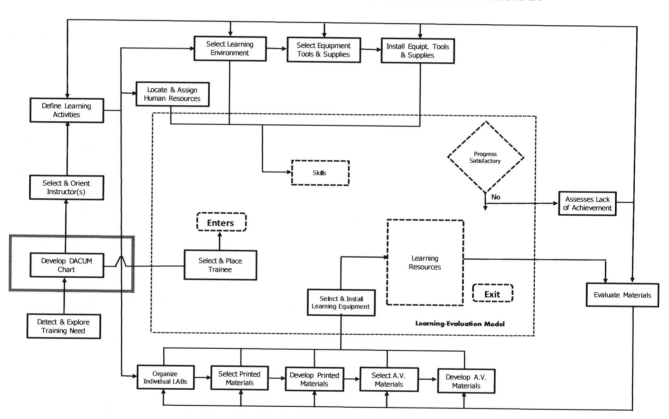

Figure 7-1. Development Model for DACUM Learning Program

As with most training programs utilizing behavioral objectives, the accurate specification of these objectives is critical. The reasons for this are obvious. First, the learner must have a clear and relevant statement of the training program objectives. The learner must know what skills the organization expects, in order to isolate suitable learning experiences as well as assess his or her own performance in a realistic way.

Second, if the chart is not well defined, the organizational representatives participating in its development will be dissatisfied, feeling that it does not adequately reflect the skills of the occupation. They may be left in doubt as to what the training program will produce and ultimately have difficulty in assessing the product to determine whether it fits their needs or, if not, in what way it is inadequate.

This chapter deals with the rationale, procedures, and specific techniques for development of DACUM charts. The intent is to provide a guide for those who wish to study the process in detail, perhaps preparing themselves for the role of co-ordinator of DACUM chart development committees. Detail is provided regarding desirable and undesirable characteristics of charts, along with descriptions of problems that may arise out of inaccurate application of chart development techniques.

The DACUM chart is, in effect, a form of occupational analysis conducted to determine requirements for a training program for the occupation. The DACUM analysis differs from conventional approaches to analysis in the following ways:

1. **Only observable behavior is identified.** Knowledge content is assumed to be supportive to the acquisition of the stated behavior and, therefore, need not be defined in this initial stage. This is preferable because undue concern with knowledge specification leads to specification of more knowledge than is actually required by most learners. If knowledge specification is not removed from the analysis process it tends to get primary emphasis and detracts from the task of identifying what people actually have to do.

2. **Skills are stated within the context of the DACUM rating scale**, and, as a result, the DACUM definitions take on their own unique characteristics. In other occupational analysis approaches it is assumed that someone will eventually produce achievement tests and performance criteria that will indicate whether the skill has actually been acquired to some predetermined standard. Various kinds of skills in various parts of the occupation will receive different specification treatment because it is assumed that someone else will later provide the needed specialty through the tests.

3. **The analysis is conducted by the industry** or other eventual users of the training product, with the DACUM chart an external specification of program goals, as opposed to the more prevalent practice of internal analysis by an instructor or instructors.

4. Because of (3) above **skill definitions encompass more activity** than the typical teacher-specified skill definitions.

5. **The analysis is conducted by means of dynamic group activity**. Under the direction of a co-ordinator, the industrial representatives learn to function as a team on each portion of the assignment as well as on over-all organization and structuring. No member is allowed to work as an individual as in some analysis approaches where individual writing assignments result in much preliminary specification that is difficult to integrate.

6. **The analysis results in a format that is directly applicable as a curriculum**. In most other forms of occupational analysis, it is necessary to embark on a lengthy and sometimes difficult task of converting analysis specifications to a format useful for the training program.

ORIENTATION

Orientation takes place during the first one and one-half to two hours of the first morning of a DACUM development workshop. It is a rather flexible, informal, non-technical presentation planned to provide a conceptual overview of DACUM rather than an introduction to a variety of technical details. It is designed to provide a framework or model within which the committee can function over the remainder of the workshop period. In the absence of this model, committees have tended to require additional time to complete the task, repeatedly raising questions or expressing doubts about various aspects of the system and failing to function as a cohesive unit. On the other hand, attempts at making the presentation too technical or formal have also resulted in difficulty. Each individual can approach a technical detail from a different vantage point, and as a result members begin to disagree later on in the workshop. But each individual can readily identify with the basic concept.

No effort is made to have each committee member agree with every point stated. An effort is, however, made to expose all to the same concept and to allow all to integrate into a unit to work within the same framework.

Introduction of participants is kept to a minimum at this point as it is important to get on with the assignment. The committee members must quickly learn that they are not involved in a typical meeting with its formalities, work pace, etc., and must adapt to a new approach to getting a task completed.

The only introduction to DACUM itself on beginning is to specify briefly where it has been applied and explain that it appears to work well in terms of reaching goals of designers and implementers and that it seems to have a good deal of relevance for their own occupation as indicated by the request by the sponsoring agency responsible for the workshop.

Brief reference is made to the historical background, how DACUM originated (See Chapter 1) in an effort to improve learner identification with the training program and, hence, motivation, how the techniques were subsequently, investigated by the Canadian Government, and how they were introduced to the Canada NewStart corporations.

At this point, the co-ordinator begins the conceptual orientation to the process by relating a story about the development of a training program. Used as an example is a highly visible occupation that contains a number of good examples of various classes of skills or operational behaviors. The story illustrates how the original goals of a program may become somewhat aborted along the way, showing how it can change direction and continue to develop in the wrong direction while attempts made to improve it lead it further away from the original objectives, which basically were to provide persons with the skills necessary to perform competently and to provide industry with a needed resource.

The occupation selected for illustration is a rather simple one in terms of identifying its skill requirements and training needs. Nevertheless, it serves a useful purpose in allowing the committee members to see how someone could abort the training program and how the instructor and persons in the occupation became involved in some rather funny activities and situations, with the result that the committee can chuckle about what is happening, while, at the same time, they are gradually acquiring a concept of what can occur and are reflecting on their own occupation, noting similarities which could easily lead to similar departure from original training objectives.

The co-ordinator, because of their lack of knowledge or experience in the occupation to be examined, is not able to draw (and should avoid attempting to draw) examples from that occupation. Further, the co-ordinator must draw examples from an occupation with which both the co-ordinator and the committee members are somewhat familiar . Such examples will help the committee members reach decisions within the framework of their own occupation.

It is important to run through the entire story (in italics, following) before stopping for questioning by committee members. If they interrupt with questions, they may have difficulty in grasping the concept. Therefore, the co-ordinator should ask them in advance to refrain from questioning until it is indicated that questions are in order.

As previously mentioned, it has been found that there is little value in a "canned" or formalized presentation. Some committees grasp the concept quickly, others require more time in orientation. Whether or not they have grasped the concept will be revealed by their questions and initial attempts at comparing their own occupations to the one from which examples have been drawn.

Sometimes it becomes apparent, because of the nature of the occupation or the specific committee members selected, that certain features of the concept do not apply to their circumstances or do not particularly appeal to them. It is necessary, therefore, that the presenter remain alert to committee reaction to detect signs of disinterest or concern. The co-ordinator can then take a different approach and draw on different examples that might help the committee to become better oriented. It is necessary for the co-ordinator to think on the fly and select only those elements for presentation that will contribute to understanding on the part of the committee.

The following is the story which has been found useful in leading committees to think about the weaknesses of the traditional method of developing an occupational training program and to become aware of the need for something better:

The story begins with the realization by industry of a need for training in an occupation, let us say Heavy Equipment Operation. The need may result from technological change or from changing working conditions. The need is expressed to a training institution which agrees to provide training and begins the process of establishing a training program.

Because this is the first training program for the occupation, the institution has no precedent to rely on in selecting location, facilities, and other resources and in planning the program. Because there are no trained instructors available, it is necessary to select someone from the occupation, ideally someone who is competent in the skills of the occupation and who also has supervisory experience and prior success in training new employees on the job.

Because it lacks knowledge of the occupation, the institution must rely heavily on this instructor in planning and developing the training program even though the instructor has no skill or prior experience in developing a training program. As a result, the instructor will likely attempt to replicate in the training environment the conditions, equipment, and other resources found in the job site.

The instructor begins training the first group of learners in much the same way as new operators were trained on the job site. The instructor attempts to have on hand an adequate number of a variety of major pieces of equipment to allow each trainee to be occupied in operating one of the pieces of equipment at all times. The instructor spends time dealing with the trainees as individuals, helping each to get started in new assignments, and allotting most time and attention to those persons who need more help. The instructor spends relatively little time with those trainees who are able to learn many of the skills through having an opportunity to practice them.

Because the learning environment is realistic and well equipped the instructor has little difficulty in providing each individual with adequate skills, even though the learners may have arrived with diverse educational levels and work experience backgrounds. Because of the realistic working conditions, the instructor is able to determine when each individual becomes competent and relays this information to his former colleagues to assist the learners in obtaining entry jobs. Because of the similarities in the environments, the learners quickly adapt to the work environment and perform to the satisfaction of their new supervisors.

However, during the second or third repeat of the program the instructor becomes concerned about his or her own efficiency and the efficiency of the training program. First, the instructor becomes concerned over the fact that it was necessary to repeat some of the information presented for most or all learners. The instructor decides that it would be more efficient to present this information to them as a group and begins to plan and install presentations and courses accordingly. Second, the instructor begins to wonder if the learners would not learn a good deal more if provided with much additional information. This necessitates the preparation and presentation of lectures and demonstrations along with prescribed reading of supporting printed materials. Difficulties encountered by self-learners in achieving in groups influence the instructor to add audio-visual presentations as well as courses in physics (mechanics), mathematics, and communications designed to assist the learners in occupational information presentations and related study.

After performing well in the occupation, the graduates of the first class will eventually demand some kind of recognition for the new competence. Their concern might be satisfied by interest shown by a suitable licensing body. These bodies normally grant accreditation on the successful completion of a qualifying examination. In developing a suitable examination, adequately discriminatory questions have to be drawn from the theoretical or knowledge portion of the occupation as opposed to the relatively simple practical side. With a likelihood that the graduates will have to complete this examination before gaining entry to the occupation, the instructor places increasingly more emphasis on presentations and related study in order to assist them in qualifying.

As each new dimension is added to the program, proportionally less time is allowed for equipment-operation skill development. The instructor also gradually changes, and ceases to be a foreman who serves as a role model and information source and becomes an instructor specializing in presentation of theory and knowledge.

Over a time a number of difficulties occur with respect to the learners and the graduates of the program. It is found that more and more learners do not complete the training program. Some find it difficult and drop out while others are counseled to leave and select another alternative because it is apparent they do not have the interest or aptitude for this kind of learning and qualification. To its surprise industry experiences a high turnover rate with the program graduates. Many, including those most highly qualified in terms of examination grades, work as heavy equipment operators for only a brief period of time and then leave to seek more technical positions. Some are found in more advanced training programs at a trade school or technical institute.

Eventually a study team is assigned to look at the program and its problems. It finds that few learners have completed the program and successfully passed the qualifying examination if they had less than a grade 10 education. It recommends establishment of a grade 10 prerequisite for entry to the program. On looking at the graduates and the work environment, it decides that the job structure is badly organized and recommends that industry revise its jobs to increase upward mobility for the graduates. Industry rechecks this notion for it requires a work force to operate the equipment. Therefore, industry decides that the program is not going to provide the manpower it specifically requires and takes steps to recruit and train its own operators on the job.

After telling this story, the co-ordinator discusses what went wrong and how this could have been prevented:

1. It would appear that the instructor had difficulty in specifying what he or she really wanted the trainees to achieve, and had difficulty in making this the sole

objective of the training program. A solution would be a set of behavioral objectives in the form of an accurate identification of the requirements of the industry.

2. It proved to be too difficult to assess or evaluate learner performance in terms of the instructor's original poorly defined goals. There are few instruments available that allow one to measure achievement in flexible, diversified skills in diversified occupations. Required is a universal method of evaluating job performance in much the same way as it is evaluated in industry.

3. It is necessary to develop procedures that would make it easier for the instructor to keep sight of the original objectives and provide training in much the same way as they did with the initial group of trainees. This prevents drifting into program modification and development activities that lead away from the objectives.

At this point, the co-ordinator opens the meeting for discussion and questions, and must read reactions carefully. If committee members tend to agree with points raised in the story, if they concede there is danger of falling into the same pitfalls in training for their own occupation, if they note that this has already occurred in such training programs, the co-ordinator can forego much further exploration of the concept. If, however, one or two or all of the committee fail to see the application to their own situation, it is necessary for the co-ordinator to provide additional detail or examples that will help them to see the concept.

Following this discussion, the co-ordinator begins to describe the DACUM solution to this set of problems. The co-ordinator does this in the following way:

1. Using one of the existing charts as an example, the co-ordinator shows the committee the arrangement of General Areas of Competence, the nature of skills, the way they are defined, the level of detail required. The co-ordinator describes the concept of treating the chart as a profile or map, which reduces the level of definition required of each skill.

2. The co-ordinator describes the rating scale. They shows how the definitions apply, how the baseline level relates to the young newly accredited worker in a skilled trade, and how the other levels apply. The co-ordinator runs through a description of a typical occupation, describing how the employer or manager of an organization would evaluate employees and their skills using the rating scale.

3. The co-ordinator describes the way in which the rating scale expands each of the skill definitions. He or she illustrates the relationship between the implied introductory words "The individual must be able to" and the skill definition as contained in the block and any one of the levels in the rating scale. The co-ordinator indicates that these combined form a rather detailed behavioral objective and how they must keep the rating scale in mind while they are constructing their skill definition: that is, once a definition is specified and considered complete, they must be able to visualize assignment of rating to an individual on the basis of the definition.

4. The co-ordinator briefly describes the Learning-Evaluation Model (see Chapters 15 & 16). This may take two or three minutes or it may take half an hour, depending on the interest and the conceptual needs of the committee. Some members are concerned about the resulting training program and have to be able to see how their work will be applied before they can proceed. Others can proceed after a very brief definition of the training program.

5. The co-ordinator asks the committee members to look at the DACUM brochure (Appendix H) and gives the committee an opportunity to ask questions.

6. The co-ordinator shows a sample diploma or record of achievement. This is the clincher for some committees as it readily illustrates to them the usefulness of the system and the chart. They can see that, if they do an accurate job of specifying the requirements of the occupation, they will ultimately receive detailed descriptions of the ability of prospective personnel stated in their own terms to a level of specificity they require.

REVIEW OF OCCUPATION

It is sometimes necessary to conduct a review of the occupation prior to beginning the first analysis activity, the establishment of General Areas of Competence. Sometimes committees are willing to proceed right on with the activity of identifying the areas of competence and do not need any prior exploration of their own occupation and what it involves. On the other hand, with newly evolving or changing occupations, it is necessary to review the field and begin to see structure and relationships in the occupation and related functions before the committee can proceed. Or sometimes this review is needed to satisfy the requirements of certain members who like to start off committee proceedings or workshop activities with general discussion. The co-ordinator should proceed on the assumption that this discussion is not needed in advance of the detailed DACUM charting but be prepared to branch off into this activity if it becomes necessary or if specific committee members recommend it.

Review usually centers around the range of the occupation and identification of its components. This is necessary in some cases because of the diversity of jobs in the occupation. For example, an occupation such as electrical technology might have as many as six different major categories of jobs ranging from technical supervision to technical troubleshooting and servicing. Because the committee members are normally selected from the diverse job categories, it is frequently important for them to be able to discuss their roles and their specific viewpoints with the other members of the committee before proceeding with the detailed task.

While the committee is participating in this sort of discussion under informal leadership of the co-ordinator, who should take this opportunity to help them visualize the relationships that exist within and around the occupation. This is most usefully done on a large whiteboard or flip chart by graphically identifying the occupation, its specialties, and the jobs or occupations surrounding it.

First, the major jobs in the occupation are blocked out with overlapping boundaries to show that they do not exist as separate entities but that their functions overlap.

Another consideration is the level of the occupation, or its location in the occupational structure of the industries that contain it. Frequently, committees have difficulty isolating their occupation in this way. Some members tend to inflate the level of the occupation while others, who currently serve in managerial or supervisory roles, may tend to delimit it. It is important to get them to agree on the level, and the graphic analysis is most useful.

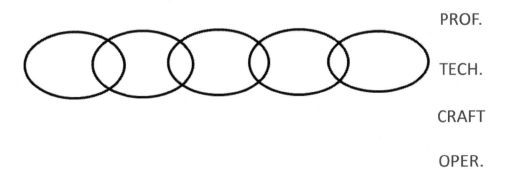

The committee should then consider the surrounding occupations. These can be depicted in a parallel band with the major categories of the occupation to show their relationship. Frequently, there are occupations at the same level that tend to overlap or interact with the occupation being examined. Specification of this relationship in advance helps the committee in its future deliberations.

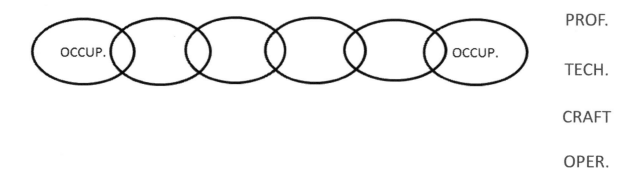

PROF.

TECH.

CRAFT

OPER.

Finally, the committee should consider occupations in levels above and below the occupation being analyzed. It is necessary to identify occupations that provide creative or managerial input into this occupation as well as the supporting occupations. This is helpful in eliminating later debate on whether or not certain skills should be included in the analysis. By referring back to the diagram, it is easy for the committee to avoid including in, for example, a technician-level occupation some of the skills that are most likely to be performed by engineers or designers and at the same time avoid placing in the chart skills that are really part of a supporting occupation.

This analysis is also useful in helping the committee recognize common functions among the occupations. For example, there are no doubt skills that are applicable for both engineering and technician-level occupations. Similarly, a technician might require some of the skills required of a craftsperson but he or she applies them in a different way or less frequently.

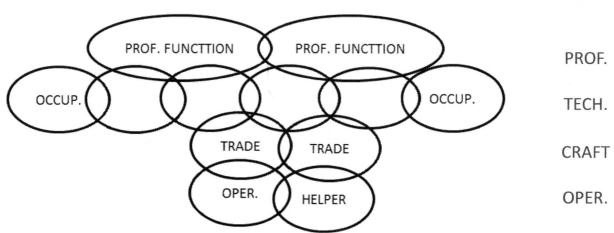

PROF.

TECH.

CRAFT

OPER.

The committee should be asked to consider the future of the occupation: What will be the major role changes within the occupation in the immediate future? The occupation may be one that is rapidly being delimited and in some ways replaced by other occupations, or it may be one that is evolving and facing an expanded role in terms of the range of tasks the person in the occupation will be expected to handle.

Finally, the committee should be asked to identify areas in which their occupation has been particularly weak. It may be too narrow, with a limited range of skills which prevents personnel from assuming responsibility. It may be weak in that it has traditionally been ill-defined, resulting in confusion about what skills are required for adequate performance. This weakness may be the result of lack of or inadequate entry training.

Whether or not the occupational review is conducted as a separate activity, many of the issues above must be resolved at some point in the workshop. In most DACUM development workshops to date it was found feasible to conduct most of this review concurrently with the establishment of General Areas of Competence.

CHART DEVELOPMENT PROCEDURE

The following procedure has become standardized in DACUM chart development and is considered essential. It is designed to provide an analysis of each element of the occupation. Efforts to construct charts without following this basic procedure have been found to result in inaccuracies, in much difficulty in analyzing the occupation and organizing the chart, and eventually in termination of the work before the analysis was complete. The basic steps in the process are: (1) development of General Areas of Competence, (2) completion of the first band (which is also a training exercise), (3) completion of the additional bands, (4) review, (5) skill sequencing and structuring, and (6) final agreement.

Establishing General Areas of Competence

The first activity is specification of General Areas of Competence in the occupation. These are merely logical groupings of all the skills in the occupation. Their selection helps the committee in its later task of identifying skills, organizing them in some fashion, and making certain that none are overlooked.

Standard ways of specifying subdivisions of the occupation (jobs that may be considered part of the occupation, subdivisions of the work within a specific job, typical grouping of skills for training) are ignored. Some of these designations may be used, but they are selected because they allow the committee to do its task with ease and efficiency rather than because they are standardized or commonly used.

Initial specification of General Areas of Competence takes approximately one hour. It may be conducted concurrently with the review of the occupation. In some cases, it may take longer as a committee may have difficulty in identifying appropriate General Areas of Competence. Or it may be accomplished in as little as 30 minutes if the members of the committee are extremely competent in the occupation and if the occupation is one in which the skills are readily identifiable. More difficulty is experienced in establishing General Areas of Competence for those occupations that contain a cluster of jobs. This is particularly true of technician level occupations.

Because the committee must begin working on the General Areas of Competence without any specific framework (that is, they are working with a blank wall), it must be led a good deal during this stage by the co-ordinator. The committee is unsure of what it is trying or expected to achieve, and frequent pauses for explanation are necessary. The co-ordinator should be looking for some sort of pattern in these General Areas of Competence, having previously noticed patterns in a number of other charts. The co-ordinator must avoid forcing a specific pattern of organization on the committee. Nevertheless, the co-ordinator should support specific patterns which confirm that the committee is on the right track.

The co-ordinator must continue the process of establishing General Areas of Competence until convinced that the committee members are satisfied that they are going to be able to cover all the skills in the occupation within the established categories. Initially, committees tend to establish a few (six to nine) General Areas of Competence, feel they have the job done, and want to proceed with the specification of skills. The co-ordinator must resist this tendency and continue to ask the committee to visualize all the skills in the occupation, the variety of jobs, and the variety of specialized activities, to be sure that there is a place for each skill in one of the established areas. The co-ordinator must insist that this be done in order to avoid the confusion and frustration which would arise if it were found that the specified General Areas of Competence were not satisfactory.

Normally, a committee will suggest too many General Areas of Competence (more than 12 or 14 have been found to be cumbersome). The co-ordinator continues to solicit additional contributions, however, and places these to the immediate right of those that have already been agreed upon. The committee may suggest 15 or 20 areas of competence. To reduce these to a workable number, it may be necessary to have the committee begin to group them into 10 to 14 clusters and then begin to create new definitions for each cluster. An excess of contributions is usually caused by the committee's inability to arrive at a suitable definition that covers a set of skills. Consequently, they end up suggesting several sub-definitions.

The purpose of this activity is to achieve a balance of skills on the chart. In questioning the committee on the suitability of their suggested General Areas of Competence, it is frequently useful to ask them to project the number of individual skills that would be contained in each. No area should remain as a General Area of Competence if it contains only three or four skills. Such areas should be grouped with others and a new definition or title established. Similarly, it is the responsibility of the co-ordinator to make sure that an excessive number of skills do not get lumped under a single General Area of Competence. In such cases, the co-ordinator will ask the committee to subdivide the skills into more workable groupings.

All of this is designed to facilitate the analysis process. A good balance of skills in each General Area of Competence or band in the chart tends to improve the accuracy of definition and the adequacy of coverage. In cases of poorly established General Areas of Competence having too few skills, there is a tendency for the committee members to struggle to subdivide these skills more finely than is required for the purpose of the DACUM chart. On the other hand, if the General Areas of Competence contain too many skills, the committee tends to try to cluster these into a smaller number of skills. An appropriate initial balance will reduce these problems.

The co-ordinator must be alert to see that committee members do not specify as General Areas of Competence what should be specified as single skills. They are as yet unfamiliar with the process and may have difficulty distinguishing between skills and General Areas of Competence.   The co-ordinator must question suspected contributions to avoid much structural change later.

Cards should be written for suggested General Areas of Competence as quickly as they emerge. The committee is faced with the blank wall and needs some encouragement. Even though initial suggestions may be badly stated or may not look like fully developed General Areas of Competence, the co-ordinator should place them up as quickly as possible, with the intention of structuring, reorganizing, or restating them. When the co-ordinator asks them to structure or change the relationship of the dozen or so General Areas of Competence, they begin to think of the General Areas of Competence as part of a whole and often detect other skills which they have overlooked. The primary purpose of structuring is to organize the General Areas of Competence into appropriate groupings and to place these in order in the vertical alignment. For example, General Areas of Competence applying to administrative skills might be grouped together, those applying to use of hand tools, technical equipment, and test equipment might form a second group, and those that deal with analytical problem-solving skills might be a third group. Once the committee is able to structure the areas in this way, the co-ordinator can feel assured that it has arrived at a reasonable set of categories suitable for at least beginning the process of determining or identifying the skill makeup of the occupation.

In most workshops, it is necessary to change one or more of the General Areas of Competence during the course of constructing the body of the chart. Sometimes, this need is detected in struggling to include a much larger number of skills in one General Area of Competence than was originally expected, or in encountering a General Area of Competence that includes fewer skills than was anticipated. The committee will often suggest that a reorganization of some sort must take place. This is relatively easy once the structure is established, for there is no need to reorganize the entire structure of the chart.

Two examples of the kind of change necessary are clearly indicated on the chart for GENERAL NURSING PRACTICE:

a) It was necessary to make a change to create the General Area of Competence COMMUNICATE EFFECTIVELY AND ORGANIZE NURSING. During the course of the analysis the committee experienced difficulty in determining in which of two existing categories they should locate certain skills. The problem was resolved by combining the categories and creating the new definition.

b) The General Area of Competence ADMINISTER SPECIFIC NURSING CARE was established well after the committee had begun to define specific skills on the chart. Difficulty was encountered in specifying different patterns of care within the existing framework of the chart. A decision was made to insert a new band in which were included all the skills dealing with planning, initiating, and monitoring a pattern of care for specific kinds of patient conditions.

While beginning to establish the General Areas of Competence (and later during the workshop) the co-ordinator can draw upon an array of DACUM charts to help the committee members visualize a pattern for establishing categories within their own occupation. In most cases it is necessary to show only one or two samples to illustrate the kinds of decisions that must be made, but in others it may be necessary to halt the proceedings for a few moments to allow the committee to review a number of charts kept on hand for this purpose. The following have been found useful to illustrate points in DACUM chart development:

<u>MOTOR VEHICLE REPAIR (MECHANICAL)</u>. This chart is located on Appendix A and subdivided into 13 General Areas of Competence. Five deal with skills applied to the servicing and repair of basic systems of the automobile:

> SERVICE & REPAIR STEERING, SUSPENSION & BRAKE SYSTEMS
>
> SERVICE & REPAIR COOLING & EXHAUST SYSTEMS
>
> SERVICE & REPAIR FUEL SYSTEMS
>
> SERVICE & REPAIR ELECTRICAL SYSTEMS
>
> SERVICE & REPAIR & OVERHAUL TRANSMISSIONS & DRIVES

Two additional bands deal with an additional system, the engine:

> SERVICE & REPAIR ENGINES
>
> REPAIR & OVERHAUL ENGINES

It was necessary during the development of this chart to subdivide the skills related to work on engines into these categories because it was felt that skills are somewhat different for the two applications, and because the modern trend in the motor vehicle repair industry is for service garages to specialize in service and repair of engines while special shops are set up to repair and overhaul engines. It was felt that the skills would best be subdivided in this way to enable the supervisor and the learner to see the distinction because the mechanic-in-training probably would perform in one or the other of the areas rather than in both. Three additional General Areas of Competence deal with general skills that would be part of the application of skills included in the seven areas mentioned previously:

> PERFORM GENERAL SHOP DUTIES
>
> USE AUTOMOTIVE EQUIPMENT
>
> USE REPAIR TOOLS AND EQUIPMENT

It is found useful in DACUM occupational analysis to isolate categories such as "use repair tools and equipment" to avoid undue repetition of skills in several bands on the chart. Skills common to a wide variety of other skills are isolated in the charts in this way. Two additional General Areas of Competence which relate to the above three are:

ADJUST AND REPLACE MECHANICAL EQUIPMENT AND CONTROLS

USE MEASURING AND TESTING DEVICES.

The skills contained in these areas are commonly applied in a variety of the jobs that have skills included in the seven General Areas of Competence that relate to the basic systems of the automobile. Finally, there is a single General Area of Competence,

COMMUNICATE EFFECTIVELY IN WORK ENVIRONMENT,

which contains all the skills related to the communication process in the work environment of the motor vehicle mechanic.

DECKHAND TRAINING. The main feature of this chart is that three of the bands in the chart are devoted to three basic kinds of fishing operation:

OPERATE TRAWL FISHING GEAR

FISH BY LONG LINE

OPERATE PURSE SEINE FISHING GEAR

Four supporting General Areas of Competence are categories of skills that would be applicable to any deckhand, whether or not he works in the fishing industry:

PERFORM EMERGENCY DUTIES

PERFORM GENERAL SHIP DUTIES

MAINTAIN EFFICIENT WORK ENVIRONMENT

STEER A VESSEL

Two additional bands relate directly to fishing operations but contain skills that are somewhat common to the three specialties of the occupation:

RIG FISHING GEAR

MAINTAIN FISHING GEAR

An additional band that is common to all of the specialties of the occupation is

HANDLE AND PROCESS FISH,

while the final band on the chart,

LEAD A CONSTRUCTIVE WORKING LIFE,

is a set of social adjustment skills necessary for the fishing deckhand to be able to adapt to the conditions of this occupation.

COMMERCIAL DESIGN. This chart has a total of 11 General Areas of Competence. Six of these are related to art technique:

LETTER AND USE TYPOGRAPHY

PRODUCE GRAPHICS

DRAW SHAPE AND RENDER

COLOR AND PAINT

USE PHOTOGRAPHY

APPLY TEXTURE AND MATERIALS

Four additional General Areas of Competence contain design skills that are generally applicable to the technique skills:

CREATE FUNCTIONAL DESIGNS

COMPOSE

DESIGN FOR AND CO-ORDINATE PRODUCTION

ANALYZE AND DEFINE DESIGN PROBLEMS

The remaining General Area of Competence,

MANAGE ART OPERATION,

contains skills needed in all the other areas.

PROFESSIONAL COUNSELLING (SCHOOL). In this chart three bands were allocated to the counseling process:

IDENTIFY AND SPECIFY PROBLEMS AND STUDENT NEEDS

APPLY COUNSELLING METHODS

APPLY SPECIAL GROUP COUNSELLING METHODS

Five General Areas of Competence contain skills related to the provision of programs:

      ADMINISTER PROGRAM OF SERVICES

      ORGANIZE AND CONDUCT VOCATIONAL AND EDUCATIONAL INFORMATION PROGRAMS

      ENLIST AND UTILIZE COMMUNITY REFERRAL RESOURCES

      EMPLOY EFFECTIVE INSTRUCTION TECHNIQUES

      DEVELOP AND IMPLEMENT PROGRAMS IN PSYCHOLOGICAL EDUCATION

An additional three General Areas of Competence were assigned to skills that are part of the specialist-consultant role of the professional school counselor:

      MEASURE AND EVALUATE

      SERVE AS CONSULTANT

      APPLY BEHAVIOUR CHANGE TECHNIQUES

Two additional bands contain the remaining skills.

      COMMUNICATE

      CONTINUE TO ACQUIRE PROFESSIONAL COMPETENCE

The First Band

After the committee has established the General Areas of Competence for the proposed chart to its satisfaction and to the satisfaction of the co-ordinator, the co-ordinator encourages it to select one of the General Areas of Competence for immediate analysis or specification of the skills it contains. Because this is a new step for the committee, the first band is a learning exercise as well as an analysis. Completion of this band can, therefore, consume anywhere from two to four hours of committee time. It is frequently necessary for the co-ordinator to stop the proceedings and review the principles involved when committee members begin to drift away from the intent.

During this stage, the co-ordinator must place emphasis on the accepted method of wording or defining a skill. The co-ordinator insists that each contribution be prefaced with "The individual must be able to ..." and tries to get the committee members to make contributions in a maximum of eight words plus connectives. Some find this difficult at first and hesitate to make contributions. The co-ordinator sometimes has to attempt to express the intent of members in his or her own words and place this skill definition on the wall temporarily.

It is at this point that the work becomes a brainstorming activity, which it continues to be through most of the remainder of the workshop. For this reason, it is important that the co-ordinator record and locate the skill definitions as quickly as possible, with a minimum of debate and negative comment. It is easy at this point to lose a committee as the members are unsure about what is required of them. It is important to work quickly and to encourage only positive contributions to set a pace for the remainder of the workshop.

Beginning from the right, the cards are placed on the wall as they are prepared; that is, in the sequence in which skills are defined. Sometimes committees want to begin ordering the skill definitions immediately. It is necessary to resist this as it tends to destroy the brainstorming process in which they are learning to participate.

While they are brainstorming, committee members will want to suggest and record skills for other bands in the chart. However, it has been found that this tends to break the analysis process. Not only does it make the analysis of the bands disjointed in terms of time, but it also allows the committee to stray from the immediate activity, which is to analyze a specific category of skills. When this occurs, the co-ordinator should suggest that skills being mentioned belong in another band and that the committee cannot involve itself in specifying them at this time. The co-ordinator should insist on continuing specification of the skills in the first band until the members have exhausted their ideas for this band.

During this initial work, the co-ordinator must stimulate contributions from each member of the committee. In most committees there are a few vocal members who may be quite expert in the occupation, and there may be others who at that point are somewhat unsure of their position and their stature with the committee. It is important that the co-ordinator solicit some sort of contribution from each of them and quickly record it on the wall to provide them with the feeling that they are a part of the committee and that their contributions are important. The longer it takes to extract a contribution from a silent committee member, the more difficult the task becomes. Reluctant members can frequently be drawn out by questions such as "You're in a different field, how would you word the skill that has just been suggested?" or "Your work is sort of specialized, are there additional skills that the rest of the committee is overlooking that relate specifically to your work?"

It is equally important that the co-ordinator begin immediately to control the more vocal members of the committee. Some committee members will begin by identifying a series of what they term skills, indicating that they came well prepared. However, because of the newness of the approach, they frequently are off track in terms of what is required. Sometimes these are committee members who feel they are representing a specific power or movement in the occupation and must make their point as soon as possible. Accepting a series of contributions from one committee member can be dangerous, as it may set a pattern for the remainder of the committee. It is best to break this pattern by soliciting contributions from other members while avoiding the listing of a large number of contributions from any single participant.

During early stages of specification of skills, there is a tendency for committee members to make skill definitions too encompassing or, on the other hand, to break skills down too finely.

The tendency to make definitions too encompassing may be due to inability of committee members to analyze skills properly. This happens when a committee member is remote from the actual detailed work of the occupation and, as a result, tends to think in terms of more global definitions.

Individuals (and sometimes entire committees) tend to overestimate their occupation in terms of the number of skills it contains. This failing has been quite consistent in all chart development activities to date. It is perhaps a natural reaction of people faced with the assignment of breaking down and sorting out the skills of their occupation. A resulting problem is that when a specific band is encountered which obviously contains a large number of skills some committee members react negatively. They believe that there just is not room on the wall or the chart to define all the skills within that band. Sometimes they do not express this feeling immediately. Some individuals attempt to have the committee agree that only more global definitions are required. Others insist that the band contains too many skills to go through with the analysis process. It is important that the co-ordinator persevere. The co-ordinator can ask committee members to go along with the process to determine if there are indeed too many skills. The co-ordinator can usually rationalize the need for proceeding by saying "If there are too many skills in this band, or as many as you think, it may be necessary to subdivide this band into two or more. However, we shall have to define the skills before we can make a decision about how to regroup them". Another solution is to indicate that the charting process does allow for a General Area of Competence to occupy two bands on a chart when it contains an excessively large number of skills. Finally, the co-ordinator may say to the committee, "You may be right in suspecting we don't have to break these skills down so finely. However, let's proceed, and, if we can specify all the skills in the way that is recommended, we may be able to look at them and find we can combine several". Suggestions of this kind tend to relieve apprehension on the part of committee members and allow the activity to proceed.

Only when the first band on the chart is complete does the co-ordinator allow work on other bands to begin.

Additional Bands

The above procedure is followed for remaining General Areas of Competence or bands on the chart.

The co-ordinator must be skillful at selecting the sequence in which General Areas of Competence are attacked. Typically, he or she selects (or encourages the committee to select) as priorities bands most likely to be relatively easy for the committee to analyze, bands that contain an adequate number of skills, and, to provide a variety of learning experience, bands that call for a variety of types of definitions.

It is easy to select a band of skills similar in definition to the skills in the first band attempted and to proceed in this sequence. The committee's work can be quite quickly disrupted if it shifts from one type of skill to an entirely different type and then has to revert back again. It is best to try to predict which bands will contain similar skills.

Each band is analyzed independently. However, after the first band has been completed, the co-ordinator can make rare concessions when committee members happen to think of skills for other bands which they do not wish to be forgotten. One way for the co-ordinator to handle this is to record such suggestions on a note pad for reference at the appropriate time. If the committee member, however, insists that a card be lettered for the skill he or she has defined, this can be done and the card can be placed to the right of the appropriate General Area of Competence. This enables the co-ordinator to record the skill without having to fit it into the chart. It is left there as a reminder when that particular band is tackled.

Committees often run into difficulty when they are required to shift from one band to another that requires quite different definitions. The co-ordinator must be alert to two possibilities:

a) The committee may attempt to repeat the prior pattern of skill definition on an entirely different set of skills. If this happens, the co-ordinator must quickly search for and suggest alternative ways of defining the new set of skills.

b) The committee can bog down due to its inability to come up with new action words that suit a new group of skills. This can happen when the committee shifts its focus from procedural skills to analytical problem-solving or design skills. Again the co-ordinator must help the committee find appropriate terminology.

The process is repeated until all bands are covered. The co-ordinator will know that the activity is complete when he or she notes that the committee seems to have exhausted its ideas and is suggesting skills for one band that have already been included in another or simply breaking down or reviewing already defined skills.

Skill Definition Review

Once it is determined that coverage is essentially complete, the co-ordinator should lead the committee through a quick review of each of the skills and bands on the chart. The main purpose is to improve quality of definition of skills. No attempt is made to restructure the chart at this time.

The suggested procedure is for the co-ordinator to place a hand on each card in sequence and solicit the agreement of the group. It is important to focus the attention of all members on the definition being discussed.

Definitions may not have been well specified earlier for the following reasons:

(a) Earlier contributions may have been poorly specified because the committee was not yet familiar with the process. The earliest completed bands require special attention.

(b) Some definitions may have been ill-defined due to haste or the need to maintain a rapid work pace in order to complete the task within the allotted time. This may have happened in cases where the committee experienced difficulty in working out a pattern for a specific band.

(c) Some skills may have been badly specified because the committee could not agree on a suitable definition, with the result that notation was made and final specification left until the review stage.

(d) Some skill definitions may have been mounted on the wall without the agreement of the entire committee. One or two members may have agreed to let them stand until the review stage. It is important that each of these definitions be reviewed critically.

(e) Some skills may have been posted without being noted by all the committee members. (Some may have let their minds wander or have been getting coffee or making notes.)

Skill definition review takes approximately one hour. In some cases it may not be necessary as the committee may have done an excellent job of specifying skills in the first place. Less re-specification is required in occupations that are less complex and that have a history of detailed skill specification. In most DACUM development workshops, this work progresses rapidly as the committee has had almost three days to think over the issues and is now prepared to resolve quickly any that may remain.

Skill Sequencing and Structuring

There are two stages in structuring of the chart:

(a) Sequencing of the skills in each band,

(b) Structuring of the final chart.

It is important that eventual users be able to see the finished work in some sort of organized structure. Work that is not systematically organized in some fashion tends to lack credibility and seem incomplete to the viewer who is searching for structure. The intent is to enable viewers to see skills in different bands in relation to each other, to see individual skills as part of a whole, and to see chronological structure.

The procedure is informal and is completed in a short time. Sequencing can be accomplished in approximately one-half hour, while the structuring process frequently takes somewhat less. The pace is rapid because of the over-all time restriction and because most of the decisions about placement of skills on the chart are arbitrary in any case. That is, there are few cases where one could establish that one skill should definitely precede another in a band.

The co-ordinator plays a key role at this stage and must work rapidly and hold the attention of the committee. The co-ordinator must also control the entire wall and ensure that individual committee members in their enthusiasm do not begin to move cards and as a result make structural changes that are not approved by the entire group.

It is frequently best, particularly if the chart is large, to have committee members stand and move along the wall so they can properly read the cards at each extremity while they are being discussed.

Before proceeding it is useful to create a blank horizontal space the depth of two bands along the center of the wall. This is done by quickly moving up all cards in the upper half of the chart and lowering all cards in the lower half. The gap allows space to shift *each* card on the wall by gradually working from the center to the top or bottom during sequencing. If there is not adequate space available, the committee will tend to avoid suggesting desired shifts and will say "They look just fine where they are". However, if it is indicated that all cards will be relocated and apparent that space is available, the committee will respond accordingly.

The committee is provided with a rationale for making decisions about sequencing of each band. They are asked to imagine, now that the definition of all the skills in the occupation has been completed, that they are working in a small operation and are the sole experts in the occupation. They are going to hire and train someone who may have a high school education and aptitude for the work but who has none of the skills on the chart. They are asked to decide, band by band, which skills on the chart they would have this individual first learn and apply in his or her daily work in order to realize an immediate return on their investment. Assuming that the learner would begin at the left side of the chart, the committee begins to shift to the left those skills they would have him or her apply almost immediately on entry. At the same time they shift to the right those skills they would reserve for themselves until the learner had developed an awareness and appreciation of the occupation and was better able to make the complex decisions related to them. In effect, each committee member is asked to look at this hypothetical situation and visualize the way in which he or she would provide skills for an individual on the job.

These guidelines are relatively easy to apply. However, there are cases where committee members become confused and lose sight of them. For example, they may drift into sequencing skills:

    a) in the order in which they would be applied in a typical job by an expert,

    b) in the order in which they have been provided in conventional training programs, or

c) in a straight simple-to-complex or easy-to-difficult order.

The problem is that, even though they have been analyzing their occupation, committee members suddenly perceive the chart as a curriculum and begin to sequence skills accordingly. The co-ordinator must periodically stop proceedings for review of the rationale. It must be explained that, for an individualized training program such as DACUM and a curriculum based on specification of skills rather than knowledge as learning goals, a different method of sequencing is required. One can see decided benefits in structuring or sequencing presentation of a large body of content for the sake of efficiency in conventional presentation, particularly to groups. The DACUM process, however, is not a group learning process, and the focus is on the skills themselves rather than on the supporting knowledge that may be required for skill development.

It is important that each band be sequenced individually with no reference to other bands. Consideration of possible sequences for other bands adds new criteria for reaching sequencing decisions and adds to committee confusion.

One band is selected as a baseline to establish the length of the chart. It is usually the one that contains the most skills. An exception would be made when a single band contains an unusually large number of skills. In this case, the skills might be placed in a double row and the band with the next largest number would be selected to establish the length of the chart.

The co-ordinator selects the first band to be sequenced. Based on his or her observation through the workshop the co-ordinator can select the one that contains skills most readily sequenced according to the criteria he or she has established. This allows the committee to grasp the procedure quickly and to proceed more easily with more difficult bands.

Some bands may contain groups of skills that are difficult to sequence because it does not much matter in which order the skills are placed, or because the group of skills would ideally be learned and applied at the same time. In such cases the co-ordinator should allow these skills to be sequenced arbitrarily.

While skills are being sequenced in specific bands, the co-ordinator should spread out the cards along that band so that it will be the same length as the baseline band. This begins to provide visible structure to the chart. It also puts the cards in such a position that they must be relocated during the next stage, which is preliminary structuring.

Assuming that the baseline band will remain static, committee members are asked to shift groups of cards in the remaining bands laterally to bring skills in those bands into alignment with skills in the baseline band. (The committee is cautioned that it is not to change the sequence previously established in each band). Sometimes this task is approached by shifting either groups or individual skills. At other times it is useful to suggest obvious gaps or blank areas that indicate that some skills should be shifted to the left while others should be moved to the right.

The final step in structuring is to have committee members spend a brief period scanning the chart vertically in some organized fashion (e.g., left to right). The purpose is to search for specific skills that may be out of place in the structure as it stands. Committee members are cautioned that no wholesale shifts in cards will be allowed. They frequently spot one or more cases where a pair of skills in two different bands are not in the same lateral location on the chart though they would normally be learned and applied at the same time. A case in point might be a skill related to use of a hand tool which should be in the same lateral location as the first skill in which that tool would be applied.

Restructuring as a result of this scanning is not extensive. Sometimes it is not required at all. However, it is valuable as a review and to ensure that there is not an obvious mislocation of any skill.

Final Agreement

Before the committee leaves the workshop, the co-ordinator should solicit agreement that the chart is a reasonably accurate description of the occupation, that it is comprehensive, and that it is adequately structured. In most cases, the committee readily agrees that the chart will stand as an accurate skill profile of the occupation. Experience to date has shown that committees consistently agree that it is much more thorough and accurate than any other description of the occupation known to them, particularly those related to training programs or curricula. One technique used at this stage is for the co-ordinator to walk to the wall and designate portions of the chart (quarters, thirds, or halves), asking the committee if it sees the skills in the portion designated as the skills that might serve, for instance, as job-entry skills, or as the skills required by a person performing in a junior or supporting capacity. Consistently the committee agrees, and this is repeated to show how an individual acquiring skills in this fashion can develop skills to a point, perhaps reach a desired level of competence or perhaps have to leave his or her training for financial or other reasons, and yet can find a place in the occupation.

Two more activities may take place before the committee departs.

a) The committee may suggest the vertical shifting of one band or more to a location adjacent to a band that has similar skills or that has a number of skills that would be applied in the same types of work. The shift is not made at this time but is noted and made during the final mock-up of the chart.

b) The committee is asked to suggest a title for the chart. This is something that is sometimes difficult since there is always a temptation to apply a training definition when what is required is a title designating the chart as an identification of the functions that are performed in the occupation. For example, an early effort to define the skills of instructors for a DACUMized Adult Basic Education Program was called "DACUM Chart for Learning Assistance and Monitoring in a Personalized Adult Basic Education Environment". This, to the committee present, was a functional definition of the work to be performed and was selected in preference to a definition including reference to teacher training, instruction, job titles, etc. The subsequent training program will likely have a training name attached to it, but the chart should not, as it is an analysis of the occupation.

SUMMARY

The purpose of Chapter 7 was to explain the charting process. This process, facilitated by the co-ordinator, begins with the orientation of committee members by providing a conceptual framework of DACUM. Next, the co-ordinator guides the committee through a review of the occupation by examining its range and components. The first major stage following the occupation review is the development of the DACUM chart by defining General Areas of Competence in the occupation followed directly by identifying, isolating, and defining individual skills for each General Areas of Competence. After agreeing upon a set of General Areas of Competence and individual skill (behavior) definitions, the committee, under the direction of the co-ordinator, proceeds to structure the skills into a desired learning sequence. Finally, the committee solicits agreement of the chart.

<u>REFERENCES</u>

Adams, R. E. (1975). *DACUM: Approach to curriculum, learning, and evaluation in occupational training.* Ottawa: Dept. of Regional Economic Expansion.

8

SKILL DEFINITIONS

The quality of the DACUM chart depends on the quality of individual skill definitions. As previously stated in Chapter 1, **skills** are the focus of the DACUM chart (versus Knowledge, Jobs, Duties, or Tasks) because they are the behaviors that enable an individual to perform competently in an occupation.

DEVELOPMENT MODEL FOR DACUM LEARNING PROGRAM

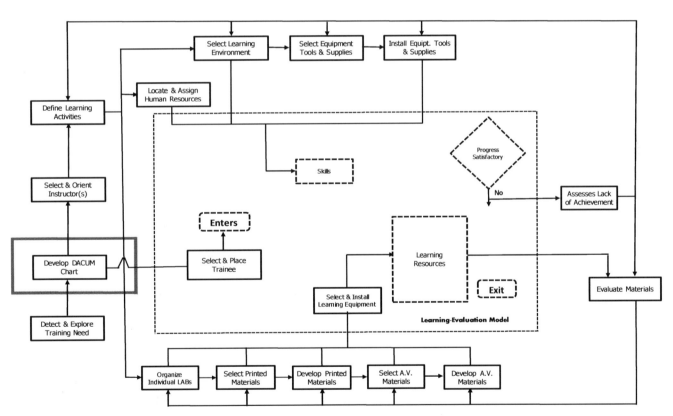

Figure 8-1. Development Model for DACUM Learning Program

Skills, unlike tasks, specifically allow for determining the level of performance needed within the occupation. On the surface, these skill definitions look quite simple, and the casual observer might assume that they are easily or hastily devised. On the contrary, each definition is derived through consideration of a number of criteria and guidelines and many are finalized only after considerable discussion.

This chapter deals with considerations in developing skill definition criteria, categories of skills, levels of skills, and mechanics of chart printing. The intent is not to provide a rigid set of controls. This tends to stifle the chart development process. The purpose, rather, is to provide a framework for assessing and refining each contribution by taking advantage of the criteria or guidelines found useful in what are considered to be the most effective and comprehensive DACUM charts prepared to date.

GUIDING SKILL DEFINITIONS AS A CO-ORDINATOR

While the committee is busy trying to sort out what is or is not required in the occupation, the quality of skill definition is controlled by the co-ordinator. The co-ordinator's responsibility is to assess contributions of members in the light of a variety of factors that indicate whether the skill suggested is a realistic skill, whether it is stated within the context of chart requirements, and whether it is well specified. The suggestions following are, therefore, addressed to the co-ordinator.

It is not necessary to provide committees, in advance, with detailed descriptions of skill categories, patterns of specifying skills, and methods of constructing definitions to cover unique problems. In fact, this detailed information may be detrimental in two ways:

1.   The information may cause the committee to become overly concerned with quality and specific criteria, resulting in reduced emphasis on brainstorming and skill isolation and identification. This would slow down the analysis process.

2.   Due to inexperience in this kind of analysis, the committee may struggle to adopt a specific pattern for skill definition that is not suitable for analysis of its own occupation. It is best that the co-ordinator make in-process judgments while learning more about the occupation and lead and assist the committee in selecting patterns based on their knowledge of a range of patterns and a range of occupations. The co-ordinator may wish to describe patterns and criteria in some detail once the committee has indicated it cannot function without this information.

BASIC RULES OF SKILL DEFINITION

Skill definitions must specify action behaviors. Each must be prefaced with the words "The individual must be able to ...", immediately followed by an action verb along with necessary objects and qualifications. The definition as it appears on the chart begins with the action verb, the prefaced words being assumed.

Early in the workshop it is necessary to insist repeatedly that each committee member preface each contribution in this way. It is a new activity for the members, and sometimes they feel that this is unnecessary. Nevertheless, the prefaced words cause them to improve contributions while in the act of stating them. This insistence also provides the co-ordinator with a quality control. If contributions cannot be stated in this fashion, it indicates that there is no skill involved or that the member is indicating a skill yet to be articulated. Repeated failure to apply the prefaced words is an indication that a committee member is having difficulty in or is avoiding stating the desired action. Other members should be requested to assist by attempting to restate the original contribution within the agreed upon context.

The action verbs may range from readily observable physical action to mental problem -solving or analytical action that can only be observed by an expert in the occupation (see Figure 8-2). There is no intent to limit the skill definitions to the more obvious easy -to-identify physical action skills, such as individual tasks or steps.

The following kinds of definitions should not be allowed to appear on the DACUM chart:

(a)   Statements of static behavior related to knowledge. The co-ordinator should not accept "... KNOW ...", "...KNOW HOW TO ...", "... UNDERSTAND ...", "... HAVE A KNOWLEDGE OF ...".

(b)   Statements of static behavior related to personal or professional role characteristics. Unacceptable are statements beginning "The individual must be able to BE ..." as in "... BE PROFESSIONAL", "... BE CREATIVE".

(c)   Statements of behavior that is affective or attitudinal. The co-ordinator should reject "... APPRECIATE ...".

Committees typically begin by wanting to specify knowledge or knowledge application. The reason may be that they can see completion of specification of knowledge elements in the three days allocated, but they cannot visualize being able to define all the skills in their occupation in that time. Some feel that the task is hopeless due to the uniqueness or complexity of their occupation, which they are certain the co-ordinator underestimates.

<u>Skill definitions must be explicit</u>. The responsibility of the co-ordinator is to engineer the committee into making its definitions so explicit that they cannot be misinterpreted and will not be confusing to each other and to their colleagues in industry. The co-ordinator must encourage constant review to expand the definition or to search for alternate words which will make it explicit.

Explicit Definitions	Potentially Misinterpreted Definitions
Write PHP code	*Know* code
Perform lock out tag out	*Understand* safety policy
Operate asphalt paver	*Use* equipment
Train first line supervisors	*Educate* employees
Verify OSHA certification	*Ensure* safety
Assign job responsibilities	*Communicate* with subordinates
Set up computer equipment	*Start* program
Monitor control chart	*Appreciate* quality
Participate in workshop	*Be* professional
Confirm product delivery	*Take* document
Calculate net income	*Do* math
Prepare administrative report	*Make* policy

Figure 8-2. Example Action Verbs

Acceptable definitions are written in eight words or less (plus connectives). At the same time, too few words may indicate that the skill is not adequately qualified. A typical contribution for skills involving machinery and equipment is "... USE ...", followed by the name of the equipment. It should be redefined to describe clearly what is to be done. This is accomplished by using a more specific action verb and by qualifying the equipment to precisely what will be utilized. On the other hand, definitions that are too long are not likely to be sufficiently explicit, indicating that the committee is still struggling for precise and concise wording.

Definitions should not be treated as independent entities while subjecting them to critical review. Each should be considered as part of a whole, as a location on a map. Therefore, in ensuring that each definition is explicit, it is also necessary to assess skills surrounding it or related to it. The other definitions help to clarify at least what the skill in question is not.

Original contributions are most frequently made more explicit by adding qualifying words. In some cases these may be additional verbs which help clarify the action intended. In others it is useful to describe the range of application to limit meaning to exactly what is intended.

Skill definition must reflect organizational function. Each skill statement must be based on the actual function that must be performed for the employing organization to help meet its over-all objectives. In other words, it must reflect what actually has to be done or achieved on the job under typical working conditions.

Two factors can lead the committee to create definitions that do not reflect organizational function. First, it may be influenced by conventional skill definitions used in contemporary training programs for the field. These may be definitions of sub-skills designed to enhance the training process and as sub-skills will not qualify for a place on the DACUM chart. Such definitions are widely used in industry even though they are inaccurate or misapplied. Second, the committee may be influenced by typical definitions found in the work environment (such as job descriptions which emphasize responsibility and authority rather than skill, or occupational or professional standards which are a measure rather than skill definition).

Skill definitions must reflect future as well as current requirements. Because of the required lead time before a training institution can produce graduates, it is necessary to treat the occupational analysis as a need projection. The committee is requested to predict what skills will be required in the immediate future. It can include any skills for which it can provide some evidence of likelihood of wide application in a reasonable period of time. Unless there is indication that the graduate will be expected to apply the skill on the job, it should not be included. A built-in control against unnecessary coverage of future processes is the difficulty the committee has in specifying the occupational skills required even though a great deal may be known about the process.

Occasionally committee members want to specify skills that are expected to be less required in the future because of phasing out of equipment or processes. They should be questioned about the probability that graduates of a program will be expected to apply these skills. One argument raised is that there are still a few applications of processes that demand the skills. It should be pointed out that new graduates are unlikely to be involved in such work. Employers would be more likely to assign experienced veterans.

Skill definitions must reflect the level of activity. Because occupations are part of a multi-level structure of industrial organizations, there is often overlap with occupations on the same level. Similarly, there are also skill overlaps, with somewhat the same skills being applied in more than one occupation. It is important to make definitions for each clear in order to illustrate differences in application.

A frequent problem is specification of appropriate skill definitions for occupations responsible for functioning of other occupations. Committees tend to specify the skill of the supporting occupation due to inability to specify skills in, for example, a technician-level occupation where the action verbs would probably be ... MONITOR ..., ... DIRECT ..., ... CO-ORDINATE ..., ... CONTROL ..., rather than ... CONSTRUCT ..., ... FABRICATE ..., or ... SERVICE ....

Skill definitions must reflect the entire knowledge application. Committees frequently become concerned over a large body of knowledge, principles, or theory that they know is important in their field, but which they feel has been neglected in the skills defined up to that time. They may even insist that some other way be devised to include knowledge, principle, or theory definitions in the chart. It is important that the co-ordinator be consistent in demanding that each contribution be made in the form of an activity or skill. At times it may be necessary to pause to reflect on the knowledge or theory that is considered so important and to have the committee begin to speculate on the kind of skills, activities, or jobs in which this knowledge would be applied. In some cases one finds that the knowledge has been overrated or overemphasized. In such cases the committee realizes that it has little bearing on the real work in the occupation when they can identify few, if any, skills. More frequently the committee will eventually find a way to specify the critical missing skills that caused the problem. Normally these will be problem-solving and analytical skills, which are typically more difficult to specify than are the more observable manual skills.

Skill definitions must reflect terminology acceptable to the occupation. The committee is charged with responsibility for articulating a set of skill definitions that will be meaningful to all persons in the occupation. Therefore, it is important that they utilize terminology commonly applied on the job.

The co-ordinator should attempt to make all definitions as precise and accurate as possible. Nevertheless, there are times when the co-ordinator will have to make a concession, when a committee insists that terminology they use to describe a particular skill *is* recognized by most persons associated with the occupation and *is* used consistently by practitioners.

In some cases the on-job terminology is unacceptable, as when it is not used in all applications of the occupation. Specific on-job terminology found in one location may not be meaningful in others. This can sometimes be resolved by including alternate words. However, if the skill is applied in a number of diverse situations, each with its own terminology, this becomes unwieldy and it is necessary to search for a suitable generic term that accommodates each situation.

Skill definitions must be measurable using the DACUM rating scale. Frequently, the co-ordinator will ask the committee to pause and reflect on some of the skills already identified (particularly when becoming concerned that specifications are not explicit). Committee members are asked to visualize assigning ratings to persons in their employ or to visualize the ratings they would like to see in persons being interviewed for a position in their firm. If they cannot visualize how they would rate specific (or even hypothetical) persons, they must either change wording to make it more explicit or break the skills down into sub-components that are in reality the skill definitions sought. A good example of this type of problem is when a committee specifies that an individual must be able to perform in some sort of results oriented activity. The difficulty arises when the results can be achieved in two or more different ways, each of which is acceptable, but ability in each of which must be known to the prospective employer.

In such a case it may be necessary to break a definition down into sub-definitions until the committee is sure it could readily interpret what the person being assessed can do in a specific work environment.

CATEGORIES OF SKILLS AND ACTION WORDS

In the interest of providing the DACUM chart development co-ordinator with a useful tool for resolving skill definition problems, the following categories of skills appearing on DACUM charts were established after analysis of a number of reasonably comprehensive DACUM charts. The intention is not to provide a taxonomy of carefully structured skill categories that must be adhered to in developing DACUM charts, but to illustrate the kinds of skill definitions that may appear on a chart and to suggest action words that will be suitable for skill definitions in a specific category if it should be present.

Three factors mitigate against designating skills in discrete categories or attempting to have the committee describe a skill contribution within one specific category:

1. It will tend to inhibit the committee in its brainstorming activities. Most skills (particularly those more complex and difficult to describe) are easier to define if the committee can be free of structures or criteria which inhibit their efforts to solve a difficult problem.

2. Many skills involve more than one of the categories described. In some cases it is difficult to isolate the category in which the skill should be located. In others the use of multiple action words (such as IDENTIFY and SELECT) would combine two categories for the same skill. In such cases the definition would include two action words although the skill is actually performed as a simultaneous single action. To attempt to segregate them would only add confusion to the analysis process.

3. Many skills on a chart partially change category as different levels in the rating scale are applied. The rating scale covers a range from rather mechanical applications of the skill to analytical problem-solving applications.

No attempt is made to weight individual skills on a chart even though they may require different amounts of learning time and have different values in an industrial environment. Each is defined individually, and other processes (e.g., training, on-the-job development, work analysis) will provide weighting which is beyond the scope of this kind of analysis.

SKILL CATEGORIES

Manipulative Skills

Some skills are manipulative or psychomotor skills. Mechanical occupations or skilled trades contain a number of these. Typically there is a band related to hand tools or associated equipment, and one or more bands related to basic manipulative trade techniques. Other occupations contain fewer of these skills.

They are relatively easy for the committee to define and are frequently the most simply stated definitions on a chart. This is because they have traditionally been well-defined, and the simple terminology used is easily understood by all concerned.

In most cases the action verbs are easy to select and are quite direct because they are taken straight from the organizational process. Typical action verbs might be ... FILE ..., ... SOLDER ..., ... SAW ..., ... OPERATE ..., ... BEVEL ..., ... SHEAR ..., ... PUNCH....

Because these skills are most readily recognized, there is less need to make them explicit. In dealing with hand tools or equipment, committees might apply the action verb ... USE .... While it is not considered explicit for application in other skills, it may be widely applied in the occupation. The co-ordinator should try to determine if more explicit action words can be found, but should concede the point if the committee insists there are no useful alternatives and they are comfortable with the definition as it stands.

Procedural Skills

A second kind of skill requires following an established procedure, with somewhat less psychomotor skill demand than the first category. These skills frequently relate to operation of pieces of equipment that demand correct procedure or monitoring rather than psychomotor skill. Such action verbs as ... SEQUENCE ..., ... FOLLOW ..., ... CONSTRUCT ..., ... ADJUST ..., ... PREPARE ..., ... LAY OUT ..., and ... SET UP ... are commonly used to introduce skills in these categories.

Analytical Skills

Most occupations contain a number of what may be termed analytical skills. These skills are frequently described as a result of committee concern that certain theory or knowledge they know is important to the occupation has not been identified. One option is to specify application of the body of theory or knowledge. However, this causes difficulty for the user of the chart in determining just how much of, or how widely, a certain body of information or theory is required. A better alternative is to insist that functions be specified and lead the committee to identify the analytical skills that underlie their concern.

Interpretative Skills

Each occupation normally contains a number of interpretative activities or skills that must be specified. Typical sources of information or standard references are available and must be used to enable decision making in other skills. These in themselves demand certain skills in obtaining needed problem-solving information. Typical action words are ... INTERPRET ..., ... READ ..., ... EXTRACT ..., and ... SEEK OUT ....

Problem-Solving Skills

Normally there is a group of skills in each occupation that constitute the heart of the occupation. That is, they are the skills that characterize the occupation, making it unique and its practitioners valuable. They are normally complex problem-solving or decision-making skills that demand excellence of performance in applying combinations of skills in the four previous categories and in applying the background knowledge of the occupation. Typical action verbs used to introduce these skills are ... PLAN ..., ... DEVISE ..., ... TROUBLESHOOT ..., ... ESTIMATE ..., ... CALCULATE ..., ... SELECT ..., and ... LAY OUT ....

Organizing, Managerial Skills

Because of the way in which occupations fit into organizational structure, many involve the practitioner in organization or supervision of work done by related or lower-level occupations. The skills are sometimes difficult to specify because the activity might be described in the same way on the job in two or three different levels or occupations. The skills at the upper level are frequently introduced with the following action words to make the distinction clear: ... ORGANIZE ..., ... MANAGE ..., ... DIRECT ..., ... CO-ORDINATE ..., and MONITOR....

It should be noted that the same action words can be effectively applied to more than one category of skills. The remainder of the definition and surrounding definitions helps qualify the action. Skills frequently cover more than one category, and action words from two categories can be applied in the same skill definition. The committee should, therefore, be given considerable latitude in its selection of action words and should not be limited to the words listed above. Each occupation has its own action words, which will become apparent as chart development progresses.

Finally, no attempt has been made at ranking the various categories of skills while listing them. Some skills in each category can be quite difficult to learn and apply competently while others may be relatively easy. Most of the first-mentioned category of skills are normally part of, or supportive to, later categories. However, in some cases skills in the later categories may be supportive to the earlier, somewhat less complex skills. The intent is to provide a framework rather than a control for decision-making.

LEVELS OF SKILL

The preceding section described the kinds of skills one might find in a variety of mixes in any single DACUM chart. It was intended to show that these categories exist but that they cannot be specifically imposed on any one occupation or chart without detracting from analysis of the occupation itself.

Similarly it is useful to illustrate the ways in which a variety of levels or strata of skills may link together. The intention is not to impose discrete categories, but to illustrate that they do exist and that it is possible to specify several levels of skills that may be applied in the same process.

Figure 8-3 illustrates how four "levels" of skills taken from a variety of charts can be assumed to be independent skills even though all the lower levels may automatically be applied as part of a higher level skill when it is applied.

At times committees have difficulty with this concept. First, they may be reluctant to state all the lower-level skills, feeling that these can be assumed as part of the definition of the higher-level skills. They overlook the fact that most lower-level skills are repeatedly applied in conjunction with several higher-level skills and must be specified independently if they are to be isolated for training and evaluation purposes. It is preferable to begin with the specification of these lower-level skills in order to be sure they will be covered. Second, on completion of specification of lower-level skills, committees tend to feel the job is complete. They overlook the more complex problem-solving skills that integrate various combinations of lower-level skills in order to achieve in the major complex tasks in the occupation. Sometimes they even argue that the chart is complete without such lower-level skiils they can see that everything is covered if one takes the position that the integrating skills can be assumed.

In such cases it is useful for the co-ordinator to describe the four possible levels.

LEVEL I – Simple, Direct Skills

This category contains those skills that are the most simple to apply and are the most directly stated. Included would be tool usage skills and skilled psychomotor applications. Skills at this level may be applied independently and do not draw other skills into the action when they are applied.

LEVEL II – Routines

Skills in this level typically involve one or more Level I skills when they are applied. They might be classified as routines in which the skill is to integrate several other skills in some organized way.

LEVEL III – Assembly

Skills in this category might be considered task-oriented skills. Application of these skills to an industrial task or project would bring in application of several routines which in turn might each include several simple, direct skills.

LEVEL IV – Over-all or Overriding

This level contains the most comprehensive skills which are job-oriented. Many may be largely organizational or managerial in that they would involve task-oriented skills, several routines, and many simple, direct skills.

It is important that the co-ordinator (and committee) treat these levels in the appropriate context. There is no guarantee that there will be many such complete linkages of skills in levels in each chart. The intent is to illustrate that they *can* and do appear.

Skill Levels

	Oil Burner Repair and	Electrical Technology	Welding Fabrication	Motor Vehicle Repair	Community Work
Level I Simple, Direct Skills	Use nozzle wrench	Identify and select auxiliary contacts	Identify gases by color, code, or cylinder identification	Select and use sockets, wrenches, screwdrivers, and other threaded fastening tools	Analyze location and accessibility pattern or service
Level II Routines	Check and adjust position of nozzle assembly	Select and identify auxiliary relays	Select gases for specific metals and fillers	Disconnect, adjust, and connect switches, springs, and mechanical controls	Identify barriers to service
Level III Assembly	Remove, inspect, clean, and replace nozzle	Coordinate protective devices	Determine gas flow requirements and set meters	Check spring tension, operation, and adjust automatic chokes	Accompany people in contacting agencies
Level IV Overall or Over-riding	Diagnose flame to determine nozzle malfunction	Layout control circuits	Operate MIG welding equipment	Disassemble, inspect, replace pairs and reassemble carburetors	Plead case on behalf of person or group

Figure 8-3. Samples of Relationship of Skills in Levels

SUMMARY

The purpose of Chapter 8 was to provide a thorough explanation of how skills are defined in the DACUM process. Skills are the behaviors that enable an individual to perform competently in an occupation. Skill definitions are guided by the co-ordinator who ensures that skills elicited by the committee specify action behaviors, are explicit, reflect organizational function, reflect future as well as current requirements, reflect the level of activity, reflect the entire knowledge application, reflect terminology acceptable to the occupation, and are measurable using the DACUM rating scale. The co-ordinator also elicits skill definitions from different skill categories and that reflect varying levels of skill.

<u>REFERENCES</u>

Adams, R. E. (1975). *DACUM: Approach to curriculum, learning, and evaluation in occupational training*. Ottawa: Dept. of Regional Economic Expansion.

Minimum Skill Profiles Chart

The main goal of the DACUM system is employer satisfaction. Determining minimum performance qualifications is a crucial activity in meeting employer expectations. The purpose of Chapter 9 is to help practitioners gain a better understanding of how to complete the final phase of DACUM Program. Specifically, an explanation is provided on how to utilize the DACUM Rating Scale and a committee of experienced experts to apply ratings to skills within a DACUM chart resulting in the creation of a new document entitled MINIMUM SKILL PROFILES CHART.

The assigned ratings are later used in the learning process by comparing learners' self-ratings to those ratings on the MINIMUM SKILL PROFILES CHART and through this process, the learner can be evaluated to determine requirements needed for graduation or certification.

The MINIMUM SKILL PROFILES (MSP) CHART is a DACUM chart, which has had added to it ratings which reflect the minimum acceptable level of performance for one or more job categories within an occupation. This chart is created by a committee of occupational experts who can distinguish between expected levels of performance within an occupation. The process to develop the MINIMUM SKILL PROFILES CHART is as follows:

1. Three or four trusted experts in the field are selected to meet as a committee

2. Committee members not familiar with DACUM and the DACUM Rating Scale are given a brief orientation.

3. The committee agrees which categories of the occupation are to have minimum skill profiles prepared.

4. An initial job category is selected to begin applying ratings.

5. The DACUM co-ordinator leads the activity by recording ratings on a clean copy of the DACUM chart.

6. The committee continues until all job categories and associated skills have been rated.

7. After the meeting, copies of the MSP chart are distributed.

COMMITTEE SELECTION

The members asked to serve on the MSP chart committee could be people who had previously served on the DACUM chart development committee, or possibly a local employer in the occupation, or an expert recommended by other members of the committee.

The MINIMUM SKILL PROFILES (MSP) CHART committee's work begins after the development of the DACUM chart. Selecting committee members is vital to the success of the DACUM system, as creating the MSP chart documents the level of performance required in the occupation. The makeup of the committees is not cut-and-dried. Sometimes it may be whatever skilled participants are available. These committees are not as large as the DACUM Chart Development Committee and usually only 3 or 4 members are necessary to create the MINIMUM SKILL PROFILES CHART. In some cases, some members of the original DACUM chart committee may end up being invited to the MINIMUM SKILL CHART committee. Invited members could be local employers in the occupation, or experts recommended by other members of the committee. The committee will work together in applying the rating scale to skills appearing on a DACUM chart under the direction of the co-ordinator.

Members of the committee should possess the following qualifications. They must have worked, or be working in the occupation, and be fully skilled in all aspects of the occupation. Typically, these individuals have risen to managerial ranks within the organization and have supervised persons performing the skills that are to be rated. If individuals selected are not managers, it is important to select persons who have an ability to distinguish accurately and confidently between different levels of performance. Finally, members should be able to devote full-time to the meeting ranging from one to three hours, depending on the complexity of the occupation.

PHYSICAL LOCATION & SUPPLIES

The meeting is usually quite informal and can be held anywhere; an office, a boardroom, or a classroom. Required supplies are: several copies of the DACUM chart, writing tools, and a tabletop surface large enough to view unfolded charts.

THE RATING SCALE

Again, the rating scale is a 7-point descriptive scale (see Figure 9-1) ranging from zero to six to reflect the level of performance demanded in the selected occupation. The rating scale focuses on the most readily available form of evaluation: observable behavior. Because most occupations, particularly new occupations, do not have already established standards and measures, observation of behavior is used more consistently and more often by employers in evaluating employees. The rating scale is used within the DACUM system to evaluate trainees in the same way that industry looks at employees and is the key link that makes DACUM work. Specifically, the rating scale is the glue that ties the analysis, learning, and evaluation together.

Since the objective of occupational training is to provide employees who can satisfy industry's need for performance in work situations, the rating scale focuses directly on realistic work situations. This avoids evaluation of performance from the traditional point of view of the instructor, personnel manager, or educator, who tends to measure in a simulated situation with artificial criteria. The description of each level is designed to reflect a level of performance typically found or demanded in an industry. The definition with the value of '3' is used as a baseline for measuring occupational skills. It describes the minimum performance normally expected in each skill of a minimally qualified person such as a Journeyman Cook as noted later in one of the skilled trades.

While the DACUM rating scale has 7-points, it is important to note here that the '0'rating is not used during the development of the MINIMUM SKILL PROFILES CHART. The definition with the value '0' indicates unsatisfactory performance. In other words, the individual is unable to perform well enough for pay in a work environment. At no time would we expect a trainee to not be able to perform a skill satisfactorily. The '0'rating is therefore reserved for self-ratings and in-process ratings of skills during the learning process. There are instances however where a MSP chart is built for several job categories within the occupation where a trainee within a specific category may not be expected to perform a certain skill. In these cases, the committee should not assign a '0'rating, but simply leave the space blank when rating the skill in that category.

The definition with the value of 'l' is a first level of successful performance. It is characteristic of an individual who is able to perform a skill, but normally cannot achieve alone. The individual may need help in each new assignment and may often run into problems that require expert assistance. The individual would normally be expected to perform only in a work environment where direction and expert assistance are close at hand and constantly available.

The definition with the value of '2' indicates that the individual is fairly capable of functioning independently in performing a skill and needs only periodic supervision or assistance. This individual could be placed in a much larger work environment where a single supervisor would be on hand to respond to periodic needs of many individuals.

Level 6	Can perform the skill with more than acceptable speed and quality, with initiative and adaptability and **can lead others** in performing
Level 5	Can perform the skill with more than acceptable speed and quality, with **initiative** and **adaptability** to special problem situations
Level 4	Can perform the skill satisfactorily without supervision or assistance with **more than acceptable speed** and quality of work
Level 3	Can perform the skill satisfactorily **without** assistance and/or supervision
Level 2	Can perform the skill satisfactorily but requires **periodic** supervision and/or assistance
Level 1	Can perform the skill but **not** without constant supervision and some assistance
Level 0	**Cannot** perform the skill satisfactorily for participation in the work environment

Figure 9-1. DACUM Rating Scale

The definition with the value of '4' is for those individuals whose performance in terms of speed and quality of work is better than would be expected as a minimal level of journeyman performance.

The definition with the value of '5' is for excellent performance of the skill. Not only can the individual perform with more than acceptable speed and workmanship, but they have reached a level enabling them to solve unique problems with initiative and adaptability. This category represents the highest level of technical performance.

The definition with the value of '6' is for the top level of employment in the occupation. The individual performs exceptionally well and has the ability to lead others in performing the skill. They are undoubtedly the type who would be considered for a supervisory or instructional role in the occupation.

DEVELOPING A MINIMUM SKILL PROFILES CHART

Committee Orientation

Usually committee members are already familiar with DACUM, having also been members of the chart building committee. But if any members are not already familiar with DACUM, the co-ordinator gives them a brief informal orientation.

Certification Categories

Next, the committee decides on the categories for which professional certification could be granted and minimum skill profiles need to be prepared. For some occupations, the committee will only be focusing on one category (job classification) and for other occupations, a few classifications. For example, a committee of professional cooks might establish the following categories: CHEF DE CUISINE , JOURNEYMAN COOK, SHORT ORDER COOK.

Creating a Minimum Skill Profile

The committee chooses a category to begin with, for example, JOURNEYMAN COOK. The DACUM co-ordinator leads this activity and does all the recording on a clean copy of the chart. Each member follows along on a copy of the chart while the co-ordinator reads each skill statement in turn aloud and asks for the desired rating level for that skill expected of a JOURNEYMAN COOK. There may be little discussion as the committee may quickly agree on a rating level of that skill. However, for some skills it may be necessary to have considerable discussion before members can agree on a minimum rating.

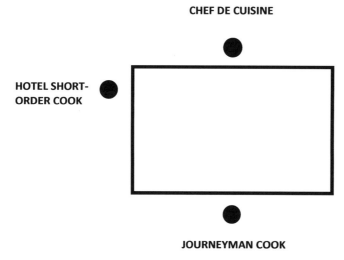

Figure 9-2. Job Category Legend

It is necessary for the members to keep in mind (all at the same time) the needs of the industry and employers, the needs of the profession in general, the future needs, the needs of competent colleagues who would have to be qualified, the needs of an occupational association as a certifying body, and of course their own individual views of what should be required for their own profession. The agreed rating for each skill is recorded in the location for each corresponding job category legend (see Figure 9-3) around the perimeter of each skill statement. Only the ratings that are applied within the job category are required. It is very likely that some job categories will be void of a rating for a given skill statement (see Figures 9-4 and 9-5).

The committee continues in the same way with each of the other categories (e.g., CHEF DE CUISINE) if applicable, doing them one at a time. The committee may review and possibly modify a rating from an earlier category that they now realize may have been a bit too high or low in relation to the others. The committee will not place undue requirements on the learner to acquire ratings in skills they are unlikely to use in their specialty.

Once the skills for all the categories are rated satisfactorily, the meeting is concluded, and copies of the newly completed MINIMUM SKILLS PROFILE CHART are distributed. This new document represents the minimum accepted skill requirements for performance in an occupation for one or more job categories.

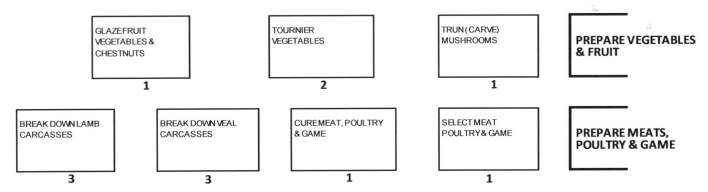

Figure 9-4. Skill Ratings for a JOURNEYMAN COOK.

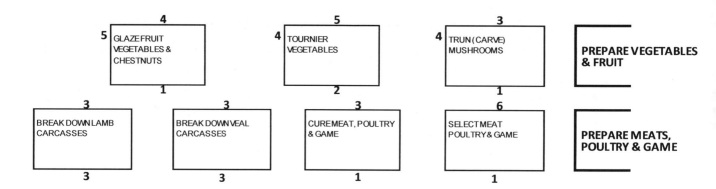

Figure 9-5. Skill Ratings for JOURNEYMAN COOK, SHORT ORDER COOK, and CHEF DE CUISINE.

USING THE MINIMUM SKILL PROFILES CHART TO EVALUATE PERFORMANCE

Comparing the learners' self-ratings to the ratings on the MINIMUM SKILL PROFILES CHART is a simple process that occurs during the Learning-Evaluation phase of the DACUM system (see Chapter 12 – 15). The process can be formal or very informal and relaxed, depending on the situation. Consider this scenario:

> *"An instructor in a community college informally observes a learner continually self-rating and improving his skills. If asked for advice, the instructor points the learner to useful learning resources and provides guidance when needed. When the learner presents new ratings, the instructor confirms that the learner is actually able to perform those skills at the self-rated levels. The learner charts his overall progress by comparing his self-ratings to the ratings on the MINIMUM SKILL PROFILES CHART. Eventually the learner's self-ratings match or exceed those on the MINIMUM SKILL PROFILES CHART, and both learner and instructor realize the learner is ready to graduate from the program."*

Another example:

> *"A supervisor in a company running a training program and her employee both have a pretty good idea that the employee is occupationally ready. Typically the employee initiates discussion about whether they are actually ready. The supervisor confirms any new self-ratings the employee may have. The supervisor compares the employee's self-rating chart to the MINIMUM SKILL PROFILES CHART and determines whether the employee has indeed completed the program."*

A further example might be:

> *"In a technological institute, a student approaches his instructor to ask for a check of his*

ratings, to compare his latest ratings to the MINIMUM SKILL PROFILES CHART. He believes he's getting closer to qualification. The instructor tells the student he still has to improve ratings and performance in two or three skills. The opportunity to practice these skills might not be available at this institute. So the instructor might contact colleagues in the occupation who are expert in the missing skills and invite them in to help assess the learner's performance in these skills. Conversely, the instructor might send the learner out to the colleague's work environment to help improve his performance. The colleagues are happy to assist because they may be interested in hiring the student once he qualifies."

Sometimes the process may be very formal. Here's an example of a set of step-by-step instructions for using the MINIMUM SKILL PROFILES CHART in certifying members of an association (see Chapter 16 – TERMINATION AND CERTIFICATION).

CERTIFICATION PROCEDURE:

1. The applicant approaches a representative of their occupational association, indicating they would like to self-rate and apply for certification.

2. The applicant is given instructions on how to self-rate.

3. The applicant will self-rate on a clean copy of the DACUM chart.

4. If the applicant has any questions regarding how to proceed, they can contact any already certified member of the association.

5. Once self-rating is completed, the applicant should have their ratings looked at by their boss (if skilled in the field), a colleague in the association, or one of the certifiers in the association. Ideally, the applicant might discuss it with all three. Any one of them might be able to spot general errors in self-rating.

6. The applicant is next provided with access to a copy of the chart titled MINIMUM SKILL PROFILES CHART. Placing that chart, and the self-rated copy together, the applicant can compare their ratings with those in the category for which they would like to be certified.

7. If all the self-ratings at least match those of the minimum skill profile for the category, the applicant should immediately contact the association representative, to set up a rating interview.

8. If even a few of the self-ratings are lower than those indicated on the MINIMUM SKILL PROFILES CHART, the applicant will realize

improvement is needed in those skills. In the meantime, the applicant may contact the association to indicate which skills are weak, indicate when the applicant thinks their skills will be raised to an acceptable level, receive advice on how to go about improving the skills, and tentatively establish a future time and place for the RATING INTERVIEW.

9. Or if the applicant finds that many of the self-ratings are lower than those required for the category in which they wish to be certified, they may decide to, in the meantime, apply for a lower category if one is available. The applicant should contact the association to arrange for a RATING INTERVIEW.

10. But if the applicant finds that some skills are too low for even the lowest category, they have no choice but to improve performance in those skills and re-apply when each of their skills match the ratings in the MINIMUM SKILL PROFILES CHART for the category.

It is important that all parties realize this is a performance-based system. Only those who have performed at the desired levels can be granted approved ratings and the associated certificate. If the applicant has never performed at the required rating level, they cannot receive the certification.

If applicants lack ability in certain skills, it is mainly up to them to improve their performance in those skills. No one else can do it for them.... although all parties involved can pitch in and help.

11. RATING INTERVIEWS will be conducted at a time and place that is convenient to both the interviewer and applicant.

12. During the course of the RATING INTERVIEW, the interviewer records their impressions of the applicant's skill levels on a fresh copy of the chart, called a MASTER COPY. It becomes the official one for that applicant.

Briefly, the RATING INTERVIEW procedure is a careful questioning by the interviewer of the applicant's self-ratings. Questioning is done only to the level needed for the interviewer to be confident the agreed-upon ratings accurately reflect the applicant's ability to perform. It is not a 'third degree' or inquisition designed to put pressure on the applicant and perhaps trip them up. Neither is it an oral examination where the applicant is expected to spout out all the information they know about a subject. Instead, the role of the interviewer is to help the applicant describe their ability -to-perform as accurately as possible. The interviewer is a professional simply helping a professional colleague determine their own competence. In the interview they review each of the applicant's rated skills one-by-one. The applicant indicates the self-rating, and the interviewer may question when, where, or under what circumstances the performance took place, to see if the performance is accurately rated. If the interviewer is already familiar with the applicant's ability in the skill and agrees with the rating, there is no need for questions. Such interviews go very quickly. But if the interviewer knows little about the applicant's work, the interviews may take 2 hours or more. The interviewer may have to ask a lot of questions to be satisfied that the applicant performs as well as rated. During the interview, the applicant may change several of the self-ratings, suddenly realizing that their competence in a skill is lower than they had self-rated. Or the applicant may become convinced by the interviewer that their competence in a skill is indeed higher than they had self-rated.

13. If after the interview the applicant indicates they still feel they qualify, the association representative will check the approved ratings on the MASTER COPY against those on the MINIMUM SKILL PROFILES CHART for the certification category. If they all match or exceed the minimums, the association representative will attest to this fact on an appropriate form and file the applicant's MASTER COPY for future action.

14. At the next meeting of the association's certification committee, the applicant's MASTER COPY along with other information will be presented for the approval of the committee. They will question the representative on the applicant's background and may ask for an explanation of unusual ratings. On the other hand, the representative may at this time request help from the committee in making a final judgment on the applicant. The representative may be concerned about some aspect of the applicant's skills. When the committee is satisfied, the representative has done a thorough job of assessing and documenting the applicant, the applicant will be considered qualified.

15. When the committee is satisfied the applicant indeed qualifies, a copy the applicant's MASTER COPY, along with any others, is forwarded to the chair of the association for preparation of the certificate document.

16. The certificate is then presented to the applicant.

17. After a copy is made, the MASTER COPY will be returned to the representative for use in approving further ratings if and when the applicant decides to begin working on a more advanced certificate.

18. By following the same procedure, applicants can periodically have their certificate upgraded to reflect increased skill levels, or they can apply for and receive a new certificate at an even higher category.

**Note:** It is expected that occupational associations will concentrate on certification for the more advanced categories, for example MASTER CHEF and SAUCIER, leaving the JOURNEYMAN COOK profile to serve as guidelines for training institutions and government certifying bodies.

SUMMARY

This chapter provides direction in developing a MINIMUM SKILL PROFILES CHART. The goal of the DACUM system is employer satisfaction and the rating scale is used to identify expected levels of performance by expert workers, supervisors, or employers. This chapter explored the selection of a committee, physical location and supplies needed for the meeting, the DACUM Rating Scale, committee orientation, certification categories, and creating the MSP chart. Finally, the use of the MSP chart to evaluate performance both formally and informally was presented.

REFERENCES

Adams, R. E. (1975). *DACUM: Approach to curriculum, learning, and evaluation in occupational training.* Ottawa: Dept. of Regional Economic Expansion.

10

INSTRUCTOR SELECTION AND DEFINING LEARNING ACTIVITIES

After the DACUM chart is developed and each skill isolated, planning, co-ordinating, and monitoring program development for a DACUM learning environment can take place. This enables program developers to treat each as an independent entity for each stage of development. This chapter discusses the Instructor Selection and Orientation and Define Learning Activities elements of the Development Model for DACUM Learning Programs (Figure 10-1) and what they tend to affect.

DEVELOPMENT MODEL FOR DACUM LEARNING PROGRAM

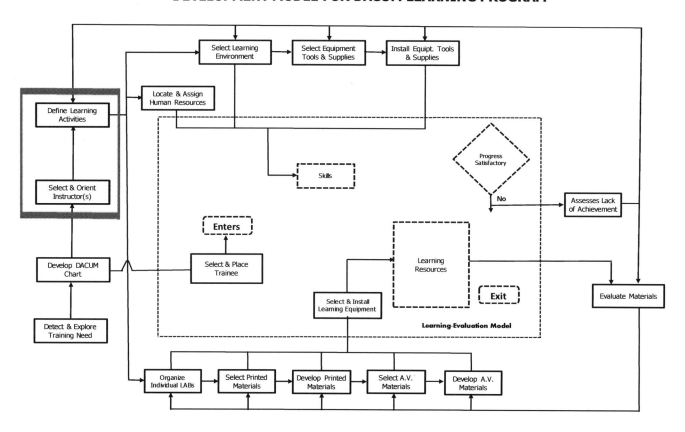

Figure 10-1. Development Model for DACUM Learning Program

It should be pointed out that the model applies skill by skill in terms of program development. If a chart contained 215 skills, this model would be applied 215 times in planning the program within the DACUM framework.

INSTRUCTOR SELECTION

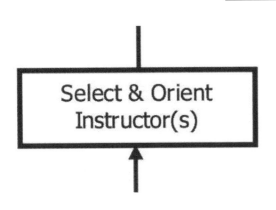

Once the DACUM chart is completed (as described in Chapters 5-9) program organizers or administrators can begin the process of instructor selection. Or this may be done in advance of chart construction. In some cases training staff is on hand because DACUM is being applied in a program conversion. In such cases, orientation to the system should be kept general and to a minimum in order to avoid the intrusion of too many preconceived ideas about the system and how it will operate in the new program. These ideas inhibit application of the system in an optimal way since they make more difficult a clear look at the elements of the program and its installation.

In the same way, it is possible to determine if all the skills on the chart are going to be adequately covered by a team of instructors. Each individual's competency can be assessed to ensure that the entire range of skills is adequately covered in terms of technical capability.

Potential instructors can share in the assessment process. One technique is to have them entry-rate themselves. If it is convenient, it is possible to have someone familiar with their work assist them in arriving at ratings and verify that they possess the skills to the degree indicated.

Additionally, using the chart, it is possible to call upon persons in, or familiar with, the occupation and the industries of which it is part to assist in nominating persons with the required background.

Instructor Selection Criteria

Demands in terms of instructor capability in the DACUM system are somewhat different from demands in more conventional training programs, although many of the characteristics of the incumbents may be much the same. Specifically required are:

a) *Expertise in the occupation as indicated by extent of ability to cover the chart.*

b) *Evidence that the applicant is a "veteran" in the occupation.* This is not necessarily related to length of time in the occupation. Some relatively young persons may be known for their ability to handle a wide range of assignments.

c) *Responsibility in the occupation.* In order for the instructor to relate the requirements to new or developing learners, organize useful learning experiences, and assess acceptable performance, there should be some evidence that the instructor was able to handle a responsible position in an industrial environment demanding the application of much the same skills.

d) *Capability in directing the work of others.* Because the DACUM learning environment replicates or simulates industrial job conditions, many learning activities should be group or team projects. The instructor should have demonstrated some ability to lead teams in prior work experiences.

e) *Imagination in adapting techniques in occupations.* There should be some evidence in the instructors' s industrial work that the instructor is imaginative in applying the skills or techniques of the occupation to a wide range of tasks. The instructor will be required to do this in the learning environment while helping learners identify applications for skills they desire to acquire. Similarly, this expertise will be replicating skills, in initially specifying learning activities and in simulating and replicating skills, projects, and work in the learning environment.

f) *Interest and ability in developing others on the job.* It is important that the instructor like to work with people in terms of developing their skills on the job.

g) *Ability to assess skill performance.* The instructor should have been in a position in industry where they were required to make on-the-spot assessments of skill performance. Persons with supervisory experience typically have this ability, as well as persons who have spent considerable time as members or leaders of project teams. The expert in the occupation who usually works alone might be unsuitable even though he or she might be theoretically and technically competent.

On the other hand, there are certain characteristics commonly required of instructors that are **<u>NOT</u>** required, or are less required, in the DACUM system. These include:

a) ***<u>Ability to handle group presentation.</u>*** One of the traditional requirements of an instructor is the ability to present lectures, demonstrations, etc., to groups of learners. Normally required are a good range of verbal skills and confidence in speaking to a group. Little group presentation is applied in the DACUM system. In most situations it is discouraged because most DACUM instruction is intended to be provided on a one-to-one basis or to a very small ad hoc group.

b) ***<u>Ability to prepare and evaluate tests.</u>*** One would normally be concerned with finding persons with at least potential ability to construct a variety of evaluation instruments. Often this necessitates a requirement for prior instructor training in a formal program. Such instruments are not used in the DACUM system.

c) ***<u>Ability to organize instruction.</u>*** Normally, there is a need to recruit instructors with ability to plan training programs, establish instruction sequence, and schedule and organize presentations. There is also a concern about the ability to describe these in the form of curriculum outlines and training plans. Such abilities are usually developed through formal instructor training. Again, these abilities are not required in the DACUM system.

d) ***<u>Ability to create instructional materials.</u>*** Conventional programs, especially those which are information-based, require instructors to prepare a variety of instructional materials suitable for delivery to groups of learners. They must be able to create materials that will either support or fill gaps in available modes of presentation. Because of the flexibility of the DACUM system, this is not required. The instructor can draw on a variety of sources of information, hence need not have this kind of technical competence.

Primarily, the need is for someone who is responsible, competent in the occupation, and able to transfer their abilities to the training environment.

Selecting Instructors from Present Occupational Training Staff

It is difficult to tell in advance how well an instructor is going to adapt to the DACUM system. One needs to see actual performance in operating the system or in system development activities to determine whether or not the instructor can identify with the process and adapt technical competence to this new model.

There are three problems in the selection of instructors for work in the DACUM system (or for determining whether or not the system can be applied in a present training facility using its staff resources):

a) There may be a lack of certain technical skills. If they were initially selected on the basis of suitability for performing in the conventional instructor role (e.g., demonstrating fundamental skills to beginners, lecturing on theory), they may have been taken on with the knowledge that they had little practical experience in applying a number of the skills of the occupation. They may not be technically capable of devising and providing learning experiences, monitoring learner progress, and assessing learner achievement in those skills.

b) There is the possibility, particularly in well-established programs, that some instructors will have been away from the industrial environment for a considerable period of time. Some may lack knowledge of the way in which new techniques and concepts have been applied in the occupation, as well as of current demands of the occupation on the employee. The instructor may be aware of these, but may not have the in-depth knowledge or experience that would enable the instructor to apply them in the learning environment.

c) Some instructors may not be able to identify with the DACUM process or may show a marked lack of enthusiasm for the system. If they continue to feel this way, it is unlikely that the system will be well applied. The appropriate procedure is to involve these persons in workshops, discussions, and review activity, and allow them time to observe on-going programs and program results.

In installing the system for the first time in an institution, it is wise to select as pilot or demonstration applications those departments that contain instructors who can quickly identify with the process and who exhibit a willingness to apply it as designed. Their program may then serve as a model for others who are reluctant or somewhat skeptical.

Selecting New Persons for the Instruction Role

It is also important to detect how the new instructor feels about the DACUM approach. This can be done by presenting some of the concepts and encouraging the instructor to react. This is relatively time-consuming, but it is considered essential. In spite of the fact that an individual may know a good deal about the program and agree to participate in it, they may arrive with certain reservations or preconceived ideas about how it will operate. Instructors may see only certain desirable features of the program that will be useful in applying the sort of technique the instructor intends to apply anyway. This causes the instructor to overlook some of the other techniques that might be deemed more essential by program organizers. It is important to check out each element of the approach through a complete orientation and review to be sure that new instructors are willing to apply the program as it is designed.

There is also the problem of recruiting staff within the limits of employment structures of institutions. Due to salary scale or other factors, it may be necessary to employ persons who are not yet fully occupationally competent. Where this is necessary, it is important to clarify at the outset exactly how competent the person is in each of the skills on the chart and determine which skills can be upgraded or improved and how this can be achieved.

INSTRUCTOR ORIENTATION

Once an instructor is selected, it is important to provide them with an orientation to the DACUM system. The following looks at the components of instructor orientation including a review of the DACUM system and rationale, and review of the DACUM chart. This section will also address the completion of instructor orientation, as well as potential problems that may occur during orientation.

Review of System and Rationale

The first step in orientation of instructors is to provide them with a thorough review of the rationale for the DACUM approach and the models which describe development and operation. This has been done in the form of a workshop-discussion presentation which lasts two to four days, depending on the nature of the program and the personnel involved. It is important in providing this that the instructor be exposed to an overview of the entire training system in order to become familiar with each kind of developmental and operational decision that the instructor will be called on to make in their first activities. The review is conducted through visually supported oral presentation with discussion and questions. Examples are selected from another occupation or training situation. The instructor is encouraged to learn principles, develop concepts, and observe and assess techniques for developing and installing a program for another occupation. Usually the program selected is hypothetical and is based on an occupation that is highly visible, somewhat limited in number or scope of skills, and for which training time would be short. This enables the new instructors to visualize and discuss the entire development of a program and the progress of a learner through the program within a reasonable time span. During such reviews or presentations, discussion of issues related to the program in which the instructors will actually be instructing is limited or prohibited. It has been found that if this is not done they become concerned about specific skills and have difficulty in visualizing the way in which the components of the DACUM system will combine to produce a workable training program.

Review of DACUM Chart

The next step is a thorough review of the chart. In some cases, it may have been possible to make a video recording of all or part of the chart development workshop. If this was done, instructors can observe and assess the discussions that took place while identifying the skills of the occupation. This makes it easy for them to relate the chart and eventual program to their own work experiences. Normally, someone from the occupation or a program organizer tries to orient the instructors to the chart through a short presentation. Sometimes this can be done in an hour or so, while in other cases it requires two or three days of discussion related to the occupation, the nature of the chart, and why it was constructed in the way in which it was. Ideally, the appropriate person for this assignment is the person who co-ordinated the DACUM chart development workshop. The co-ordinator can relay the reasons for including certain skills and the discussion that took place in arriving at specific sets of skills or specific structures in the chart. The instructors will have to study the chart quite carefully to develop a mental image of the meaning and scope of each skill. If necessary, the instructor can question the co-ordinator (or committee members) to obtain clarification of some of the skills. Normally, the occupationally competent person has little difficulty in quickly interpreting the meaning of the skills on the chart.

Completion of Orientation

There are two sets of conditions for completion of instructor orientation, depending on the stage of development of the training program.

1. ***Orientation during program development:*** If the program is yet to be developed, the instructor will be oriented to many of the details of the DACUM system while participating in development work. It is easy for instructors to move into this development work quickly and apply personal experience to the selection of learning activities, equipment, tools and supplies, and information resources.

   Program development activities are carefully monitored by someone designated as a program development co-ordinator. This co-ordinator will take every opportunity to use the technical competence of the new instructor. At the same time the co-ordinator will take every opportunity, when an issue arises, to halt the proceedings for a review of the DACUM philosophy, principles, or techniques in order to assist the instructor to learn more about the system and the program. While primary concern is with developing resources and facilities, much of the discussion centers on how the learner will use these resources and how the learner and instructor will function in the learning environment. This continues through the entire development of the program, from initial planning through first generation operation of the program.

   It was found useful in the programs to have key development staff work in close contact with the co-ordinator while developing the program. This was arranged by having them occupy adjacent office space and assigning both, for a period of a month or two, to the planning and development of the program. Co-ordinator participation was reduced as program staff demonstrated their ability to reach decisions on their own within the framework of the system until such time as the program was installed in its own location and operating without extensive monitoring.

2. ***Orientation during program operation:*** If the program is already operating, instructors will go directly from initial orientation into the learning environment. This is relatively easy as the DACUM learning environment is similar to the work environment and has the added advantage of putting new instructors in a learning position similar to that of the trainees. In instructors relationships with trainees they are able to consider trainee needs in the light of the instructors experience and is more likely to avoid applying resources and practices unsuitable to this kind of learning.

In the other DACUM programs conducted, it was seldom necessary to bring in new instructors during actual operation, as these were one-shot demonstrations. That is, they were operated through one training cycle and then disbanded as there was no provision for operating training programs on a continuous basis. As a result, most staff remained for the life of the program.

When it is necessary to bring new instructors into an on-going program, they should be brought into the training environment as quickly as possible. There is little likelihood that instructors can be oriented and trained as part of a group. Therefore, instructors initial orientation must be planned and conducted on an individual basis. It may consist only of an opportunity to read about the system, a short orientation to the principles of DACUM, a chance to observe other programs in action, and then a short period observing the program of which instructors are to be a part and discussing principles and techniques with present staff. It has been found that new instructors can adapt readily to the program with little prior orientation if they have competent models in the form of other instructors.

Some effort should be made to designate another instructor to back up the new instructor for a brief period in reaching decisions in relating to learners, selecting learning assignments, monitoring performance, and establishing achievement through ratings. This arrangement should not continue for more than a few days since it could create reliance on the person assigned as backup or monitor.

If a change is necessary in a single-instructor program, the problem is greater. The new instructor must move into the operating program and take charge immediately. In this case it is recommended that someone familiar with the DACUM system (a co-ordinator) be assigned to work relatively full-time with the new instructor for a month or so until becoming acquainted with the resources and techniques of the program. Nevertheless, the new instructor can begin to perform immediately on entry if this is demanded. Because of the way the training system is organized, learners can continue to perform independently of instructor assistance for a period while the new instructor adapts to the new role. The new instructor will, however, need assistance in negotiating assessments of performance and ratings with learners.

Problems in Orientation

Most problems in orientation become evident only when instructors have had opportunity to apply DACUM principles and techniques in program development or operation. It is sometimes difficult, on the basis of discussion only, to detect lack of identity with the program and determine whether or not orientation has been successful. Lack of orientation will, however be quickly evident through the nature of the activity the individual creates and becomes involved in and the nature of the decisions reached as part of program development or operation. This provides the co-ordinator with an opportunity to take some form of corrective action. Normally, this corrective action is to stop proceedings and discuss the issues in question, as well as the program philosophy in some detail, in an effort to provide instructors with a further opportunity to orient themselves to the objectives and principles of the program.

Persons who experience difficulty in orientation and require more assistance might be classified in the following ways. These are not necessarily distinct categories. The same individual might have more than one of these characteristics.

1. ***The instructor who is reluctant to follow the DACUM model.***

   This frequently can be the individual who on selection or assignment to the program was interested in the DACUM process and who, in orientation sessions, seemed to identify with it quite readily. However, on being exposed to the techniques and principles that must be followed in applying the system, the instructor begins to encounter issues and conditions not expected. On being confronted with these, the instructor begins to lose an identity with the approach. The instructor is characterized by the tendency to apply other components or principles which results in a program that becomes incohesive.

2. ***The instructor who originally opted for a different role.***

   Based on learning experiences and impressions of occupational training programs, the individual may have initially decided to become an instructor because of certain desirable features or an image held of the conventional instructor role. The instructor might have been attracted to the training field by the prospect of lecturing, demonstrating, being an authority in the learning environment and generally controlling the learners and the environment. It frequently comes as a bit of a shock to such a person to find that they must function in a supporting capacity.

The instructor can take a great deal of initiative in planning and developing resources, but the actual learning process is essentially organized and managed by the learners. The instructor must respond to them rather than they to the instructor. This is sometimes difficult to accept. It is frequently necessary to review the entire philosophy of the DACUM system, particularly those parts relating to the needs of learners.

3. *The instructor who has been conditioned by success in another system.*

Some individuals who move directly from another mode of training into a DACUM-based training system have difficulty identifying with some of the DACUM techniques. They have become comfortable and competent in the use of components in other systems that appear to work very well. There is reluctance to give up these techniques in the interest of selecting alternate techniques that fit much better into a new training system that is complete within itself. If this motivation is strong, the only recourse is to allow the instructor to function in the best way and attempt to test the techniques within the DACUM framework in the hope that he or she will realize where they must be adapted or changed to fit the new concept.

4. *The instructor with personal pride in prior resource and program development.*

The creative instructor in any system will, over a period of time, develop program resources or entire components or parts of programs. The instructor will have a personal pride in these, and they will represent considerable work. The instructor will be reluctant to drop them even though they do not fit the DACUM model. It is difficult to relinquish the fruits of painstaking work and begin to work with a system that must be developed in another fashion.

Extensive discussion should take place, particularly relating to the selection and application of learning resources and their effect on the individual learner and independence in learning. Prohibiting the inclusion of components or resources may result in outright rejection of the DACUM approach. It is frequently better to help the individual take advantage of prior work by helping the instructor adapt the resources so they can be used effectively by the individual learner in the new system.

5. *The instructor with extensive teacher preparation for more structured directive training systems.*

> This individual has the greatest difficulty in adapting to the DACUM learning system through orientation. Primarily it is because this instructor already has a well-established learning and instructional model upon which components or ideas are built or assessed as they appear. The instructor has difficulty taking a good look at the DACUM system because parts of it conflict with their own well-thought-out model, and, as a result, the co-ordinator must normally spend more time to help them adapt to the system in a fully committed way. Each system is built on a set of assumptions. Due to training in one system the instructor had to adopt its set of assumptions. Now the instructor is called on to adopt a much different set of assumptions. It is difficult to adopt these and apply techniques designed to work toward objectives based on them.

> This does not imply that all former instructors are unable to adapt to the DACUM system. On the contrary, if they can overcome difficulties in identifying with the system, they normally become the most effective DACUM instructors. The point is that problems must be identified early during orientation so that recognition can be given to their views and feelings and steps can be taken to help them adjust.

In orienting new instructors, program organizers or co-ordinators must be prepared to encounter a different set of characteristics.

1. *The new instructor who is deluded by DACUM.*

> Some persons, particularly those who have not had experience in learning systems, will see only the most highly visible characteristics of the DACUM system and will be deluded into perceiving it as an almost automatic solution to training problems. They lack the experience to assess the worth of its components when compared to other systems and do not study the system in depth. Such persons appear to be well on their way during early orientation and frequently run into difficulties only when they start to participate in developmental or operational activities. Frequently, there is a let-down followed by a resentment of the system or several of its components.

2. *<u>The new instructor who opted for the traditional instructor image.</u>*

In spite of the fact that new instructors can be partially oriented to the system during job interview and visits to the training institution, some individuals will find it hard to relinquish the traditional image of the instructor as a lecturer or demonstrator or authority figure, When such an individual is encountered, emphasis during orientation should be on the new role, how valuable it is, and what it means to the learners, as opposed to the traditional role and what it sometimes lacks for the learners.

3. <u>The new instructor who takes advantage of the flexibility of the DACUM model.</u> This tendency is sometimes difficult to detect. The individual will participate in development or operation and will reach decisions quickly and begin developing materials. Because of the flexibility of the system, the instructor feels he or she can install what they want to and their personal preferences override the unique requirements of each skill and of the learners who will be attempting to master these skills. For instance, the instructor might have a bias toward a particular medium or mode of presentation which would show up in the development of materials. The instructor can, however, complete a good deal of work before this is detected, and it is a difficult tendency to change.

Formalizing Instructor Preparation

Formal preparation of persons for work in a DACUM learning environment has been developed. These are directed at developing instructors who will be working in an occupational training program. The intention of this type of workshop is to develop the capability of these potential instructors, first to assist in DACUM chart development and, second, to undertake the role of co-ordinator of DACUM-based program installations.

Formal instructor training, while beneficial, isn't a necessary component of the program development model. Some persons need little, if any, preparation for the new role of instructor in the DACUM training environment. The person with a good range of ability in the occupation, who is well adjusted personally, who has a good perspective of other persons in the occupation and their performance requirements, has no difficulty in adjusting to the process. Therefore, it may not be necessary to organize any full-scale training program for instructors. Instead, a supportive or remedial program could be designed. This will allow instructors to begin working in the DACUM system and continue to develop their learning-environment competence while they are working. A DACUM chart for instructors is provided in Appendix C and should be a useful guide in developing materials and devising learning experiences to enable instructors, first, to prepare themselves quickly for entry to the learning environment, and second, to assess their skills so they can develop competence in the areas in which they are weak.

DEFINITION OF LEARNING ACTIVITIES

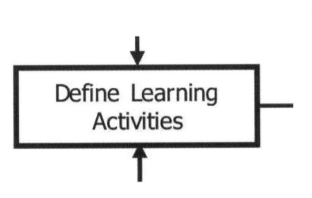

The next step, after initial orientation, is to define learning activities that should be provided to enable the learner to apply and develop skills and demonstrate competence. This is the most critical component of program development. If done well, the result will be an imaginative, stimulating training program.

The intention is not to produce hard and fast specifications of specific learning activities. Instead, it is to activate instructors to consider the range of potential learning activities so they can respond when need arises. In some cases the result may be a tentative listing of potential learning activities for each skill. In other cases these may not be recorded but will be discussed in detail and mentally stored for future reference.

Skill	Learning Activity	Location	Equipment	Supplies	Instructor Responsible	Printed Materials
Sample Skill	1. Activity 1 2. Activity 2	1. OJT 2. Other				

Figure 10-2. Program Development Grid

One useful way to list learning activities is to lay out a large grid on which all program development notes are recorded by component of the development model (See Figure 10-2). The skill definitions are listed in the second row, with planning notes in the columns below. These columns can be completed as work in these areas is undertaken. Once the learning activities are tentatively specified, it is sometimes useful to proceed immediately with completion of the grid. It will be possible at this time to note for many skills what equipment or supplies will be needed, sources of printed materials, computer-based resources, or demonstrations that should be available via video.

Defining learning activities must be completed, however, before proceeding with the further stages of program development as the nature of learning activities will have a bearing on the occupational and learning resources which will be required. They will tend to narrow the range of potential resources that might be applied.

Definition of learning activities must be completed without undue consideration to subsequent steps or decisions and is best handled in the form of brainstorming focused strictly on defining activities. Concern over where the activity would be located, the cost of equipment and supplies, absence of certain resources, or the dissimilarity to accepted learning methods will all negatively influence the process and result in the rejection of excellent activity ideas. For example, the best learning activity for a certain skill might be one that can only be provided feasibly in industry, while the development team is concerned with an in-house training program. Subsequent decision-making in further development steps will resolve this matter. At this time alternative suggestions will be weighed. Some ideas for learning activities may have to be rejected if it is found, on further analysis, that it is not practical to provide them.

If possible, several alternate activities should be defined for each skill to provide opportunity for the learner to apply the skill repeatedly in different problem situations in order to improve competence or prove the learner warrants a higher rating.

A single multi-skill activity can be noted for several skills, provided there are also single-skill activities prescribed for these skills. The learner requires single-skill activities for early learning efforts. Later the learner will be able to cope with (and will be more interested in) larger multi-skill activities or projects in which the learner can learn to integrate the individual skills developed. The latter kind of activity is usually more similar to the nature of skill application in industry.

In isolated cases the only activities available might be multi-skill. This can happen when an industrial committee has identified a skill which is never performed independently but which had to be isolated for analysis and rating purposes. It is important in such cases to identify several multi-skill activities. It may also be necessary to simulate an enabling learning activity to help the learner develop initial skill. Because it would not be considered an occupational "activity", successful performance would not warrant a rating, which could only be granted through successful application of the skill in multi-skill occupational activities. Enabling learning activities should only be suggested when absolutely necessary.

The following classes of learning experiences are categorized in order to provide a picture of the potential scope of activities that might be included in a DACUM learning environment. They are ranked in order of desirability as learning experiences and in terms of how they might help the learner adapt to the new work or occupational environment. Therefore, they are also ranked in order of the degree of direct application or transfer from a work to a learning environment. Efforts to define learning activities for each skill should begin with the first-mentioned kind of activities. Subsequent categories should be considered only if difficulty is encountered in providing an adequate number of acceptable learning experiences for each skill.

1. <u>Directly Applied or Transferred Work Activities</u>

Many activities of the work environment can be transferred to the learning environment. Generally speaking, these are the most useful kinds of learning activities and should be emphasized in specifying learning activities for the DACUM system.

The instructors attempt to define activities that are carried on as part of the work of the occupation and in which the learner can apply the skills in conditions almost identical to those encountered in the work environment. It is often best to assume the learner will be learning via O.J.T. This removes the worry about defining activities that seem unfeasible because of preconceived difficulty in transferring them to a learning environment. Later, efforts can be made to modify the learning environment or the activity.

Many of the skill definitions are self-explanatory, and direct activities are easy to specify. For example, it is relatively easy to visualize establishing learning experiences for each of the skills specified on the DACUM chart for Housekeepers. In some cases the definitions of the skills themselves indicate the learning activity that should take place. In the skill ANALYZE FABRICS FOR WASHABILITY, COLOUR-FASTNESS, AND HEAT LIMITS, one can readily visualize that each of the learners would have to have an opportunity to select and sort batches of laundry to isolate fabrics that require different washing care. Having learners select and identify fabrics from sample swatches contained on a panel board or in a booklet or from photographs would not be considered as realistic as a learning experience. Similarly, in the Oil Burner Repair and Service DACUM chart, for the skill CEMENT AND SEAL DOORS AND OTHER OPENINGS ON HOT WATER FURNACES it is relatively easy to visualize having learners perform this task in much the same manner as craftsmen in the job environment. All that is needed is one or more furnaces that require this treatment. If there are not several available, it may be necessary to consider having to destroy the completed work and return the equipment to its initial state of disrepair so that each learner has an opportunity to work at the skill and raise his skill level through repeated performance.

Learning experiences should be as realistic as possible. In the Housekeepers example one would expect that the learner would have to care for a typical collection of clothes such as might be used by a family or business and that these clothes would be soiled when they are being analyzed and sorted for laundering. Realistic learning experiences are provided for most of the skills on the Housekeepers chart by having members of the project staff live in the learning environment. This creates a need for the learners to perform regular housekeeping skills in an acceptable time period. They will encounter situations they would encounter in a normal housekeeping environment in replacing strewn articles to their proper locations, sorting out laundry, etc.

2. Directly Applied or Transferred Components of Work Activities

While in some cases it is difficult to visualize how an entire work application of a skill would be directly transferred to or replicated in a learning environment, it is possible to transfer components of the work experience to the learning environment and to handle other components of the skill by simulation.

For example, in planning the Oil Burner Repair and Service program it was deemed necessary to provide learners with activities that would allow them to apply a number of skills required in balancing a hot water heating system. The initial idea of heating a portion of the training center with hot water was rejected as impractical. Heat exchange was simulated by installing a large water container outside the building and heating the water with an actual hot water furnace installed for training purposes. The container could be rapidly drained and replenished with cold water to create simulated conditions for system balancing while retaining the mechanic's real work with the heating unit.

The two kinds of learning experiences described above are the most used and are the starting point for any analysis. When these are exhausted, the following classes of learning experiences can be considered, especially as conditions are noted which prevent the provision of more realistic work experiences in the learning environment. There is a tendency for developers (particularly experienced instructors) to begin by selecting from the following categories. They are more familiar and are considered acceptable for conventional programs. Nevertheless, initial selection of these kinds of learning activities causes developers to overlook the more realistic work activities of the occupation. The resulting training pattern is difficult to change when it becomes apparent that more realistic experiences must be provided.

3. <u>Simulated Activities</u>

As noted in example 2 above, it is possible to simulate some of the work activity in converting it to learning activity. However, care should be taken to ensure that the activity is not needlessly simulated, resulting in a learner experience that is less than meaningful in relation to the work the learner will enter.

Mechanical simulation (as opposed to replication) has been little used in other DACUM programs. It is relatively expensive and time-consuming to set up and is impractical in many cases for one-shot training programs. It is used more appropriately in occupations for which advanced technology has made available suitable learning and operational simulators (e.g., flight simulators, police training simulators, refrigeration or electrical simulators).

Most simulation in these programs has been in providing realistic job conditions for certain skills and in providing direct learning experiences for potentially dangerous work environment skills and communication skills through role-playing. For example, police officers can demonstrate realistic firearm skills through the use of detailed simulators. For communication skills, the instructor usually adopts the role of the supervisor or foreman in directing team work activities in the learning environment. As some learners progress, they can also begin to fill this role.

A useful simulation in a fisheries training program was to mark out a full-scale plan of the training vessel on the floor of the net loft. This allowed learners to become familiar with vessel terminology and take positions on the vessel as directed by officers. It also enabled trainees to be more comfortable and sure of themselves once they were aboard the training vessel.

4. <u>Created Projects</u>

It is possible to create special projects for the purpose of providing opportunity for application of a number of skills. These projects are not actual industrial activities since they often result in a product that would not be demanded of the craftsman in industry. Usually they are designed to integrate a larger than normal number of skills in a single project which the learner can be expected to complete in a reasonable period of time. In conventional training they are used to ensure that the learner will apply several specific skills that may be applied in the work environment only in a handful of difficult or time-consuming activities.

Such projects are devised only when it is difficult to replicate real work activities in a learning environment or when it is not feasible to provide such activities to an O.J.T. learner in a work environment. Completion of the industrial activity may be too time-consuming, or it may not be considered wise, due to safety or other considerations, to allow a learner to try to perform without some prior controlled experiences. It has been found, however, that these conditions are rare, and projects have been little used in other DACUM programs.

5. Lab Projects

The DACUM system does not use laboratory activities to any appreciable extent. They are used only when there is no feasible way of replicating work activities in the learning environment. They have not been used in many DACUM programs but have been integrated in a limited way in some programs developed elsewhere.

Because they are designed primarily to assist the learner in acquiring and integrating theory and information, laboratory activities are dissimilar to work activity. They usually involve requirements such as report preparation that are not requirements of the occupation. Therefore, it is hard to determine when occupational skill has increased. Rating is difficult and not too meaningful and really should not be attempted on the basis of Lab Projects unless they are part of the normal activities of the occupation.

6. Programmed Learning

Programmed learning materials have been used in a limited way in DACUM training programs. Well-prepared programs that focus on skill development would be an excellent resource for learning in this approach. However, few such programs are commercially available, and high cost of development discourages in-house preparation of materials. Such programs as are available are usually information-based and cover a number of skills. This makes it difficult to assign them to specific Learning Activity Batteries.

Programmed materials are also difficult to integrate because of the linear sequencing format commonly used. It is difficult to dissect the program to isolate a specific block of information required for a specific skill. Normally the learner must progress through preceding parts of the program in order to understand and be able to work through the sections required.

7. <u>**Information Learning Alone**</u>

Training programs are often limited to providing only information learning for some skills because the skills are felt to be relatively undefinable or because it is not felt feasible to provide suitable learning experiences in the training environment.

Information learning alone is not appropriate to the DACUM system, and attempts at inserting certain elements of this are discouraged. Because the learner cannot perform and demonstrate competence, it is not possible to grant any recognition for the simple acquisition of information. Where such a learning resource has been provided, it has had the effect of encouraging instructors and learners to guess at performance level on the indirect basis of how well information was absorbed or how well learners could describe how they would respond if confronted with a real problem. Learners may wish to acquire information but cannot be rated on its acquisition except as it increases their demonstrated ability to perform.

SUMMARY

It is relatively easy to replicate workplace experiences in the learning environment for most skills identified on DACUM charts. Therefore, directly applied or transferred activities are most widely used and there is little need to use the other less desirable kinds of learning activities. The developer or co-ordinator should be cautioned again, however, that some instructor-developers sometimes decide that they cannot provide replicated learning activities for most of the skills on their chart. They begin instead to focus initial attention on the less desirable kinds of activities which may be more familiar to them. Therefore, co-ordinator/instructor orientation is critical to ensure control and stimulation of emphasis on directly applied or transferred learning activities.

The program development co-ordinator is most valuable during this stage of program development. While the program development co-ordinator may be relatively unfamiliar with the occupation, they can still serve as a stimulator of contributions or ideas. The program development co-ordinator is not hampered by tradition or restrictions that influence the occupational specialists to adopt conventional learning activities and overlook excellent possibilities for selection of more realistic activities. The role of the co-ordinator is to generate brainstorming to identify the realistic learning activities.

<u>REFERENCES</u>

Adams, R. E. (1975). *DACUM: Approach to curriculum, learning, and evaluation in occupational training*. Ottawa: Dept. of Regional Economic Expansion.

11

SELECTION AND DEVELOPMENT OF
LEARNING ENVIRONMENT AND RESOURCES

After determining training needs, developing a DACUM chart, selecting and orienting instructors, and determining the different types of learning activities to be used in the DACUM learning program, the next stage of development is specification of the appropriate learning environment and resources for each skill (see Figure 11-1). This chapter will focus on the selection, development, and installation of different environmental and occupational resources necessary in developing a DACUM training program.

DEVELOPMENT MODEL FOR DACUM LEARNING PROGRAM

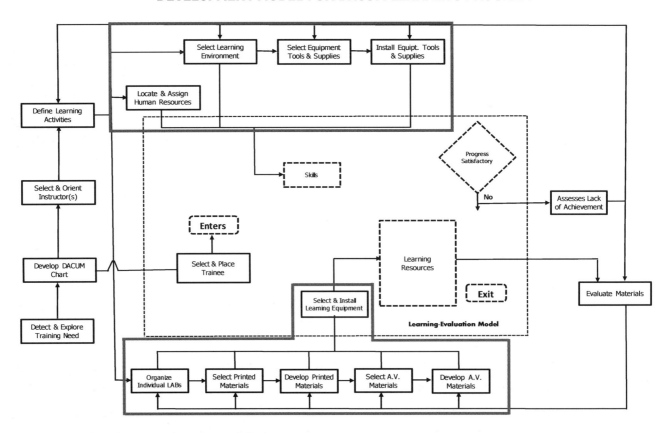

Figure 11-1. Development Model for DACUM Learning Program

SELECT LEARNING ENVIRONMENT

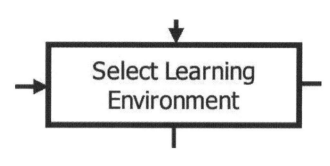

It is important that this be done on the basis of individual examination of each skill and its related learning activities. There will be a tendency to mis-locate specific skills if selection is made for groups of skills by looking at General Areas of Competence or other subdivisions of the occupational profile.

For example, in a mechanical service occupation one might assume that all communication skills could be learned in the job environment, overlooking the fact that one or two might be difficult to learn in a job environment and more suitably learned in a fully protected learning environment.

It is particularly important that the nature of optimal learning experiences be established first. There is a tendency, if this is not done, to begin by looking at suitable learning resources such as programs or printed materials. These may contain some form of learning experience or highly simulated skill application, which are among the weakest kinds of learning experience. They are not a good base on which to build as they lead developers into assuming the training must logically be provided in an in-center training environment.

Selection of the learning environment for each skill is normally a matter of deciding between the job environment and a specially created learning environment which may become a training center for the occupation or may become part of a larger institution. Each has advantages in terms of requirements of the occupation and, more specifically and importantly, in terms of each identified skill and the nature of learning experiences required for development of that skill.

Each of the two possible environments will have some characteristics that will not be conducive to the development of some or perhaps most of the skills of an occupation. In fact, one may have characteristics that make it undesirable for providing most of the skills of a specific occupation.

Some occupations do not lend themselves to extensive training in the work environment for the following reasons.

1. The work environment may be too hazardous for the individual to perform in until some basic skills are acquired. For example, initial training in machining might be better given in a controlled training environment which allows the learner to perform under close supervision where the primary concern is safety

when operating high speed equipment until the learner develops the fundamental operational skills and procedures that will ensure safe operation even in more complex operations.

2. The work environment may be too large or too busy to make it possible to provide trainees with personal attention while they are learning. Large construction sites, formerly considered to be suitable for on- the-job training, are now considered less suitable. A learner has little opportunity to begin learning to operate heavy construction equipment in an environment that demands a rapid work pace that is controlled by the pace of the entire project. Again, preliminary or basic operational skills would be best provided in a controlled learning environment.

3. The work environment may involve critical work that cannot be trusted to the unskilled due to the cost or other ramifications of learner errors. For example, a large communication network demands a high level of skill from electronics servicing personnel. The errors of an unskilled person might disrupt an entire system. Here again, it is best to confine training to a controlled environment.

4. The work may be complex and unlikely to be assigned unskilled persons without prior training. In other words, a substantial period may have to be spent in acquiring some basic skills before the learner can even begin to function in the tasks of the occupation. For example, it is difficult to conceive of an individual going to work directly in a secretarial job without having spent a considerable time developing basic typing skills. Many other aspects of the work might be developed on the job, but development of basic skills would be extremely difficult in the work environment. Similarly, there is little productive work in modern design offices that a young drafting technician can do until acquiring some basic computer aided drafting skills, knowledge of geometric layout techniques, and ability to visualize and project in three dimensions. The nature of work in design offices formerly allowed opportunities for the draftsperson to develop these skills while doing productive work. However, this situation no longer exists. Again, initial learning experiences can best be provided in a controlled learning environment in which the individual can develop basic skills at their own pace.

On the other hand, some occupations, specific skills, or learning experiences in specific occupations are not suitable for development in a controlled separate learning environment.

1. The learning environment may not be able to provide expensive little-used equipment that is, however, necessary for skill development. This might be the situation in an occupation such as stationary engineering where it may be necessary to work directly with a large power plant in order to provide learning experiences for a few skills.

2. It may not be possible to provide complex work conditions and problem-solving situations to allow the learner to apply his or her skills within a meaningful framework. For example, in the building construction industry workers in specific trades must learn to apply their skills within the framework of a hectic work pace and the frequent confusion that surrounds the negotiations and co-ordination of various trades in parts of construction development.

3. The learning environment may not be able to manage situations which demand large space or for which long periods of time may have to elapse before realistic problems appear. In occupations related to the servicing of electrical equipment or systems, it might conceivably be best to allocate to the work environment that proportion of the training that involves faultfinding and repair related to storms or other environmental conditions. This could be done under controlled circumstances by arranging for appropriate on-the-job training experiences with supervision by competent persons.

4. In some cases, it is impossible for the learning environment to provide a realistic set of environmental experiences that will allow the learner to identify with the skill application and activities of the occupation. For example, in personal service occupations it is essential that the learner come into contact with persons needing the service. In training persons for the care of the elderly, it is necessary that they have elderly persons to work with under controlled circumstances while they are in a learning situation.

Allocation of training for a specific skill to either a learning center or an on-the-job environment is considered in two ways:

1. By assuming that entire training for the skill will be placed in one of the locations.

2. By assuming that part of the training for the skill will be placed in each location. This would be done by designating an arbitrary rating level (see Chapter 9) as a dividing line to determine what should be provided in each environment. It may be decided that some skills and associated learning experiences can readily be provided to only the "2" level in a learning center. Consequently, learning

activities, achievement level, information and learning resources are divided at the appropriate level. This is opposed to the more conventional method of providing minimal experience and most of the information content in a learning -center environment and more complex experiences and little information in an O.J.T. environment.

Applying skill-by-skill analysis, it may be found that in some cases it is not necessary to create a learning-center environment at all because of the unique characteristics of the occupation or the unique characteristics of applications of the occupation in work environments that are available to the learner. Previous DACUM training programs were able to place persons in training in small firms that did not contain the pressures of the larger work environment. Since these small firms clearly could not absorb the cost of maintaining an individual until he or she became somewhat productive, support was provided, on a diminishing scale, until the learner could begin to demonstrate the ability to earn returns for the firm. These small-firm environments contained almost all the resources necessary for learning. They provided a wide range of adequate work activities that could be performed at a reasonable pace, and there was always someone, a supervisor or co-worker, who could assume responsibility for monitoring the learner in the learning and work experiences, thus providing personal attention not available in larger faster-paced work environments.

In previous DACUM training programs conducted initially or primarily in learning centers, an additional period of time was spent in an on-the-job training environment, monitored by project staff. The Housekeeper training program was conducted primarily in a large residence suitably equipped to provide learning opportunities for most of the specified skills. However, it was impractical to have children reside in the home so that the learners would be able to apply child-care skills. Similarly, it was impractical to provide useful experiences in caring for bedridden and other invalid persons. Therefore, each learner had the opportunity to spend two weeks in each of three external learning environments. One was an urban home with a number of small children, another was a rural home with a number of small children, and the third was a small nursing home specializing in care of elderly bedridden persons. In the latter case, almost all training for associated skills was conducted in the on-the-job training environment. In addition, learners had an opportunity to refine already acquired skills by applying them in a range of more realistic situations.

In the Oil Burner Repair and Service project, a learning center was created in an unused oil burner service shop. After developing adequate competence in the shop, the learners were placed in prearranged on-the-job training assignments with mechanics in the community. This enabled them to begin developing skills in communicating with customers, costing jobs, etc. It also afforded them the opportunity to refine basic skills acquired in the training shop by learning to troubleshoot and repair a wider range of heating equipment.

In another program, Deckhand Training, the selection of a learning center was almost of secondary consideration. Most of the training was provided aboard a leased commercial fishing vessel operating on a commercial fishing schedule under realistic fishing conditions. The vessel and its work pace, however, were not conducive to development of some skills requiring considerable training assistance such as gear repair and maintenance. Therefore, learners alternated between 10-day trips at sea and 10-day periods in a training center developed as a net loft, where they could acquire preliminary net-mending and repairing skills without the pressure of having to get back into operation while at sea.

It is important to recognize that the O.J.T. segments of training must be prearranged with some agency or firm to ensure that they will be provided. This is opposed to the conventional method of teaching what can be learned in the learning center and assuming that learners will somehow manage to acquire skills once they get into industry. By using the DACUM chart to specify learning experiences the individual will have to encounter, it is easy to visualize exactly where additional training might best take place and to begin to move toward this. The objective is to provide opportunity for learners to acquire specific skills and experience specific learning activities rather than to arrange time blocks of on-the-job training in the expectation that these will provide required experiences.

Once the decision is reached about optimal learning environment for each skill and activity, it is possible to finalize a number of other decisions. First, there is the decision regarding space required for a learning center. Consideration should be given to arrangement of resources and activities in the learning environment to provide ready access for learners, at the same time replicating as closely as possible the activities, atmosphere, and conditions of the work environment. The size of the learner group can also now be better established. In an on-the-job training environment it may be feasible to assign only one learner to each specific job position. The number the learning center can absorb can now be predicted, as well as a suitable learner-staff ratio.

SELECTION OF EQUIPMENT, TOOLS, AND SUPPLIES

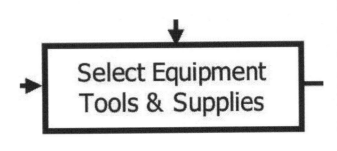

Program developers analyze each of the skills on the DACUM chart to determine the equipment, tools, and supplies required to provide the learner with an opportunity to learn. They also have additional planning information in the form of specified learning activities and environment.

If the entire training program is to be operated in an on-the-job environment, all the necessary equipment, tools, and supplies may already be available. This will depend on whether the firm in which on-the-job training will take place is diverse in its operation and not merely a specialty firm.

It is necessary to avoid planning on the assumption that a standard set of occupational resources will be used and endeavoring to determine to what extent these resources will be useful for each skill and learning activity. This often results in a rejection of some learning activities because of lack of resources, or in overemphasis on other learning activities and skills because of availability of resources. This is most apt to be a problem when an existing well developed program is being converted to DACUM. There will be a reluctance to remove expensive resources and replace them with others more suitable for the specified skills and learning activities. It is important in such cases to approach occupational resource selection by starting with the skill definition and learning activities. Only after resources have been selected on this basis should the program developer examine present resources to see how well they fit and what trade-offs may be possible without hampering learning.

The DACUM-based training program in a learning center will probably contain a wider range of occupational resources than would ordinarily be found in an occupational training environment, especially in a training environment designed primarily for group instruction. On the other hand, the more orthodox program requires more equipment and tools in order to allow learners to learn and perform simultaneously as a group. In the DACUM system, learners use equipment and tools independently because they work on different skills and activities at the same time. Any duplication will result from usage demand rather than from efforts to match numbers of pieces of equipment to numbers of learners in a group. Experience to date has indicated that costs will be no higher for resources in the DACUM system because of less need for duplication, in spite of the fact that a wider range of resources may be provided.

Most training programs, particularly at the trades' level, can readily be adapted without undue change in occupational resources. Most difficulty will be encountered for highly developed programs currently providing most learning activities as Projects or Lab Projects.

Diversity of resources is important and often easy to provide. For example, the Housekeeper training program was equipped with three different kinds of heat in the kitchen provided by an electric range and an oil and gas combination. It was necessary for learners to become familiar with electricity, oil, and gas as they might expect to encounter any of these in their work situations. Nevertheless, the arrangement of the learning environment and the nature of the learning process eliminated the necessity for duplication.

INSTALLATION OF EQUIPMENT, TOOLS, AND SUPPLIES

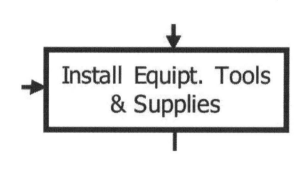

Once the nature and quantity of equipment, tools, and supplies required are established, it is necessary to plan how they will be installed in the learning environment. An important consideration is to attempt to replicate realistic work conditions. It is necessary to place more emphasis on this than on efficiency of installation.

In the previously mentioned Nova Scotia NewStart DACUM training programs it was relatively easy to replicate work conditions because of the nature of the learning environment. A fishing vessel and a net loft were the environments in which Deckhand Training took place. A large home was used for the Housekeeper training program. An oil burner repair shop was the site of Oil Burner Service and Repair training. In each case it was easy to install equipment, tools, and supplies in much the same manner as they would be installed in a normal work site.

In an on-the-job training environment, the main considerations are to be sure that the resources are on hand and that the learner will have access to them when and if needed. If the O.J.T. firm does not accept certain kinds of work, it may lack resources necessary to allow the individual to learn certain skills necessary to develop over-all occupational competence. In these cases it may be necessary to release the learner for short periods for access to these resources elsewhere. Similarly, the firm may not have obtained certain equipment and tools but may have performed a limited amount of work with outdated equipment or other less efficient resources.

It is necessary to make certain that the occupational resources of a firm are indeed accessible to the learner. Expensive equipment, tools, and materials may be locked away when not in use or may be assigned to an artisan who is reluctant to allow a learner to work with them. Negotiations must be made for controlled learner access to these so he or she may gradually develop skills that can be applied when the job demands.

The situation is much different when one plans to build a DACUM learning environment into present training facilities: that is, when the DACUM learning environment is to be part of an existing institution. Here one encounters difficulties in that the atmosphere of the institution or space available may not lend itself to replicating a work environment. Similarly, programs that are already equipped for another mode of training may require design of the resources layout. The equipment typically assembled for group learning may have to be spread out through the training environment and placed in more direct association with other equipment to provide ease of access for learners.

A further consideration in installing equipment, tools, and supplies and organizing the learning environment is the need for provision for group or teamwork activities. If these are predominant in the industry and if they have been specified as suitable learning activities, it is necessary to design suitable working arrangements and location of resources. Most training programs focus on having the individual perform independently in order to be tested individually, and resources are organized accordingly. In the DACUM approach, this becomes less necessary as the individual can work as part of a team and yet have performance, contributions, and achievements assessed independently.

LOCATION AND ASSIGNMENT OF HUMAN RESOURCES

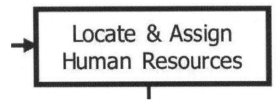

A further activity that flows out of definition of learning activities and the specification of skills on the DACUM chart is the location and assignment of human resources to the project.

It is necessary to assess each staff member's ability, interest, and willingness to perform in each skill and learning activity. It is then possible to assign primary responsibility for directing and monitoring each component of the learning program. It is important that this selection be made on the basis of ability to devise learning experiences, advise the learner of progress, aid the learner in early stages, direct team activities, and rate individual skill development.

It is also necessary to note and cover staff weaknesses. Because of the unlikelihood of locating a single person who adequately possesses all the skills in the occupation, this is particularly important in planning a single-instructor learning center or a single-supervisor on-the-job training position. It is also important when converting training programs in which all or most staff members have been away from the work situation for a period of time.

If what the staff member lacks is not too extensive and time is available, it may be possible to make up the necessary deficiencies by exposing staff to new techniques and opportunities for skill development. A program of visits to industry may do a good deal to overcome weaknesses.

A more likely solution, however, is to arrange for others to provide the necessary expertise. These would probably be industrial personnel currently applying or supervising the application of the skill in question. They may possess this expertise because they work with one of the few firms having the necessary kind of resources.

Arrangements are made to bring outside experts into contact with learners who need their assistance and advice. This can be done in two ways. First, it is often possible to invite experts into the learning environment to provide specific assistance. They should, however, concentrate on working directly with learners (even individual learners) in current learning activities rather than on lengthy information presentations. If a presentation is necessary, it should be brief, with the understanding that the expert will then circulate among the learners, examining their work, answering questions, and offering advice related to his or her expertise.

In the Oil Burner Training program three local employers were invited to provide specialized assistance not available from the instructor. For example, one arrived with a well-equipped and organized service vehicle which was opened for learners. The assistant spent a half day answering questions and discussing how to set up a vehicle, what it would require and what kinds of tools, equipment, and parts it should contain to reduce callback on service calls. Such contacts had the added effect of letting the learners know that specialists were available for consultation, and they frequently phoned or visited firms to acquire further information and advice.

The second method is simply to encourage learners to acquire individual specialized assistance and advice through visits to employment sites. In some cases the need for this kind of assistance may be extensive enough to warrant establishing short periods of on-the-job training. This was part of the reason for including the nursing home among the three O.J.T. sites for the Housekeeper project. The manager possessed skills and experience that project staff did not have and which it would not have been feasible to provide by adding another person to staff.

Experience has indicated that much additional expertise can be obtained on a voluntary part-time basis. Some experts will welcome an opportunity to work briefly with a group of learners for their occupation. Because the involvement does not demand instructional or lecture skills, most persons can readily respond. In the case of educational programs at both the secondary and post-secondary level, this practice also has the advantage of keeping local employers aware of the training program and the progress of the learners. This raises their interest in the program and results in offers of further assistance and other kinds of resources.

ORGANIZE INDIVIDUAL LABS

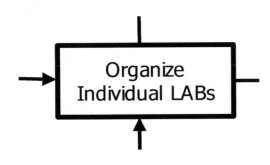

The third major category of learning resources required is the supporting learning or information resources that are necessary to enable the individual to acquire skill and competence. These are packaged into what have been called Learning Activity Batteries.[1]

[1] A more appropriate name would be Skill Development Information Resource Package. Learning Activity Battery has a connotation of including the learning activities as well and resulted in excessive inclusion of materials with built-in learning activities such as P.I., workbooks, and textbook chapter problems or assignments. Nevertheless, for convenience, they are called Learning Activity Batteries (LABs) in this book.

One package is prepared for each skill on the DACUM chart. If there are 165 skills on a specific DACUM chart, there will be 165 packages prepared for the program. In programs to date, packages have been of two kinds. In previous DACUM training projects, expanding file folders or file jackets were used. These are relatively compact and yet can been expanded to contain a number of resources if so desired. Elsewhere library periodical boxes have been used. The size found most convenient is the 4" wide box which remains open and is somewhat easier to use that the expanding file jackets.

Packages can also be created in electronic formats utilizing resources such as word processing and spreadsheet software.

It should be noted that only one package is developed for each skill. Twenty or more learners can use the same resource because they are working on different skills and require different information. Therefore, there is little need for duplication. If two or more learners are interested in working on the same skill at the same time, they can select from the variety of resources available in the package. A person using a package may take it from its shelf, spread the contents on a table, select what seems most appropriate, and pass the remaining material to someone else who is working on the same skill. When using packages in electronic format, individual packages may be stored on a server. Multiple learners may select and print any necessary materials at the same time.

While Learning Activity Batteries are developed individually by treating one skill at a time, it is useful to prepare all the packages before beginning. While analyzing one skill, information will frequently be found that relates to another and may quickly be installed in its package without the necessity of storing it for later.

No detailed analysis of the skill and its information requirements is conducted before beginning to collect learning resources. It has been found that this process can consume considerable time. It has proven to be more effective to begin immediately to search for materials that will help an individual attempting to learn the skill. The materials can be located and retrieved from information sources and installed in the package in about the same time it would take to conduct an adequate analysis of the skill prior to beginning any search.

This work should begin only after the skills and associated learning activities have been identified. If this is not done, there is a tendency to include a greater amount of information than is required. The information should be designed to be supportive to learning through involvement in learning activities. In certain cases a good deal of the information required may be inherent in the learning activity, which may not require further supporting information or other learning resources. For example, in training for operation of hydraulic controls on heavy equipment, if one started by selecting information content, this might result in extensive operation, descriptions of what they will and will not do, etc. However, learning experiences with actual hydraulic equipment will provide much of this information in a more meaningful manner, and the learner will have little need for printed or audio-visual materials which provide the same information and concepts in a different way.

Nothing is included in a package which does not relate to the skill it is to support. The skill is viewed in isolation in attempting to determine what sorts of information should be contained in the package. Therefore, it may be necessary in some cases to extract short pieces of information from a larger context if this can be done without destroying the meaning. One would not include an entire book, no matter how excellent it might be, if only a few pages were necessary to support a specific skill. This provides a measure of control or honesty to the resource development process. It prevents the developers from including information they might deem desirable for one reason or another when, in fact, it cannot be justified in terms of its relevance to the development of specified occupational competence. This is rather painful for the developers if they have had experience in operating another kind of training program which used resources in a different fashion. Persons coming directly from industry do not experience as much difficulty and can proceed with the task quite readily. Some developers of both kinds have difficulty in resisting the urge to install an impressive document or audio-visual resource that they feel must be fitted into the system. In attempting to do so, they destroy the very criteria toward which they are attempting to work.

The intention is to reduce the amount of effort that a trainee has to make to select resources pertinent to the problem. The addition of superfluous information or too great a variety of sources can only delay task achievement endeavors. The learner will spend considerable time exploring issues that may be of interest but have little to do with developing competence in a given skill. It is better for resource packages to be somewhat sparse than for them to include a large amount of excess information.

However, in the interest of self-learning and individualization of the learning process, it is desirable to provide variety. Each package should offer a choice of modes and media. This will enable the learner who does not excel in reading to use audio-visual or pictorial material. At the same time there should be printed material to give the person who likes to read an opportunity to acquire information in this way.

Learning Activity Batteries should provide information at several levels. Some materials may be technical and difficult, while others may be simple. The more difficult materials will be useful for the learner who is not satisfied with minimal information and is unable to perform unless they have all the background needed in order to begin to apply themselves.

In some cases, suitable resources will seem to apply to several skills. In such cases, if alternate resources can be found to substitute for them, they should not be placed in the Learning Activity Batteries. If they are the only resources available or a single resource is equally suitable for more than one skill, duplicate copies of these should be provided for each skill to which the information applies. Attempts have been made to develop cross-referencing systems by placing a sheet of paper in the Learning Activity Battery referring the learner to resources in another package. However, this began to become unwieldy and delayed learner achievement because of the time spent in sorting out the cross-references and locating information and materials. The learner is unlikely to retrieve and use cross-referenced information. The learner is more likely to use what is in the package in front of them.

In the initial development of Learning Activity Batteries for a program, an attempt is made, first, to provide a maximum of satisfactory materials for each skill identified in the DACUM chart. Most of these are readily available. They may be commercially available in the form of audio-visual materials or textbooks. Audio-visual materials may be available online without charge. Printed materials may be available from agencies, organizations, or companies, or from journals and other publications. Once into program operations, program staff will detect skills which demand additional information. They will then begin to supply additional resources, and may have to modify materials or develop new materials.

The initial development work can normally be completed in a relatively short time. All the packages of resources for the Housekeeper training program were assembled in a little over one month. Other programs have required similar time. More difficulty has been experienced in programs being converted, in which there were trainees and on-going staff responsibilities that prevented full-time involvement in this activity. An interesting demonstration of an appropriate approach to developing Learning Activity Batteries took place during a DACUM demonstration workshop in Moncton, New Brunswick.

> *The participants observed the construction of a DACUM chart prepared for the field of Welding Fabrication by a team of experts in the occupation. The following week, three of the curriculum specialists oriented a group of four welding instructors to the DACUM chart and the DACUM approach. They described the chart in detail and followed this with a period of discussion to assist and encourage the instructors in defining learning activities which would allow persons to develop the necessary skills. A large amount of material on the welding field was made available to the workshop participants. During a period of two and one-half days, under the direction of the new development co-ordinators, the four instructors developed initial Learning Activity Batteries for over a quarter of the 160 skills on the chart. It is conceivable that the instructors could have completed initial development in a period of two to three weeks under this kind of*

direction. Left to their own devices, without the encouragement, stimulation, and prodding of the new co-ordinators, it is unlikely that they would have completed more than a few of the skill packages by the end of the week as they would have completed more than a few of the skill packages by the end of the week as they began by overanalyzing each skill before attempting to select what were obvious supporting materials and by resisting the extraction of materials from larger contexts. The co-ordinators noted this quickly and took steps to break a pattern which would have delayed the process.

Finally, it is important to establish the location of Learning Activity Batteries within the learning environment(s). Early programs designated a single room as the locale for Learning Activity Batteries and for study and quiet discussion. This proved to be somewhat ineffective. Learners tended to remain with the task they were performing, particularly if it was some distance from the information sources. It is suggested that each Learning Activity Battery be located near where the learning activity will take place. In this way, the learner can quickly locate a package and discover whether or not it contains the specific information needed to overcome an immediate problem. If it is there, the learner is able to proceed with his or her activity. For example, in an automotive training environment, it might be feasible to have packages related to fuel injection repair skills located right in the workshop adjacent to where this bench, diagnostic, or adjusting work will take place. It is possible that materials will become soiled over a period of time, but this may be a comparatively easy problem to overcome. It is suspected that usefulness of materials and speed of growth of the individual will be increased if resources are located within reach while involved in problem-solving endeavors.

SELECT PRINTED MATERIALS

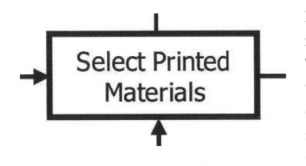

Select Printed Materials

Readily available materials are the primary resource used in Learning Activity Batteries. The reasons are obvious. First, there is a wealth of printed materials available for most occupations. Second, printed materials are much less expensive that other media for providing information for skill development. Third, printed materials have traditionally been a primary source of information for occupational training programs, and learners and instructors in training programs tend to recognize their usefulness more readily and apply them more easily.

As previously mentioned, sources include magazines, trade journals, pamphlets, brochures, manuals, textbooks, and reference books.

1. *Textbooks* in their entirety are little used and are not recommended for insertion in Learning Activity Batteries. First, most textbooks are written to accompany formal presentation. Most are theory, principle, subject-matter, or content-based rather than skill-based. They do not lend themselves readily to isolation of information required to perform in specific skills. Parts of textbooks, however, do meet this requirement. In one training program, Oil Burner Service and Repair, a textbook approach was used. However, the book was unique in that it was a service manual written about a variety of pieces of equipment or heating systems that had an excellent breakdown of information similar to the skill breakdown in the DACUM chart. As a result, Learning Activity Batteries were not created for that training program. Another drawback of textbooks is that they are not always current owing to the planning and developments lead-time required before they reach the market.

2. *Journal articles* are useful because they are usually current. Also, they are frequently problem-based, directly focused on solutions to problems the learner will encounter if the learning environment is a realistic replication of the work environment with its associated problems.

3. *Pamphlets and brochures* frequently provide excellent simple descriptions of concepts. It is easy for learners being introduced to an occupation to obtain considerable information from pamphlets or brochures related to equipment, materials, and resources available for the occupation.

4. *Industrial training manuals and equipment-manufacturer-supplied service, repair, and operational manuals* are also useful. They are normally written at a level readily understandable by learners in their first activities related to the skill.

5. *Catalogues and equipment specification sheets* are often useful resources. These allow the learner to see the variety and range of equipment and resources applied in the occupation and broaden his or her scope.

> *Because many resources used are not normally thought of as learning materials, it might be argued that some of them are not satisfactory, being too simple and direct and not leading the learner into exploration and application of theory and principle. The DACUM system, however, provides this through learning activities and does not require materials for this purpose. It has been found that, once the learner becomes self-directive in learning activities as well as in*

information acquisition, the information sources provided do satisfy the information need.

Because they are designed for self-learning, programmed instruction materials are useful for insertion in Learning Activity Batteries. They have been little used for reasons enumerated in Chapter 10. Nevertheless, it is felt that they could be valuable in a useful format.

Desired information from larger contexts such as books, manuals, reference materials, journals, etc., is simply removed or scanned for insertion into the Learning Activity Battery. It is useful to remove appropriate pages or sections of books if the material is useful for only one skill. If scanned or printed, the source of the material is noted on the copy and on the original page or pages to ensure that it can be retrieved if the original is lost.

To maintain control of the contents of the packages, a bibliography is recoded on the outside. This permits instructors to check periodically to make sure all the resources are still in the package. If materials as missing, the bibliography leads them back to the sources from which the information can again be retrieved. These sources are normally installed in a small reference library for the training environment. This permits a learner who is interested in further exploration of a topic to trace the extracted piece of material back to its source to see if there is further information available which will satisfy their need. These reference libraries are also useful for learners who simply want to learn more about the occupation or one of its components.

Much of the materials suggested (journal articles, pamphlets, brochures, equipment specification catalogues) is seldom used in traditional training programs since most programs operate on a system of presentation which requires that materials and other resources fit the pattern of delivery. Experience in installing the DACUM process in on -going training programs has revealed that most occupational training instructors have accumulated a variety of free literature and other information which they normally cannot fit into their delivery system. These may be presented once to one class of learners and then relegated to a storage box. Using the DACUM approach, all these resources, provided they are seen as useful for development of one of the specified skills, are readily fitted into the self-delivery system.

DEVELOPMENT OF PRINTED MATERIALS

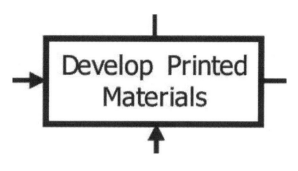

While printed materials are generally the most commonly used of the resources for Learning Activity Batteries, there is relatively little need for instructors to develop such materials. This is important as development, editing, and production of effective printed learning materials is usually a complex and lengthy task, and instructors have little time for this activity. In the DACUM system their contributions are usually confined to simple initial development and redesigning or restructuring of materials.

One useful kind of material the instructor can develop (particularly the instructor recently removed from the industrial work environment) is a listing or description of applications of skills. Frequently, skills are applied in a variety of diverse situations, and it is important that the learner be able to visualize these situations in order to understand when to apply given skills. In some cases, it is difficult to find supporting printed materials that adequately cover a range of these applications of a skill. The instructor may even add descriptions of how the skill is applied in specific circumstances. This broadens the scope of the learner's vision in terms of the occupation and its skill applications.

Instructors or program developers can also develop simple information or job sheets. These may merely condense or relate or integrate materials in Learning Activity Batteries. They may be lists of procedural steps in solving problem or completing a task assignment.

It is frequently possible for instructors to redesign or modify materials. Available material for some occupations often requires a high level of reading skill. A good example is the use of university level textbooks for technical institute level programs because they contain the required information and there is no suitable alternate reference source. It is easy for an instructor expert in the occupation to read or study a piece of material and draft a simplified version. It may be simplified in terms of reduced volume, or it may be simplified by reducing it to terminology that is more understandable by the novice. Similarly, it is possible to upgrade printed materials. In the Housekeeper project, development staff had to upgrade materials prepared initially for junior high school students. These made frequent references to the work in terms of school projects and to the role of the graduate of the program as a "good mother's helper". These had to be modified to make them suitable for adult learners.

It is also possible for instructors to re-cluster or regroup segments of printed materials from various sources. For example, it is useful to cut out illustrations from magazines, journals, pamphlets, and other sources and paste them up with appropriate clippings of printed descriptions, definitions, or other information into a new single information source. An excellent example of this was a series of single sheets prepared for a School of Nursing comprising a professional artist's renderings of specific conditions of the human body along with what were by themselves sterile definitions clipped from a textbook.

SELECTION OF A.V. MATERIALS

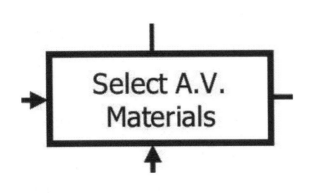

Use of audio-visual materials is most desirable. Not only do they provide alternate media and modes of presentation, but they permit learners to observe and model desired performance. While they could rely on the instructor to model this performance for them, the individualization of the program will place excessive demands on instructor time if such resources are not available.

Some commercially available presentations (e.g., videos) are excellent, and some occupations are fortunate in having a wealth of such material available for training purposes. Unfortunately, most occupations do not have this resource available. Either there is an absence of available audio-visual material for the occupation, or the available materials are unsuitable for the DACUM format for the following reasons:

1. Few visual materials available commercially are single-skill focused. The developers of the materials are often looking at a wide market. They may have designed the program for a specific population but then broadened its appeal in the hope of obtaining wider distribution. This applies even to many of the so-called single-concept audio-visual materials such as short videos. Frequently even these are not found to be single-concept but have been expanded to reach a wider market.

2. Much available material is not adequately explicit. Many presentations which one would expect to contain simply a skill demonstration or a set of procedures include considerable additional (and for DACUM proposes extraneous) information.

3. Many materials are directed at an audience altogether different from the audience in a training program. This audience is usually the biggest market that developers and distributors of the material could predict. As a result, it is found that learners do not identify with the material.

4. Materials are usually expensive and for this reason also are not used as widely as they might be. Program developers are reluctant to provide funds for audio-visual material that only runs for a few moments.

5. Materials available on loan or without charge are often not available for the period of time required. If borrowed, they must be shown at a specific time regardless of the interest or development level of the learners.

In summary, audio-visual materials are not extensively used in the DACUM learning environment. For some programs they may happen to be available. In any event a search for such materials should be made to avoid the cost and effort of producing materials.

DEVELOPMENT OF A.V. MATERIALS

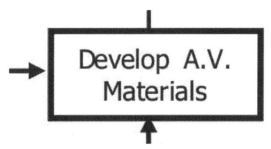

Where there is a lack of suitable audio-visual materials, it may be necessary for the development team of a DACUM training program to apportion time and resources for their development. Certain occupations involve a good deal of what may be termed "technique" in which the physical performance or movement of the skilled performer is critical. Examples of this may be found in fields such as nursing where technique is critical to avoid contamination. In such occupations or for specific skills in such occupations it is essential that there be provision for capturing technique in the form of formal demonstrations or provisions for observation of skilled persons performing.

Video was a most useful tool in some of the previous DACUM training projects. In the Housekeeper training program, for example, the project manager had a mother and baby visit the training center so the mother specialist could demonstrate proper bathing, diapering, and clothing procedures. The project manager video recorded the entire proceedings, including learner questions and repeat demonstrations. This was done for the benefit of other learners who were not present at that time or had not yet entered the training program. Other materials for that program were developed spontaneously. The project manager detected a need for training in surveying a household of which the housekeeper is to take charge while the parents are absent. Using a portable video recorder, she visited a convenient household and had the householder role-play the mother who intended to leave shortly on a trip and was introducing the housekeeper to the household. The project manager interviewed her as they went through the house, determining where specific articles were located: food supplies, canned goods, medical supplies, a list of emergency telephone numbers, and list of information that the householder would specifically prepare for a housekeeper before departing. This presentation proved to be effective in the learning environment as it allowed apprehensive trainees to view the procedure several times before venturing into a similar situation.

Video was also used in a spontaneous way by the project manager of the Craft Training program. As part of his function, the project manager frequently visited specialized handcraft operations in the region and took advantage of video-recording equipment to capture interview-demonstrations with working craftspeople. The craftspeople continued working while the project manager recorded it, at the same time asking questions about the work, the products, their value, and the materials and tools required to begin working in this craft specialty. This proved useful as a means of exposing learners confined to a learning center to a wider range of applications of handcraft work.

A well established learning resource is video tutorial instruction. Primarily the learner is presented with an object with which to work and an activity to be accomplished. The learner is aided by a video tutorial prepared by an instructor who adopts the posture of a tutor looking over the learner's shoulder while he or she is working. This allows the learner to proceed with the activity while being able to refer to someone explaining conditions, decisions needed to reach, and criteria that will indicate when the learner is reaching or not reaching the desired objective.

Typical training presentations, as a class, are designed to focus on presentation. On the contrary, the key to the DACUM environment is its focus on learning, not on the presentation to the learners.

In summary, in spite of its initial higher installation time, video recording is recommended as the most useful type of instructor- or staff-developed audio-visual material. In fact, its versatility will cause one, if a choice must be made, to opt for this over all other possible resources with the exception of audio-tutorial presentations.

SELECTION AND INSTALLATION OF LEARNING EQUIPMENT

Once optimal learning resources and processes are established, it is possible to begin to assess the desirable mix of learning equipment for the learning resources. Sometimes it is necessary to trade off desirable learning resources or to achieve a balance within limits of available funding. For example, one may decide to do without certain available visual materials in the interest of allocating resources to the selection of other equipment that will be more widely used.

Learning furniture should be selected and arranged on the basis of the nature of the learning process, learning materials, and location of learning resources for each program. The DACUM system lends itself to the use of individualized study spaces such as study carrels. The carrels provide privacy for individual study or concentration on a project and a home base or office for storage of materials related to projects under way. Hexagonal combinations have been used extensively in a circular or conference arrangement for group discussions as well as for individual work space. Typical classroom equipment and formal seating arrangements are not used with the DACUM system. Adequate overhead shelving should be provided for Learning Activity Batteries (LAB), along with a suitable table or counter space underneath. The table is required so that learners can, if they wish, use the materials in that location. There should be room to spread out several LAB's.

It is important to recognize that most viewing and learning will be individual. Computers, tablets or laptops must be provided for these learners, for individual close-up viewing. The most useful equipment, when one assesses potential frequency of use, cost, and ease of resource development, is the tablet. Because these are available at reasonable cost it is possible to provide several to permit learners to be involved with different kinds of programming at the same time. Desktop computer and laptops are considerably more expensive, but are more versatile for rapid production of materials and simulations. In selecting electronic learning equipment consideration should be given to the number of playback installations required to provide learners with ready access most of the time.

Space should be as open as possible consistent with the kind of work environment that exists for the occupation. Learning equipment should be located where it will be most used. Because of the individualization, noise and other factors are less of a problem because the learner can use earphones. Previous DACUM programs were installed in somewhat ideal space (e.g., a large house, a fishing vessel and net loft, and an oil burner repair shop). Unfortunately, most programs must be installed in institutional facilities designed for formal instruction, normally a series of classrooms or labs of uniform sizes. Lack of space leads to the isolation of Learning Activity Batteries and supporting equipment in another room away from the occupational learning activities. This results in less than desired use.

Finally, it is important to provide free access to learning equipment by the learners. They seldom respond if they are expected to retrieve needed equipment from centrally controlled storage or if they must rely on someone else to operate it. Because the recommended equipment is not complex, each learner should learn to operate it as soon as possible after entering the learning environment. Experience has indicated that usage is high and that learners are capable and do not mishandle equipment to the extent of causing damage. They consider it a privilege which they do not abuse.

PROGRAM REFINEMENT

The DACUM system is designed to encourage continual development and refinement of resources while the training program is in operation. Resources are selected in the initial development stage on the basis of instructor or developer judgments. It is impossible to determine their effectiveness until learners have been exposed to the program and demonstrated whether or not they can learn using these resources. Effectiveness and need for change can then be determined in two ways:

1. By observing and assessing skill performance. An instructor who notes a lack of achievement in a specific skill, can cycle back through the model to look for causes in the following sequence. An instructor will...

    1) examine the learning activities specified for that particular skill to determine if they provide the experiences necessary for learning and if they are meaningful to the learner. The instructor may decide the activities are inappropriate and begin to devise more meaningful activities. On the other hand, the instructor may decide the activities are satisfactory and proceed to ....

    2) evaluate the learning environment to determine if it is the right site for development of the skill. The instructor may decide to shift the activities to an O.J.T. site which provides more realistic problems and conditions. Or the instructor may decide to transfer the activities from an O.J.T. site

to a learning center which is safer and where the work pace is less hectic. If the activities site appears satisfactory, the instructor will...

3) assess the adequacy of equipment, tools, and supplies. The instructor may decide that some equipment is too sophisticated or complex for learner operation. Certain specialty tools or other materials may not be available. However, if it is found that these resources are available, the instructor begins to....

4) check their accessibility to the learner. There may not be adequate numbers of certain tools and pieces of equipment to take care of demand, forcing learners to delay progress on a project or task. Tools and supplies may be difficult for the learner to obtain because of requisitioning and control procedures or because they are centrally stored at a distance from the learning activities. If these seem to be satisfactory, the instructor can....

5) assess the adequacy of human resources. The instructor may discover that no one has been specifically assigned to be responsible for monitoring the activities related to that particular skill. Or the instructor may discover that no one on staff is particularly expert in the skill and that no external resources have been located and recruited. If adequate human resources seem to be on hand, the instructor can....

6) examine the usefulness of the Learning Activity Battery. It may be discovered that it is not clearly labeled for ease in information retrieval, that it is not located in close proximity to learning activities for the skill, or that there is no suitable place to spread out the materials for study. If the LAB's and their location are adequate, the instructor would begin to ....

7) examine the printed materials to determine if they are adequate. The instructor may find there is not enough material, that it is not well illustrated, that it is not clearly written, that the vocabulary level is too high, or that the material contains too much superfluous information. The instructor may begin to search for alternate, better materials, or may begin to....

8) develop alternate materials. This may be done by modifying materials by changing reading level, adding clear illustrations, and removing superfluous information, or it may be necessary to prepare new materials

that support, clarify, or integrate existing materials. If the problem does not appear to be with printed materials, the instructor can....

9) assess the effectiveness of audio-visual materials. The instructor will re-examine the skill to determine if it requires specific kinds of audio-visual material such as action demonstrations or visual sequences. If these are unavailable or inadequate, the instructor may search for alternate, better sources, or may begin to....

10) develop audio-visual materials that will allow the learner to proceed independently. The instructor may decide to prepare a recorded presentation of key sequences, may also quickly prepare a video-recorded demonstration of a skill action or technique. If these resources are adequate, the instructor can....

11) assess the adequacy of learning equipment. The instructor may find that certain equipment is too complex and frustrating for learner use, that there are too few units of specific equipment to accommodate the volume of materials and usage level, or that the equipment is inaccessible to learners when they want to use it because of excessive control or improper location. The instructor will then have to replace pieces of equipment, add duplicates of others, or make the equipment more accessible to the learner.

2. By observing the learner who is attempting to use Learning Activity Battery materials.

The instructor is in the same area, can closely observe learners who are studying and note any reactions that indicate that they are having difficulty and that the quality of resources may be the cause of the problem. They may be frowning, look frustrated, look puzzled or bewildered, or they may merely lapse into daydreaming.

The instructor can question individual learners about specific needs and preferences in learning material and then begin to assess the material being used to see if it fails to meet these needs.

It is important, however, to be sure the learner is preforming within the framework of the Learning Evaluation Model (see Chapter 12) and is tackling learning in the recommended sequence. It is pointless to assess the effectiveness of supporting materials if the learner has not yet been involved in an activity that can be supported. There is a tendency to overemphasize this kind of analysis and provide resources that further allow the learner to begin by reading or study and result in LAB's that are even less suitable as DACUM resources.

This evaluation process is on-going. It occurs each time a learner encounters specific difficulty with skill achievement or with using learning resources. Therefore, program development is never complete. The initial development activity merely starts the ongoing process.

SUMMARY

In this chapter, selecting and developing the most beneficial resources and environment for use in the DACUM learning program was presented. Special care must be given when determining whether the environment should be on-the-job or in a specially created learning environment that fosters learning for on-the-job skills. Once the environment is selected, each skill on the DACUM chart should be analyzed to determine necessary equipment, tools, and supplies needed for training keeping in mind that learners work independently to acquire skills competency. When the required equipment, tools, and supplies are decided upon, they need to be installed in the learning environment to replicate realistic working conditions and that the tools are available for easy access to the learners. Next, Learning Activity Batteries are assembled for each individual skill and contain learning and informational resources necessary to allow the learners to acquire the skills. Once the environment and resources are in place, the learning program can be implemented and refined during the implementation process. Program refinement is an on-going process.

REFERENCES

Adams, R. E. (1975). *DACUM: Approach to curriculum, learning, and evaluation in occupational training.* Ottawa: Dept. of Regional Economic Expansion.

LEARNER ORIENTATION

Learner orientation gives the learner insight into the nature of the DACUM training program and to provide learning experiences to help hone learning behaviors throughout the program. Chapter 12 begins the learning process of the DACUM system which is guided by the elements in the Learning-Evaluation Model (see Figure 12-1).

LEARNING-EVALUATION MODEL

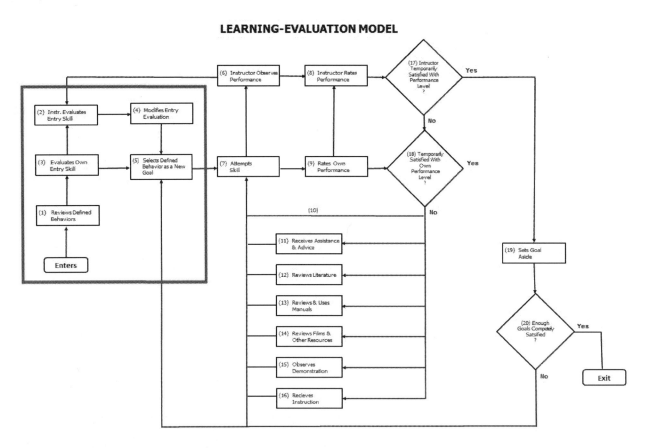

Figure 12-1. Learning-Evaluation Model

Since the learner will not be familiar with this kind of training, it is necessary to have a well-planned orientation procedure. The recommended procedure is not lengthy, with the primary purpose to provide the learner with some insights into the nature of the program. An additional purpose is to provide the learner with learning experiences which will help develop learning behavior that will be maintained through the program. Following will be a discussion of each orientation element of the Learning-Evaluation Model along with the process for implementation.

Lengthy, highly-organized presentations have not been found suitable for these purposes. They are inconsistent with the kind of training experience for which the learner is being prepared, and the learner has been found to experience difficulty in making the transfer from formal orientation to self-directed learning behaviors.

It has been felt by some that a transition period might be required between former learning experiences, such as a high school, and the DACUM learning experience. This has not been proven to be the case. But some orientation is required. Ideally, initial orientation should be brief, but orientation should continue after the learner has actually entered the program, at which time they will be sufficiently familiar with the system to raise questions and discuss issues. Many aspects of the program will become meaningful only when the learner is confronted with a real problem. At that time the problem can be treated as an orientation or adjustment problem.

It is important that the orientation procedure be individualized in the same manner that the learning program itself is individualized. The system is designed for staggered entry and exit to accommodate and take advantage of individual learner needs and preferences. Therefore it is likely that the learners will be entering as individuals or in small groups and will require individual orientation.

One problem encountered to date is that learners have been required to enter DACUM training programs on a group basis. This was due to project budgeting, the organization basis of programs, and the requirements of institutions in which DACUM has been applied. While this causes undue pressure during the initial cycle of a program and results in organized group entry procedures, this condition may not be as severe in later cycles. Later entrants to the program find that it now contains experienced learners. The new learner can observe the experienced learner's performance and begin to model their behavior to develop an approach to learning.

Ideally, the learner should be involved in learning activities and completing learning cycles by the second or third day in the training program. Orientation will continue for a considerable time as the learner encounters problems, but the DACUM learning experiences should begin as soon as possible.

ORIENTATION TO LEARNING ENVIRONMENTS

Enter

On entry to the program, the learner is provided with a tour and description of the facilities. This is important, if there are several rooms or locations, to enable learners to find their way around once becoming engaged in learning activities. The new entrant is shown the skill development resources (e.g., pamphlet, manual) available in the learning environment. The learner should have major pieces of equipment described in order to learn their use and function. The new entrant is also shown the location and nature of equipment, tools, and materials of the occupation that are available for use. This kind of orientation can be provided on a one -to-one or small-group basis by the instructor. It is possible, however, to delegate this responsibility to an advanced learner if so desired.

During this early phase, which should take no more than an hour or two, the new entrant will see learners performing in the environment. It is helpful to the new learner to be able to see others attempting to use the LABs, talking to instructors, questioning, rating themselves, and involving themselves in study related to skill achievement. The activities of the learners can best be explained by one of the instructors, but, again, it may be possible to select an advanced learner for the task.

ORIENTATION TO THE LEARNING PROGRAM

Reviews Defined Behaviors (1)

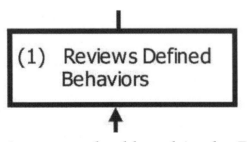

The next step in orientation is to introduce the learner to the DACUM chart. It is important at this time to indicate to the learner that the chart is not only a curriculum guide but will eventually become a record of achievement.

The instructor should explain the DACUM chart to the learner, describing each element of the chart and, if necessary, interpreting terminology. The instructor should describe where the chart came from, who produced it, and the general intent of the committee. The instructor should also discuss the General Areas of Competence, how they were arrived at, and what they mean in terms of providing a structure for the skills on the chart. The instructor should then describe each skill independently, proceeding along bands, periodically pausing to draw relationships between skills and describe how they fit into the over-all structure. It is important to refer regularly to the General Areas of Competency to provide the learner with a framework into which they can fit specific details. The instructor should proceed with this description without stopping for extensive questioning by the learner. It is more important at this stage for the learner to obtain an overview of the chart.

Once this overview is completed, questions should be encouraged. If questions are not forthcoming, the instructor may expand on a point or two, ask for comments on specific skills, or ask for estimates of how long it will take to be satisfactorily trained in all the skills.

The introduction to the DACUM chart should not take more than an hour or so provided the instructor does not dwell at great length on specific skills and provided the learner does not interrupt the initial presentation with extensive questions concerning one or two skills. Questions will be much reduced if the learner has an overview first. In its absence, new learner questions frequently relate to what they do not know about the rest of the chart rather than to the topic in hand.

Rating Scale Introduction

The instructor next introduces the learner to the rating scale and describes how he or she can use it for entry rating. The instructor first describes the categories in the rating scale, pointing out the differences in performance ability and how the learner gradually is less dependent on the instructor as they progress up the scale.

The instructor next focuses attention on the baseline '3' category in the rating scale, explaining that this is the minimal level of competence expected in most occupations and what would be described as the minimal journeyman level in some trades. The instructor then begins to relate each of the other categories in the scale to this baseline by describing the kind of performance one would expect from persons in each category and describing how all levels of performance from '1' to '6' are acceptable in some way in different work environments. It is useful at this point to describe a typical work environment for some other occupation that clearly illustrates the different skill levels that might be found. It may be possible to review, without reflecting on their ability, known performance and skill levels of workers in the occupation in the community.

The learner must next be made aware that the rating scale is a device that allows both the instructor and the learner to look at performance as it would be looked at by the employer in a job environment. It must be made clear to the learner that they are not expected to make personal judgments about one's own ability to perform. Instead the learner is to make judgments about how their own ability to perform would be assessed by a real or hypothetical employer. When this issue is overlooked during the orientation, learners often feel frustration during early rating activities, until becoming more aware of what is expected of them.

Finally, the learner is shown how to record entry ratings by enclosing a number selected from the rating scale in a small diamond in the lower left corner of the skill block (see Figure 12-2). The learner is also provided with a supporting information sheet to which he or she can refer (see page 258). New instructors are also provided with a rating information sheet that helps to clarify procedures they must follow (see page 259).

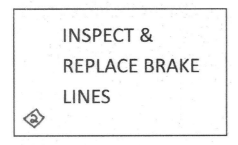

Figure 12-2. Skill Rating

Evaluates Own Entry Skill (3)

To provide the learner with a sample of the rating procedure, the learner is asked to identify a skill on the chart in which they feel somewhat competent. The instructor then asks the learner to study the skill definition within the context of the General Area of Competence, scan the rating scale, and select the level that most adequately describes their current ability.

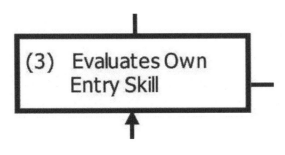

The instructor stresses at this time that the learner must have actually performed this skill. Ratings will not be given on the basis of prior reading about the skill or observation of other persons performing. The instructor will then question the learner about the learner's performance in the skill and try to verify the accuracy of the rating. If it is not accurate, the instructor can show the learner where there were inaccuracies. It may be necessary to repeat this procedure for one or two additional skills.

When it is apparent the learner is ready to self-rate without help, the instructor should describe the rationale for the entry rating procedure. The instructor should point out that it is important that the learner's entry profile be established so the instructor can begin to help the learner acquire missing skills. The instructor explains that the necessary information can be provided in an hour or so using the entry rating procedure, while it would take several weeks to set up and conduct realistic performance tasks to provide the same kind of information. The instructor also explains that the establishment of entry ratings permits the learner to make the most of training time as the individual will not be expected to work toward competences already possessed.

The learner is asked to take their chart to a secluded place in the training environment and go over it in detail, recording an entry rating for each skill perceived to have been adequately demonstrated in another environment. The learner is advised to be as honest and realistic as possible and only record ratings for skills he or she is reasonably certain they possess. The learner is also advised that he or she should not be overly concerned if somewhat unsure of the actual rating level that would apply, because their profile will be immediately reviewed with the instructor who will assist in either confirming or modifying their ratings. Nevertheless, the learner is asked to commit to a rating in each applicable case.

Self-rating should take no more than an hour or so. Learners with little prior contact with the occupation or similar work will require little time (perhaps 20 minutes) as they will have few, if any, skills to rate. Most learners will have little difficulty with self-rating. They can quickly select a rating level for each skill in which they have some proven competence. Those who can complete the self-rating with reasonable accuracy are well on their way to becoming self-directed learners.

The occasional learner will encounter difficulty in self-rating. Some of the perceived causes for this are as follows:

1. While becoming over concerned with rating, the learner may begin to lose the meaning of skill definitions and begin to apply a different meaning than that which originally understood. This is caused by failure to look at each skill within the context of the total chart. If the learner looks at each in isolation and

without the qualification of the other skills, it can take on a different meaning than that which was originally understood .

2. A learner may be frustrated by simply not knowing the meaning of many of the skill definitions, and begin to doubt the meaning of those in which they thought they were already skilled. (This problem should not be treated with undue concern for it is to be expected that new entrants will not appreciate most of the definitions of skills in the occupation until they are well into their training program.)

3. The learner may lose the meaning of the rating process and categories. This will happen if they begin to look directly at their ability rather than look "through the eyes of an employer".

4. Learners may lose sight of the fact that they have to physically perform the skills. Instead they begin to rate their ability based only on what they "know" about the skills. The learner becomes discouraged if they later detect they were wrong, and must eliminate or revise a number of erroneous ratings.

5. The learner may fear or dislike self-evaluation and have difficulty in facing and completing the task.

6. In rare cases, the learner may deliberately overrate of underrate him-or-herself due to other pressures. In a previous NSNS program, one learner significantly overrated himself because of misguided advice from someone unfamiliar with the program: "You better rate yourself high or they won't let you stay". Another underrated because of reluctance to face the instructor and later be forced to lower the ratings. This individual decided to play it safe.

The foregoing problems can be readily resolved and should not cause concern because they are due to be discussed immediately by the instructor. Of immediate importance is for the learner to begin self-rating. The instructor should not respond too quickly by providing assistance that will permit the learner to avoid making the desired kind of decisions. If the instructor provides too much assistance, the learner may be able to pass through this stage of orientation without having had to conduct a self-rating, think seriously about their ability, or think seriously about the meaning of the skill definitions. Furthermore, the learner will not have derived the satisfaction of successfully completing what he or she might have believed was an impossible skill, and will lose the benefits of the resulting confidence in self-assessment that is essential for their success in the learning program.

If the learner has real difficulty, the instructor can intercede and provide further explanation and assistance. A useful approach is to provide further information about the skills and their meaning and then depart before the learner records any self-ratings. If the learner is having difficulty in understanding the rating scale, the instructor may help the individual with only one or two additional skills and then depart before the learner can get assistance with others. In difficult cases it may be necessary to ignore the learner for a time. This has been found to cause the learner to reach decisions. Whether or not the decisions are entirely accurate, it is necessary to cause the learner to take this first step.

It is important to provide orientation in stages as outlined above. This involves providing specific information directly followed by activity. It has been found that provision of an entire overview prior to taking some of the first actions results in a shifting of emphasis by the learner. For example, if the learner is presented with all the details of self-rating before reviewing the chart, he or she tends to think too far, worrying about the forthcoming self-rating. As a result the learner may not listen to, or study, skill definitions with appropriate care. Later it is difficult to replace their rating-emphasized meanings with the intended skill-definition meanings.

The preceding orientation procedures and early entry-rating activities may be conducted as a group activity if several learners enter the program at the same time. For example, it is possible to provide the review of definitions and description of the DACUM chart, orient learners to the rating scale, and provide early rating examples as a group activity.

When soliciting sample ratings of skills from a group, it is important that several persons suggest self-ratings for only a small number of skills. That is, ratings should be solicited from several members of the group for each skill rather than allow each individual to assess themselves on a new skill. This ensures that only two or three skills will be discussed in this way and each learner will have to self-rate him alone on all the remaining skills. When many skills are used as examples, it has been found that some individuals will be unduly influenced by sample self-ratings provided by someone else.

Instructor Evaluation of Entry Skill (2)

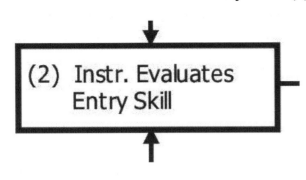

The remaining portions of the entry process must be conducted on an individual basis. In a previous DACUM program, where instructor review of entry ratings was conducted as group activity, it created confusion for the learners. The learners tended to be influenced by ratings which other learners within the group gave to themselves. As a result they did not focus on their own skill and the rating which they felt it warranted. More important, the advantage of individual instructor-learner counseling sessions to review ratings was lost. The instructor maintained a dominant role in the group activity and the learners lost an opportunity to interact with the instructor on a one-to-one basis. At the same time, the instructor did not acquire valuable information about the learner that he or she would have obtained in an individual counseling session.

Once the learner has completed their initial self-evaluation, he or she can arrange for an interview with the instructor to discuss self-recorded ratings. This allows the instructor to determine where the learner is on entry and the kind of program best suited for each individual.

Entry of learners in groups causes difficulty at this point, particularly in single-instructor programs. While it is important that the instructor conducts an initial interview with each learner as soon as possible, there tend to be difficulties when trying to start previously rated learners in their first learning activity while still determining what to do with learners that have yet to be rated. If intake is restricted to small groups of three or four persons, this difficulty is reduced.

It is important that interviews be conducted with some measure of privacy to allow the learner to express views about their ability. The interview should be conducted face-to-face across a table on which the learner can spread their own DACUM chart and the instructor can spread the master copy of the chart for that learner.

It is useful to begin by asking learners to describe their reactions to the rating process, whether he or she found it easy or difficult and which areas of the chart caused difficulty. This enables the instructor to allocate interview time to those skills or areas the learner found difficult to rate and, conversely, to confirm quickly those ratings for skills the learner found it relatively easy to access.

After the learner has described their reactions, the instructor begins a skill-by-skill questioning of the learner's self-rating. The instructor questions the learner on whether they actually have performed the task and seeks information on where it might have been performed, under what conditions, who supervised the performance, whether the supervisor was also competent and applied the skill well, etc.

Receiving this information skill by skill, the instructor can begin to make a judgment about the learner's ability to perform in each skill . If the instructor agrees with the learner's initial self-assessment, the instructor records their entry rating on the master chart in the same fashion in which the learner recorded it. In most cases, with most learners, most ratings will be unchanged. Few learners have difficulty in accurately describing their entry ability.

In some cases the instructor may doubt the learner's ability to perform to the level he or she has indicated and wish to assign a lower rating. The instructor describes the reasons for this decision and records the lower rating in the entry diamond shape in the master chart. The learner may decide to revise their self-assessment on the basis of what the instructor has said and erase the original rating, replacing it with the one the instructor has assigned. On the other hand, the learner may wish to let their self-rating stand on their own chart. The instructor should assure the learner that this is permissible and that the instructor will quickly change his or her entry rating on the master chart at the learner's request once the learner has had an opportunity to apply the skill in the training environment and the instructor has had an opportunity to observe their performance.

In other cases the instructor may want to assign a higher rating on the basis of information gleaned during questioning. The learner may have underestimated their ability or overestimated the complexity and difficulty of the skill as it is normally applied in an occupational environment. Again the instructor can record this higher rating, stating the reasons for the decision. The learner may agree that they have underrated themself and replace the initial rating with the higher one assigned to the master chart by the instructor. On the other hand, the learner may wish to let the rating stand until they can prove, when given the opportunity to apply the skill in the learning environment, that they can perform at the higher level.

In rare cases the instructor may wish to reserve judgment altogether until more information has been collected or an opportunity to observe the learner in action. This may occur when the learner has apparently applied a similar skill in quite a different environment to a high level on the rating scale and the instructor is unsure about the learner's ability to perform to this level. In such cases it is pointless for the instructor merely to provide a lower rating. It is best that the instructor make some temporary notation on the master chart indicating that he or she should take the first opportunity to observe the learner's ability to perform in this skill and then provide the entry rating at that time. (The instructor should not make this a practice merely to avoid decision-making during this interview process. It should be reserved for relatively rare and difficult circumstances.)

Cases of strong disagreement are rare. When these occur, it is often best to prepare an on-the-spot performance assignment so learner may either demonstrate competence or prove to oneself that they cannot perform to the level indicated by their rating. An expert instructor should be able to develop quickly a situation that the learner can resolve in a short time if he or she indeed has the skill. It is important, however, to ensure that the assignment demands the required level of occupational performance. Asking the learner to verbalize about their ability or asking them to solve a training-related pencil-and-paper problem will not resolve the performance issue.

Modifying Entry Evaluations (4)

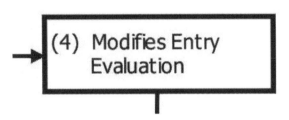

During the entry evaluation interview, most learners will choose to modify initial ratings for skills for which the instructor has provided a different rating. In some cases this may be due to increased honesty about performance when faced with an expert in the occupation who can readily spot inaccuracies in ratings. More likely changes will come about as a result of increased knowledge about the occupation, the nature of the skills, and the level of skill required for performance in the occupation at each rating level. This perhaps will have been the learner's first opportunity to discuss their own competence and the requirements of the occupation with an expert.

On the basis of the entry procedures, the learner should now have a fairly accurate idea of where they stand in relation to the occupation and their entrance into the program. The learner will be able to begin to make decisions about how much he or she has to achieve in order to reach satisfactory rating levels for performance in the work environment and can begin thinking about how to achieve these levels in the learning environment.

Selecting a Defined Behavior as the New Goal (5)

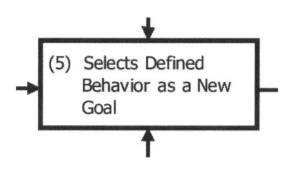

(5) Selects Defined Behavior as a New Goal

Before leaving the entry rating interview, the learner should be encouraged to select one of the skills on the chart as their first learning goal. It may be one in which they have already acquired some skill as indicated by their entry rating, or it may be one which the learner has never had an opportunity to acquire but which is appealing before entering the training program and influenced their decision to enter this particular occupation.

It is important that the instructor require the learner to make a choice about their first learning skill in order that they may begin immediately to develop a self-directed approach toward problem-solving and learning. Some learners will resist making this choice so early in the program, professing that they do not know enough about the occupation. Others may want to be led and may expect the instructor to provide much more directive assistance and guidance than the instructor is willing or able to provide in the DACUM learning environment. It is better for the learner to make an arbitrary choice than to leave the interview without having made any choice at all.

Most learners will readily select a skill that is of interest, and it usually is one that will permit quick learning achievement and resulting immediate reinforcement in the form of a new or increased skill rating. Learners typically select skills from the left side of the chart and normally begin on one in which they already have some skill and/or knowledge.

If the learner chooses a more complex difficult-to-achieve skill, the instructor has two possible courses of action:

1. If the skill is considered unattainable by the learner at that point in time, the instructor can discuss this problem with the learner and solicit selection of an alternative that will be easier to achieve. This course of action should be applied only in extreme cases for learner initiative can be quickly extinguished at that point.

2. The instructor may have to decide to take steps to modify the learning experiences for the skill to allow the inexperienced learner to achieve. The instructor will have to visualize and develop quickly ways of providing parts of the resources or steps or subskills so the learner can perform. This may occur in

cases where the selected skill is one that is normally applied only in combination with other skills.

If the learner has difficulty making a choice, the instructor can substantially assist, but must not take the initiative away from the learner. One way is to solicit several alternative choices from the learner while avoiding a final decision on any one. Subsequently, the instructor can help the learner narrow the choices. Another way is to recommend a few alternatives to the learner and provide encouragement to select one of these through elimination. Yet a further solution is to show the learner the available equipment and possible learning activities. Sometimes this will stimulate the learner to select an activity which the instructor can then show as leading to one of the goals on the chart which the individual can adopt for their choice. Finally, in stubborn cases, it may be necessary for the instructor to respond with equal stubbornness. If the learner refuses to make a choice and it appears he or she is set on making the instructor perform instead of the learner, it is frequently best to avoid the learner until he or she does choose. One severe case occurred in a previous program. A learner refused to make this kind of commitment. It was apparent that the learner was the kind that typically would talk the instructor into doing their work. Once the learner decided this was not going to work, this individual rapidly become more self-directive and one of the best learners.

INTRODUCTION TO THE LEARNING-EVALUATION MODEL

At this stage, the learner should be introduced to the Learning-Evaluation Model (see Figure 12-1). At first glance, it may appear too complex for the new learner. It has been found, however, that learners adapt to it quickly, and it only takes a few moments for the instructor to describe the way in which learning will take place and the respective roles of learner and instructor. (It is useful to have the Learning Evaluation Model displayed in a central location as a basis for discussion when the learner later encounters difficulty in adapting to the training process.)

The process of introducing the Learning-Evaluation Model should be as follows:

1. The instructor shows the learner the various stages of entry rating that the individual has proceeded through on the model, ending with the initial selection of a skill.

2. The instructor should use the model to show the activities that will take place each time the learner encounters a new skill and each time he or she attempts to increase their rating.

3. The instructor should next isolate the learning process as it is described in the model. The instructor may run through the diagram two or three times, using examples of specific skills and related activities that might be required to achieve these skills. The instructor should emphasize the decision-making involved in concluding that a currently satisfactory skill level has been achieved and that another skill or group of skills can be attempted. The instructor should also point out to the learner that some of their skill development will take place through work activities or projects incorporating combinations of skills but that the learner must look at each one independently in deciding how he or she will acquire the skill.

4. The instructor should describe their own role in the learning environment, stressing that it is to help develop the program, to counsel the learner who has run into difficulty, to monitor the learner's performance, to help the learner assess how well they are achieving, and to act as a technical resource by providing information of a technical or occupational nature. The instructor should point out that he or she will not:

    a) Make judgments about the learner's ability to perform unless the instructor sees actual performance. (The learner should make the instructor aware of such performance to be sure of receiving a rating.)

    b) Make any ratings until the learner first brings the skill profile or self-marked DACUM chart to the instructor .

5. The instructor should also describe desirable learning behavior that will be an outcome of the program and should point out that the training program requires the kind of behavior that will be required of the learner when they enter a work environment in which the learner must continue to learn if they are going to progress in their job or career. It is useful at this time to contrast this model of learning behavior with the conventional learning behavior and describe how it can result in cessation of learning once the learner leaves the training program and cannot locate and use resources in the conventional way.

6. The final step in orienting the learner is to involve them immediately in self-satisfying or rewarding learning experiences that are also ratable. The instructor may not select goals for the learner, but the instructor may help the learner select a project or assignment that will enable them to begin to apply the

selected skill and assess their achievement. The needed equipment, tools, supplies, and a project idea are often in the learning environment ready to be used on demand, and the instructor can help the learner in identifying and locating them.

In some cases it may be necessary for the instructor to partially develop or partially complete a project or application for the learner so that he or she will have an opportunity to apply the selected skill. This occurs in cases where a good deal of work on the project is necessary before the skill can be applied and in cases where the application of the skill in useful activities demands the application of several other skills at approximately the same time. This form of assistance would not detract from the possibility of rating the learner on their achievement in applying the selected skill.

It is important that the instructor encourage the learner to begin to learn by attempting a task, particularly if the task is one that does not require a good deal of background information before the learner can proceed. In this way the learner is able to experience the process of attempting an activity, determining what information or resources are required while attempting to locate them in the LAB's, and then proceeding to attempt the activity once more with the benefit of the new resources the learner has selected. The instructor should direct the new learner to the various information sources available in the learning environment for the selected skill, encouraging them to use the instructor as a learning resource .

Once the learner has increased their competency sufficiently to warrant a new skill rating, the instructor should encourage the learner to record the achievement on their DACUM chart. It is important that the learner be required to take this first step to set up a pattern of learning behavior that will continue throughout the training program. Once the instructor has encouraged the learner to take this step, the instructor can have the learner's rating verified on the master chart. At this point, since the instructor has been closely involved with the learner's initial efforts, the exchange between instructor and learner may be a bit unnatural. Nevertheless, it is essential that this procedure be followed to establish the proper pattern.

Once this cycle has been completed, the learner is encouraged to choose a new learning goal. The individual may decide to improve their rating on the same skill or may select another that he or she will encounter for the first time.

Consistent application of this orientation procedure has provided the best results. Learners adapt readily to the pattern once they know that it is demanded of them and that it is applied consistently by the instructor.

Orientation may continue through the duration of the training program. Whenever a learner loses the pattern or encounters a new kind of problem, the instructor should spend a brief period of time relating the problem to the pattern established in orientation and then allow the learner to return to their task.

SUMMARY

In this chapter, learner orientation was discussed. Learner orientation gives learners insight into the nature of the DACUM training program and to give them learning experiences to help hone learning behaviors throughout the program . The orientation process should be individualized. Learners should be given a tour of the facilities, given description of their environment, and introduced to their DACUM chart where they will document their progress through self-ratings. Following self-rating is the entry evaluation interview where agreement is reached between the instructor and the learner. After agreement, the learner selects a defined behavior as a new goal he or she wishes to acquire in the performance stage of the DACUM training program. Next, the Learning-Evaluation Model is presented to the learner so he or she understands the various stages of performing activities. The learner is now ready to begin the journey of acquiring the new set of skills by immediately attempting the chosen activities .

REFERENCES

Adams, R. E. (1975). *DACUM: Approach to curriculum, learning, and evaluation in occupational training*. Ottawa: Dept. of Regional Economic Expansion.

13

THE LEARNING PROCESS

Once the learner has been oriented to the learning environment and program, it is time to proceed through the learning process. The way in which the learner attempts to achieve, or is expected to achieve, is indicated in the lower right section of the Learning-Evaluation Model (see Figure 13-1). This chapter will deal with the learning process elements in the model and will be distinct from the evaluation process as discussed in the following chapter.

Initial learning activities take the form of simple, readily achieved skills. The learner will now begin to opt for more complex skills and higher rating levels and encounter more complex skill development problems.

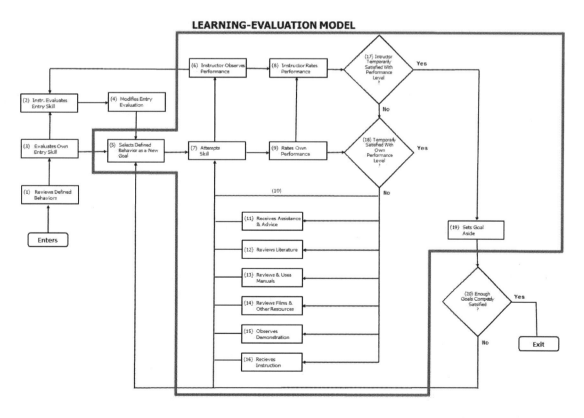

LEARNING-EVALUATION MODEL

Figure 13-1. Learning-Evaluation Model

SELECTION OF GOALS

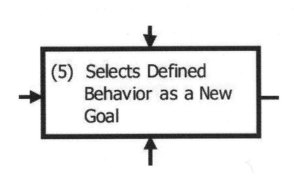

(5) Selects Defined Behavior as a New Goal

Following the learner's initial selection of a learning goal on entering the training environment, a number of factors will influence the selection process. The sequence in which a learner selects specific skills or learning modes is usually a matter of personal choice. This perhaps will be influenced by the instructor through the in-process rating interview sessions. Nevertheless, the learner will primarily select these goals on the basis of their appeal.   For example, choices may be influenced by color, rapid activity, or the prospect of working with large or sophisticated equipment. In some cases these goals may be such that they allow learners to demonstrate a newly acquired skill to their peers.

It is important that the instructor capitalize on this intrinsic motivation once it becomes evident. This imposes a demand on the instructor in that he or she must not only be alert for such motivation, but must also be ready to respond to satisfy the initial interest of the learner in each new skill or stage of development. In some cases it may even be necessary for the instructor to partially organize the project skill or resource required in order that the learner may experience achievement and satisfaction.

The need to develop an adequate skill profile will also influence learners, particularly as they near the end of their time in the training program. The learner's increasing knowledge of what is required to enter a specific job or specialty in the occupation will cause the individual to make special efforts to acquire specific skills. These may be skills that did not interest the learner initially but which now have become important as the learner needs to exit from the program with a record of achievement becomes evident. Through counseling, the instructor can stimulate motivation by pointing out skills in which the learner still must improve to meet the requirements of a specific career choice.

In some cases the selection of skills for achievement is more influenced by the nature of the problem, project, or skill that the learner wants to complete. In finding ways of applying skills while learning, the learner must locate useful activities in which to apply them. These activities, if they are fairly meaningful, will demand the inclusion of other skills as part of skill achievement. This causes the learner to develop skills simultaneously when, in effect, the individual was only interested in certain skills when first selecting the skill or problem. In some training programs this may be the most prominent method of selecting skills. For example, in the Oil Burner Training

Program, used heating units were cycled through the training center to provide opportunities for learners to gain experience in troubleshooting and repairing equipment. This was the primary learning experience and one that demanded application of almost all skills on the chart at one time or another. The learner was led or influenced by the condition of the equipment because the specific need for repair, in fact, required the individual to apply specific skills.

At times skills may be instructor assigned, as when large projects demand team activity. This makes it necessary for the instructor to assign individual learners to various skills in order to complete the project.

For learners in on-the-job training the selection of skills is almost entirely controlled by the work on hand. While there must be some measure of control to ensure that the learner does not slip into a job category in which they will apply only a limited number of skills, it is also important to allow response to the immediate work requirements. Generally, work in small firms or small departments of large firms is quite varied, and one can reasonably expect to encounter adequate opportunities for development of most skills in the occupation within a reasonable time.

Finally, later in the program, the learner will no doubt choose new skills or decide to increase the level of performance in skills already attempted on the basis of increased knowledge of the occupation as well as increased realization of the value of having a well-rounded background in the occupation. Critics have questioned the wisdom of allowing the learner latitude, particularly early in the program, in selecting skills and planning their own development. Critics feel that learners may inadvisedly overlook or avoid specific sets of skills with the result that the learner will be impeded in their career advancement efforts once out of the training program. This, however, has not proven to be the case. Learners have tended to select a wide range of skills and to strive for rather complete coverage of the chart rather than focus on some specific skill or skill clusters to the exclusion of others. It is felt that increased involvement of the learner in specific skills at advanced levels will in turn expose the individual to the value of similar achievement in many of the other skills on the chart.

SKILL SELECTION AND ATTEMPT

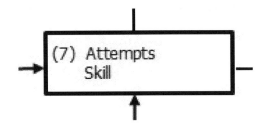

The learner increases skill and ratings through performance and applies the same procedure whether attempting to acquire a new skill or increase their level in a partially developed skill.

It is the learner's responsibility to select the skill, to locate a skill or project in which it can be applied, and to begin the learning process by immediately attempting to achieve. Ideally, this is done without reference to available learning information resources. The learner chooses these resources only after finding they need the skill and then has a much better idea of the specific kind of information is required.

The learning environment must be well equipped to permit this learning approach to succeed. If adequate equipment, tools, and supplies, as well as realistic learning experiences, are not available, the learner is not able to perform and learn by "discovery" and will be forced to begin by reading and then attempt to apply what was learned in a limited project or exercise.

Sometimes the learner does not require any learning resources beyond the occupational resources and an opportunity to attempt the skill. They may need to make repeated attempts to acquire the skill, but do not require typical learning resources. For example, an equipment operator learner may have to learn how to operate hydraulically controlled equipment or attachments. Some learners may require only an opportunity to operate the equipment in a controlled environment in order to discover how it works, its usefulness, its capacity, and its operational limitations. They may not need any information related to the theory of hydraulic units other than that which they can obtain through discovery.

On realizing they cannot progress, learners can often identify exactly what is required and can go directly to specific information resources to extract exactly what is needed to make further progress instead of having to review and study in detail all the available or prescribed information resources. The learner may alternate between attempts at performance and search for information several times each time basing the search on information needs detected in the previous attempt. In this way the learner uses only those resources, and spends only that time, needed to solve his or her unique development problems for the specific skill. This self-directed approach to learning should be of decided advantage to the learner if it continues to be their learning behavior once they enter the work environment. A further advantage is that the learner immediately integrates all acquired information into direct action. Information which is immediately applied is more likely to be retained and applied in similar situations than information which is acquired merely in the hope of applying it when opportunity arises.

Selection of suitable skills or learning activities is important. Sometimes selection is controlled by factors such as those mentioned in the previous section, but often skills have to be selected or developed on the spot. The learner may select a single skill which can be applied in a potentially wide range of available activities, or may select a skill they have already exhausted the limited number of applications available and must create or devise their own. The instructor should encourage the learner to select their own skills. If learners can develop this ability, it should be a decided benefit in their future work where they will be more able to see jobs to be done and will more readily determine which of their skills to apply; in other words, the learner will be more likely to be a self-starter. (Employers in an Oil Burner Training program commented that the learners were extremely adaptive on the job. Instead of returning to the shop when they encountered an unfamiliar problem, they improvised to get equipment in operation until they could return with advice or missing resources to complete the job.)

Frequently, however, the instructor must assist in selection of skills. This assistance is needed in the early stages in a training program or when the learner first encounters a new skill. Because of the learner's unfamiliarity with the occupation, skill, or typical applications of the skill, they may not know where to begin, and will usually ask the instructor for suggestions or advice. The instructor should limit assistance to encouragement and suggestions of way in which the learner can seek out appropriate skills and explore them further. The Instructor may direct the learner to the Learning Activity Battery to locate a list of possible applications of the skill, or may direct the learner to examine the occupational resources in the learning environment to see if they are suitable for completing suggested skills. The instructor should approve or help modify learner suggestions rather than make direct suggestions .

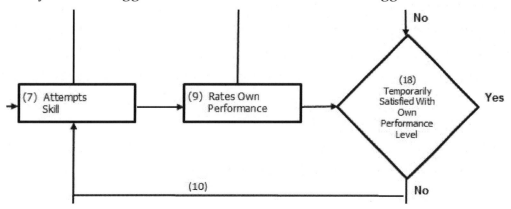

Some learners are reluctant to begin selecting and attempting skills, particularly in the early stages of the program. They wait for the instructor to select or create skill lessons for them. The instructor should withhold assistance but should encourage the learner to take the initial steps. If the instructor takes the initiative, he or she may gradually have less and less time for more important duties because the learners demand more assistance of this kind.

Just as the development of realistic learning activities is considered the most critical component of program development, the approach of beginning to learn by attempting to perform is considered the most critical of the operational components for learner achievement.

If the learner, in attempting a skill for the first time, decides their performance is not adequate for an increase in rating, they can continue to learn by attempting the repeat the skill. Many skills can be acquired this way, particularly those involving repetitive psychomotor skill applications. The learner needs an opportunity to apply the skills repeatedly.

Most attempts at learning skills will be repeated several times. This is because most learners will not achieve or satisfy their need to apply the skill adequately in a single attempt, particularly if that attempt is one in which the primary concern is with learning rather than performance. Additionally, the nature of the requirement for specific rating levels for that skill may demand several diverse performances before one can be sure that the level or performance is likely to be repeated in diverse applications of the skill.

ASSESSMENT OF PERFORMANCE

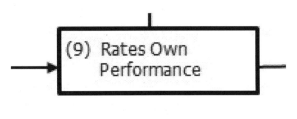

Each time a learner completes a skill, he or she must make an assessment of how well they performed by viewing their own performance through the eyes of an employer. The learner compares it to that of employees in the occupation in the community, and attempts to establish a skill rating level on this basis.

This is not a difficult task. The learner knows whether or not the skill was satisfactorily completed and, therefore, if the skill was reasonably well applied. Often successful skill completion is evident in the construction of a product that works as designed or in troubleshooting and repairing a piece of equipment that now performs to expected specifications.

While many assessments result in the learner's deciding that an increase in rating is not earned, it is important that the instructor encourage the learner to record an increase when it is merited. The learner should have their chart near at all times so new ratings can be recorded while the performance is still fresh in their mind. Ratings would not be as accurate if decisions were left until the end of the day or week or other convenient times. Delay would add further dimensions to the decision process, such as issues to follow which should be discussed during the rating interview, or subsequent complex applications of the skill.

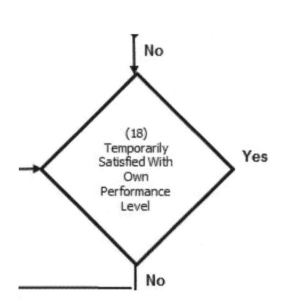

When the learner makes an initial positive decision about their performance level (in the form of an increase in a self-rating), they will also decide whether or not they are satisfied with that level at that time. The instructor influences this process a good deal, although the decision remains the learner's.

By offering comments while observing the learner in skill achievement or through raising issues while discussing ratings, the instructor can provide additional or alternate decision information that will cause the learner to reassess their own position with regard to satisfaction.

The learner may decide to cease attempting to develop the skill at that time if satisfied with their performance and encouraged by the instructor. The learner may be forced to apply the skill again in other activities in the training environment, but will not concentrate of further refining the skill until this happens. In fact, the learner may prefer to delay further refinement until one or more of the more useful or interesting activities becomes available. Sometimes the learner may even be satisfied with a low level of achievement and decide to cease attempting to refine the skill for the time being. Because of slow achievement the learner may feel that it has become too boring or time consuming.

In most cases, however, the learner concedes that additional work is needed on the skill to be reasonably sure that they can apply it in diversified situations. If the learner decides that his or her current performance is not adequate, the learner must make a decision about the way in which the various kinds of additional learning resources are going to be used to improve performance. Logically the learner applies these resources in the order in which they are listed in the Learning-Evaluation Model.

USE OF INFORMATION RESOURCES

The most readily available and adaptable source of information for anyone attempting to acquire skill competence, in a work or a learning environment, is someone expert in the occupation and in the skill being attempted. Written materials and other resources tend not to be pertinent to immediate needs. The resource person can, however, assess the learner's position on an independent basis and provide information, assistance, or advice suited to the learner and his or her individual problem. In fact, the expert worker's main effectiveness in information-giving may come from the ability to direct the learner to appropriate fixed or programmed resources.

If the instructor is skilled in the occupation, he or she will have background knowledge on which to draw in helping the learner. Even more important, the instructor serves as a role model of the supervisor in the work environment. Consequently, the learner learns to solicit information and advice from a source similar to that which will be available in work environment. However, the instructor must be careful not to become a self-imposed source of information. The instructor must become cast in a dual role in which he or she directs large activities such as a supervisor would in the work environment and at the same time is approached by individuals who are encountering difficulty and need additional information in order to proceed.

The instructor is not the only human resource available. Other learners, particularly those nearing completion of training, can be a valuable source of assistance and advice. Because of the individualized nature of the DACUM program, learners develop different skills in different combinations at different stages of their development. If the program is operated on a staggered entry-exit basis and the environment is well equipped, there is always another learner in the environment who has already experienced the skill development activities being encountered by the new learner. This was well illustrated in the Oil Burner Training program because physical space was limited and trainees were assigned as teams to work on troubleshooting and repair skills, providing much opportunity for use of this resource. Skilled learners willingly contributed time and effort to assist others. This was a useful experience for the "teachers" also as they were forced to organize and verbalize their knowledge.

Experts working in the occupation are another source of information and advice. Learners in the DACUM program work directly with specific skills that have to be completed and problems that have to be solved. These are everyday matters for the expert working in the occupation, and it has been found that experts willingly respond to requests for information or assistance. Again, this was illustrated in the Oil Burner Training program. Learners were encouraged to contact local experts by telephone or visit to obtain specific information or advice. Some learners were reluctant to do this at first and appeared to respond well only when another learner took the initiative and returned with needed information. This was considered a valuable learning experience leading to desirable information-seeking behavior on the job.

In some cases, it is possible to contact an expert in some other occupation or specialty. In larger training institutions there are often instructors in other departments who can provide specific advice or assistance toward the solution of problems and the development of skills related to their own field. Again, it is important that the learner initiate these contacts, although it is possible for the instructor to pave the way by discreetly contacting the expert to inform him or her that a learner may be in contact. The instructor can then encourage the learner to make the initial contact. The suggested procedures are designed to encourage the learner to seek information from experts in the occupation.

The most frequently used learning resource is printed material. This may be because there is a proportionately larger percentage of written than other materials in Learning Activity Batteries. It may also because learners are accustomed to using printed material and are able to retrieve information without having to take additional steps as must be done in using audio-visual materials. (Manuals as a resource are excluded from this discussion and included in the next category.)

When the learner is involved in a skill and is attempting to apply a specific skill, he or she frequently encounters difficulty because of a lack of specific information. This may be theoretical information about the skill, it may be background information about a variety of applications of the skill, or it may be information describing a specific technique.

The learner takes the Learning Activity Battery, spreads the materials out on a table, and skims over it to find a single resource that will provide the information needed to continue to work on the problem.

Ideally, the learner should spend only the time and effort necessary to acquire the minimal amount of information required to proceed. The instructor should encourage this. In some cases, however, once the learner gets involved with the package of learning materials, they may wish to review all the contents and study some materials in depth to enable them to proceed with the development of the skill without repeated referral to the Learning Activity Batteries.

The most useful materials for the learner are those which provide the most direct information. Product websites, pamphlets and brochures which describe equipment, concepts, techniques, etc., are valuable for this purpose. Those that are well illustrated, with a minimum of text, are most frequently used. Simple, direct materials such as directions for use are frequently used. Also useful in this category are selections from handbooks or other reference material designed to provide problem-solving information.

Often the most meaningful resources are simple descriptions of the occupation, its skills, and their application that one might find in trade journals or magazines related to the occupation or its associated industries. These articles tend to focus on unique problem-solving situations and success stories. These allow the learner to see potential applications of his or her new skills.

The most difficult-to-use resources are technical specifications, sections of textbooks, some programmed information, etc. Such sources frequently contain much information that the learner does not need to continue to develop competence in a specific skill. The needed information is difficult to extract and apply to an immediate problem. Nevertheless, these materials are often useful as additional sources of information that may appeal to some learners.

In some cases learners enter the training program wanting to begin work on each skill by immediately reviewing all available literature or other resources in the Learning Activity Battery. The instructor should be alert to detect these cases. It may be necessary to counsel such persons about the effectiveness of the development and

problem-solving response they are going to require once they enter the work environment.

Manufacturer's service and repair manuals and company operational or procedural manuals are frequently excellent learning resources in the DACUM environment. The reading level required to use these materials is normally not high, and they are easily understood by the learner. They provide clear, step-by-step procedures which enable the learner to process provided the learner can follow directions.

Manuals, however, are much less used than one would expect. They are necessarily designed to relate to a specific procedure, piece of equipment, or process. Unless the learner is working in very similar circumstances, they are likely to be of little use. As information resources, they are not readily transferred to another skill application. They are only applicable to the learner when selecting a problem or skill activity that will use the specific processes procedures or equipment covered. Such cases may be infrequent and can only be increased by controlling the nature of activities or problems in order to limit them to those that are well supported by the manuals. This is not consistent with the principles of the DACUM system. Nevertheless, manuals are extremely useful when and if they apply.

Because the learner is expected to obtain information only as required by the skill development activity, he or she must acquire audio-visual information on an individual basis. Therefore each learner must be able to operate the necessary audio-visual equipment learning resources. This is not an extensive skill as it has been found that learners quickly become competent in operating standard audio-visual learning resources such as computer-based presentations, web-based applications, and other digital resources, particularly those designed for individual rather than large-group presentation. Learners receive assistance in learning to operate equipment from other learners who have already acquired this ability or they can learn by observing their performance. Where more complex equipment and operational procedures (simulations, etc.) are called for, it has been found useful for the instructor to make a video tutorial describing the various stages of operation of the equipment. This can be located adjacent to the equipment so the learner can acquire this information and the necessary operational skills when they are needed.

An advantage of learner operation of equipment is that resources can be used when it is most meaningful to the learner. Presentation of audio-visual materials to large groups often provides information that they may not be current or immediate to a problem and it is doubtful how much is acquired and retained in this way. Another advantage of individual operation is that the learner is able to review material as many times as necessary to gather the level of information required to proceed with skill development. Information that presents only concepts or ideas often needs to be seen only once. Presentations involving controlled action, intricate procedures, or much detail may have to be viewed several times in order to acquire mastery.

Audio-visual resources are used most frequently during early stages of skill development. This is where the learner most needs to observe physical action and visual presentation of specific information. Both these tend to provide basic as opposed to specialized skills and information. Learner emphasis normally alternates between printed materials and audio-visual resources at various stages of an individual's development while in the program. At times the learner will acquire most information by viewing audio-visual materials while at other times will tire of this activity and acquire it principally through printed materials. This presents no problem as long as use of one type does not become the sole learning resource. This will create difficulties as the learner encounters skills which demand use of alternate materials.

While it is expected that the learner will use audio-visual resources to advantage during early learning experiences, it is desirable that he or she draw more frequently on the kind of information sources normally found and used in the future work environment, particularly as the learner begins to approach higher levels of skill competence. In most occupations these sources are other persons, manuals and technical references, journal articles and examples of the work itself. Few work environments provide extensive opportunity for continued learning using audio-visual materials.

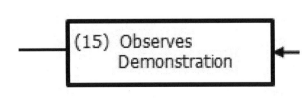

In order for the learner to master technique and procedures, it is frequently necessary to observe demonstrations. However, these are rarely, if ever, group demonstrations of the sort one would find in conventional training programs. The only time group demonstration might be provided is when two or more learners encounter the same sort of difficulty with the same skill at the same time, and then the instructor should limit the demonstration to those who are going to obtain immediate advantage from it and should avoid deliberately involving other trainees. Other learners could no doubt be encouraged to observe the demonstration at the same time but would not likely gain as much from it as they would not be working on the demonstrated skills at that time.

This is one place when the self-directedness and learner focus of the DACUM system can begin to break down. If an instructor becomes concerned with the amount of repeated demonstrations that must be provided for individual learners, the instructor may attempt to resolve this by grouping learners as closely as possible and providing demonstrations for the groups. This places the instructor in a directive role and provides a more comfortable role for some learners since they cannot be expected to act and reach decisions while performing. At the same time such activities can easily draw other learners away from meaningful activities.

Most opportunities for the learner to model expert behavior are provided informally. The instructor may encounter a learner in difficulty and illustrate correct techniques or procedures in order to address the learner's difficulty. Often all that is required is a brief demonstration of only the part of the skill that was causing the learner most concern.

Learners can obtain information and technique by observing instructors performing in the skills of the occupation in the learning environment. It has been useful in some programs for instructors to become involved in their own projects while learners are involved in theirs. For example, in a Craft Training program instructors sometimes worked at developing their own handcraft products. This permitted learners to observe at first hand the way in which they applied techniques and the pace at which they worked .

Finally, other more advanced learners have been found useful as models of skill behavior. Beginners in the program tend to model performance of other more advanced learners quite carefully. Provided there is some measure of instructor control to ensure that techniques are demonstrated properly, there is no harm in encouraging this activity. It has been found that advanced learners welcome the opportunity to demonstrate their competence to other learners who require this kind of assistance.

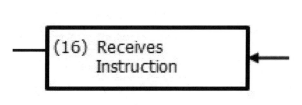

Formal instruction, in the form of lectures or other group presentation, is the least likely learning resource to be found in a DACUM environment. Need for this resource depends on quality of initial program development and adequacy of other kinds of learning resources.

Because of the diversity of the learning environment and of the skill profiles of the individual learners at any given time, such presentations become meaningless. It is doubtful just how much information the individual learner will retain until he or she has an opportunity to integrate it in a skill application.

Again, such presentations only take place if two or more encounter the same sort of difficulty at the same time and ask the instructor for assistance. This might be for the purpose of allowing them to integrate a number of pieces of information related to a concept they must acquire, it might be to help them visualize an entire procedure which is comprised of a number of individual steps or skills, or it might be to provide them with a more comprehensive and technical description of principles, guidelines, or theories that relate to specific skills in the occupation. The participants in this case usually are encountering difficulty in using the resources collected for the purpose in the Learning Activity Batteries.

This resource is seldom used and then only with small groups, hence need for classroom space is eliminated. This frequently causes difficulty when adapting facilities, including classroom space, to a DACUM learning environment. Often this space, because of its shape and location, is not readily adaptable to requirements of the new program .

SETTING ASIDE GOALS

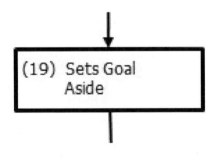

(19) Sets Goal Aside

The learner may set aside specific goals while in the training program. It is not necessary for the learner to continue to work toward mastery of a specific skill or set of skills before proceeding to others. A number of circumstances may cause the learner to set specific goals aside:

1. The learner may be satisfied with the achievement of a specific skill rating and wish to improve performance in other skills.

2. The learner may wish to set aside a skill with which they are having particular difficulty .

3. The instructor may note frustration through lack of achievement and encourage the learner to try other skills and leave the difficult one for a later time, when ready to attempt it again .

4. The immediate project on which the learner is working may not provide further opportunity for applying the skill. Lack of suitable projects at that time may force them to forego any further activity on that skill until encountering additional projects that demand its application .

5. The learner may have achieved about all that is possible with available resources, and it may be necessary to postpone further skill development until entering the work environment, where more challenging problems might be encountered.

6. The learner may have reached a satisfactory level of competence for entry to the occupation. Once the learner approaches the '3' level of competence, it is pointless to continue to refine skills which have not yet adequately achieved .

7. The learner may have reached their own level of competence in a specific skill. It may be apparent to both learner and instructor that the learner does not have the ability to progress further in this skill, at least at this time in their development, because of a lack of ability to acquire more complex information, concepts, and problem-solving techniques, or because of a physical handicap preventing the learner from further refining psychomotor skills .

SUMMARY

Chapter 13 presents the learning process of the DACUM system. To begin this process, the learner selects a skill, locates an activity or project in which it can be applied, and begins by attempting to achieve a given level of performance in the skill. Each time a learner completes a skill, he or she must make an assessment of how well they performed by viewing his or her performance through the eyes of an employer. The learner compares it to that of employees in the occupation and attempts to reach a satisfactory level of competence. The learner may decide to cease attempting to develop the skill at that time if satisfied with their performance. The instructor, expert worker, or other learners serve as a resource during the process. Learning materials come primarily from print as well as manuals, audio visual, or demonstrations while formal instruction is seldom used. Finally, the learner may set aside specific goals while in the program if he or she is satisfied with their performance, is frustrated, is having particular difficulty, has a lack of projects, or has reached their own level of competence.

REFERENCES

Adams, R. E. (1975). *DACUM: Approach to curriculum, learning, and evaluation in occupational training.* Ottawa: Dept. of Regional Economic Expansion.

EVALUATION – THE RATING SCALE

Evaluation is a critical part of any occupational training program. For DACUM developers to evaluate they must assess the intent of the program and what the program actually achieves assuming that the goal is employer satisfaction. The DACUM rating scale is the basis for evaluation. The next four chapters focus on the evaluation of the learners within the DACUM system. Chapter 14 begins this emphasis by presenting the rationale for the rating scale, explaining the rating scale, presenting typical distributions of ratings, and utilizing the rating scale.

RATING SCALE RATIONALE

The DACUM system incorporates a new approach to evaluation based on a rationale and set of assumptions which are meaningful to learner, instructor, and employer. In order to take a fresh look at learner evaluation in occupational training, it is necessary to assess the intent of occupational training programs and what they actually achieve.

Historically, occupational training programs have attempted to assess needs of employers and to direct training activities toward satisfaction of these needs. It is suggested that, in this process, standards and criteria have been developed which are at best only peripherally related to these needs.

Typically, trainers or program planners have tried to develop programs within the context of currently accepted learning objectives. These have ranged from no requirement at all to extensive written examinations and from evidence of successful employment on completion of a training program to highly structured and rigidly criterioned performance tests. The more rigid and acceptable these became in terms of behavior measurement conventions, the more likely they were to become less relevant to the specific job environment and its conditions. One cannot help but note the absence of such evaluation processes in industry in other than the largest and most wealthy organizations where a staff of specialists may be engaged for this purpose. Consequently, both the learner and the employer who must eventually assess employee achievement are hampered by the fact that the learner has been working toward goals that may not be highly relevant to the nature of the work and the work environment.

The basic assumption in the DACUM system is that a goal of occupational training is employer satisfaction. If this assumption is reasonable, it would appear that, historically, trainers have been identifying criteria and applying measures that do not adequately reflect this goal. Therefore, it was assumed in developing the DACUM system that a new method of identifying and measuring employer satisfaction would have to be developed as a companion to the DACUM curriculum process.

To develop instruments and methodology, it was necessary to observe how employers typically view skill performance. (The word "employers" here includes supervisors, foremen, etc., who are skilled in the occupation. Excluded are persons in related staff functions such as Personnel which may have a different set of job criteria.)

Occupationally-skilled employers or supervisors typically observe and assess performance in a very informal yet hard-nosed way:

1. Supervisors are able to sense their satisfaction or dissatisfaction with a skill being performed. A number of factors might be combined simultaneously, such as the speed with which a task is performed, the quality of work that is visible, and the usefulness of the product being built, yet good supervisors are able to make judgments about their satisfaction with performance involving a number of such assessment factors.

2. Supervisors assess performance by observation, followed by a rather subjective expert decision or judgment. They seldom administer tests, and, in other than the most simple repetitive or operative jobs, they seldom have an opportunity to measure performance in terms of production or quality of product.

3. The occupationally competent supervisor can tell when a good job is being done while observing and monitoring work. In other words, the supervisor can tell a good job when seeing it.

4. Good supervisors typically avoid making judgments about performance on the basis of isolated instances. They have to be shown that the individual

can apply skills in a variety of situations before conceding that performance is satisfactory.

5. While professing otherwise during curriculum review meetings, good supervisors seldom make judgments about ability on the basis of the employee's knowledge. Again, they have to be shown that the individual is capable of performing and achieving before granting recognition.

6. Technically competent supervisors are able to observe and assess mental problem-solving skill performance not observable by those not expert in the occupation. They can detect whether or not, or how well, an employee is applying design or problem-solving thought processes that are not directly observable in action or not directly visible in the end product.

7. The occupationally competent supervisor does not need rigid performance criteria to assess adequacy of performance. Adequacy is exhibited in the speed and quality of application of skill and the results of the work.

8. The good supervisor appreciates the fact that most rigid criteria developed for training programs are not really part of the job. For example, few executives are concerned about the typing speed of their secretaries. They know when they are satisfied with the speed of production of a memo, a formal letter, or a project proposal or brief. They are little concerned about whether the secretary can type at 60 or 80 words a minute.

9. Most supervisors readily express their concern about educational-type measurements and entry qualifications. They recognize that there are some persons who are not able to qualify for entry to the occupation but who perform reasonably well on the job once they are able to gain entry. They realize, too, that there are persons who more than qualify but who do not seem to be able to produce or fill job requirements. Finally they recognize that there are persons who minimally qualify but who become outstanding once in the job environment.

THE RATING SCALE

After constructing the first two or three DACUM charts, it was decided to attempt to develop an instrument or rating scale that would adequately cover the range of skills in the charts and that would reflect the way in which supervisors or employers observe and assess performance in a work environment.

An initial attempt was made at establishing a go, no-go instrument. This was quickly rejected for the following reasons: First, examination of skills identified on the charts indicated it would be difficult for instructors to make a fine distinction between the person who was minimally qualified and the person who was not. Second and more important, it was recognized that persons can be absorbed into the work environment at quite a range of levels of ability. These levels would appear to be based on decision-making capability and ability to work independently.

The seven levels on the scale were established by attempting to define categories that would distinguish between observable levels of performance at work. Not applied was the conventional practice of deciding there should be five, seven, or nine levels, and then attempting to create that many specific definitions.

It was decided to create as a baseline for the rating scale a category which would describe the minimal level of competence expected in each skill of a minimally or newly qualified performer in the occupation. This might be the journeyman who has recently qualified in one of the apprenticeable trades. This level is characterized by an individual's ability to apply skills in the occupation in making relatively standard applications without assistance or direction from others, this category eventually become the '3' category on the rating scale.

Below this baseline are three levels. First, there is the '0' level which indicates unsatisfactory performance or no exhibited performance. This level is characterized by the individual or employee's inability to perform this task in a work environment well enough to receive pay for that specific application. Given much additional time, the learner may be able to complete the activity but cannot perform adequately even in a mechanical sense, even though they may be provided with direct supervision and considerable assistance. Another example of '0' level performance would be the do-it-yourselfer. This individual produces high quality work in renovating his own home. Friends and neighbors comment glowingly about the high quality work produced (e.g. tiling a floor). But, despite the high quality workmanship, the do-it-yourselfer could not be paid to do tiling work on a paying job, likely taking three or four days to do what a good qualified worker could complete within a day.

The first acceptable level of performance is '1'. The person in this category is characterized by an ability to perform mechanically complete tasks well enough to receive pay. However, due to lack of information or decision-making ability, the individual must work under direct supervision and receive considerable assistance in such activities as selecting the job, laying out the job, determining what resources or procedures to use, and determining when the job is adequately complete. The second satisfactory level of performance is the '2' level, which is characterized by the individual's ability to mechanically perform and also to become partially involved in decision-making processes through increased knowledge. At this level the individual would require less constant direct supervision but would still require access to someone more expert than themselves who could make decisions and assist with initiation of diverse applications of skill.

There are also three levels of increasingly acceptable performance above the baseline level.

At the '4' level one would find the kind of performance expected of the more mature person in the occupation, who has had an opportunity to apply skills in a number of different situations. Through experience they have increased their ability to apply the skills with more than the minimally required level of speed and quality. The work is obviously more polished, and they complete routine assignments quickly and efficiently. The '5' level is the highest technical level of competence in the occupation. This is the level that characterizes the performance one would expect of an individual with considerable experience in the occupation who is capable of solving unique problems when standard resources and conditions do not prevail. The person with this ability would be considered to be an expert or troubleshooter in the occupation. At the '6' level one would find the individual who possesses abilities required at the other levels and also has the ability to verbalize about the skills, enabling them to lead others. This is the level of competence required of supervisors, foremen, or instructors.

It is useful to illustrate the meaning of the levels in the rating scale through an example of the kinds of individuals one might expect to find in a specific work environment. The following example describes a hypothetical Domestic Appliance Repair business which employs a number of persons trained for the occupation in a variety of jobs in a service center and in external customer contact work.

The manager of this hypothetical firm would assign persons with level '1' ability to jobs in which they would be under direct supervision of someone else, ideally the supervisor. They would be mechanically capable of disassembling, reassembling, and repairing standard domestic appliances. Nevertheless, because they lack decision-making ability, they would be confined to bench work in a location where they could be directly observed and assisted by the supervisor or another more experienced mechanic.

A person with '2' level ability would also be assigned to the service center, where he or she would have an opportunity to get periodic assistance and monitoring from someone more expert, possibly the shop supervisor. However, the individual could be assigned to work in an adjacent room and take charge of a specific kind of routine work that they have demonstrated they can handle and may also be periodically assigned to work as a helper to a fully qualified mechanic on a service vehicle.

At the '3' level one would find the mechanic who can be relied upon to inspect, troubleshoot, service, and repair a piece of equipment on their own. This individual might be found working in the service center overhauling and tuning major pieces of equipment or might be assigned to work out of a service vehicle specializing in making service calls to residences on request.

A person working at the '4' level would likely be assigned to a variety of work in the service center or in a service vehicle. Able to work quickly and leave the job in good condition, this individual would probably be selected to handle all work provided by customers who are known to be hard to satisfy, customers who want a mechanic to be in and out of their residence quickly, and customers who would be likely to complain if call-backs were necessary.

A person performing at the '5' level would handle jobs presenting uniquely difficult problems. This employee would be adept at installing, tuning, and servicing equipment recently on the market about which little is known regarding performance and the nature of problems likely to be encountered. Similarly, this individual would be assigned to service, troubleshoot, and overhaul equipment seldom encountered in the normal course of work about which there might be little information in the form of specifications or manuals. They are capable of analyzing and solving unique operational problems.

At the '6' level, one would find the supervisor in the firm who is capable of directing the work of others and helping less competent persons increase their competence. If this person were to changes jobs, he or she would possibly become an instructor in the training program designed to prepare new entrants to the occupation.

TYPICAL DISTRIBUTION OF SKILLS

To apply the rating scale it is necessary to consider the distributions of skills that one may find in individuals or groups at different levels of skill development in the occupation. These descriptions and accompanying figures have been found most useful in orienting learners, instructors, and other raters to the rating process.

Distribution of Persons in Occupations

As indicated in the preceding example, persons perform at various levels in an occupation. Most perform around the '2', '3', and '4' levels, with relatively few performing at the '1', '5', and '6' levels. There would be no one employed whose rating, in terms of over-all performance, was '0'.

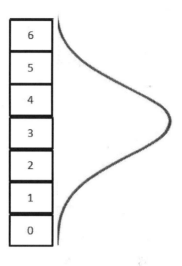

Most occupations have some jobs at the entry or minimal performance level that can be filled by the person with general '1' or '2' level ability. Some occupations, because of the nature of the work and skill demands, cannot absorb persons with less than '2' to '3' levels of ability in most skills, however, these occupations are rare, and it is expected that only a few skills may be critical in this way.

Distribution of skills in the Typical Practitioner

One would expect to find a wide range of skill levels in an individual who might be considered typical of those employed in the occupation. Most skills might be at the '2', '3', or '4' level, but some might be at the '5' level and a few at the '6' level. Similarly, they might be able to perform only at the '1' level in some skills because they have not had an opportunity to apply and develop them. In some cases, there may be skills that the well-qualified performer in the occupation cannot perform at all. These would be rated at the '0' level. The diversity of application of modern occupations makes it extremely unlikely that persons will be able to perform all skills in their occupation at the '3' level or better.

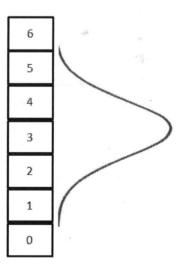

Distribution of Skills of the Learner on Entry

When entering the training program, it is quite likely that the learner will be rated at the '0' level in most skills in the occupation. However, if given an opportunity to gain some skills during previous periods of other work activity, they may have acquired some skills demanded in the occupation. The learner's profile would indicate most skills at the '0' level, a few at the '1' level, and perhaps rare skills at the '2' or '3' level. (The latter might be expected to be skills commonly applied to a wide range of occupations, such as selection and use of hand tools.) One must also consider the possibility that the learner may have a somewhat higher profile because they had an opportunity to work in the occupation in a helping or junior capacity. In such cases training time will probably be reduced.

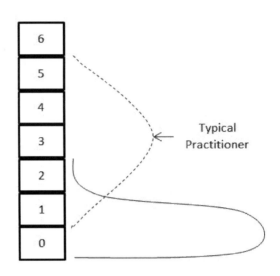

Distribution of Typical Learner Skills on Exit

The typical learner exiting from the training program will have a skill profile somewhat below the minimal '3' level required for recognition as a journeyman at a minimal level of qualification in the occupation. Most training programs provide the learner with necessary skills to enter the occupation, but it is generally conceded that the learner will have to spend a period of time working in the occupation applying his or her skills in a greater variety of situations to meet the requirements of the definition for the '3' level. The learner who terminates with the illustrated profile should be able to perform to their own, and their employer's, satisfaction. The additional competence required of a more seasoned employee will be acquired on the job.

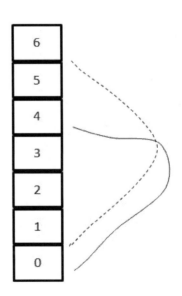

It is important to recognize that, like the practicing craftsperson, the learner may exit from the program with a '0' rating on one or more skills on his or her DACUM chart. This does not prevent the learner from entering the occupation, but it does indicate that they will have to find an entry position where the missing skills will not be demanded or at least not before having an opportunity to develop them.

Distribution of Skills for Exceptional Learners

Occasionally one will encounter an individual with extremely high aptitude for developing the competence necessary for the occupation. In spite of the fact that most entrants to the occupation will have to expect to work for a period before they can achieve '3' level competence in most of their skills, this individual may demonstrate adequate performance to warrant '3' and perhaps '4' level ratings in many skills before leaving the training program (provided there are resources and experiences available in the learning environment which will allow the learner to achieve in this way).

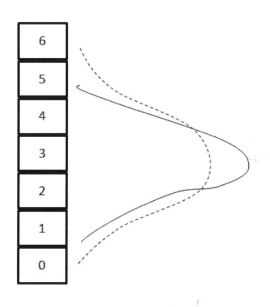

Distribution of Skills for Minimal Level of Job Entry

In most occupations, it is possible for a learner to exit from a training program with mostly '1' level ratings and still gain entry to the occupation. This depends on the nature of the occupation and its skills and, more importantly, on the kind of firm or organization they enter. Frequently large firms with adequate levels of supervision can afford to absorb learners at the '1' level who can mechanically perform tasks required under close supervision and who can be expected to grow in the occupation. The smaller firm must usually be more versatile in applying the skills of its limited personnel. It cannot absorb persons, who perform at the '1'

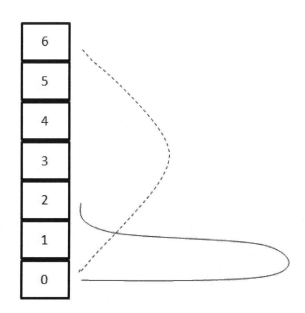

level and must demand recruits approaching the '3' level who can be expected to grow quickly in the occupation and fill a versatile role in the firm.

USE OF THE RATING SCALE

It is recommended that this instrument (which combines the rating scale with the DACUM chart of skill definitions) be the only or major instrument applied for measuring learner achievement in the DACUM training environment. The rating process demands considerable commitment and difficult decision-making from both learner and instructor. It is important to avoid installing other less needed measurements that will detract from the usefulness and meaning of this rating system, particularly in the eyes of the learner. Most learners have previously been exposed to a variety of evaluation systems which were applied at least in part as a directive control of learner achievement. If these are applied in the DACUM learning environment, some learners become apprehensive, lose sight of the DACUM learning objectives and their relative value, and do not involve themselves in the rating assessment process with full commitment.

DACUM rating assessments are based on performance. There are three levels of observation that can be applied in making assessments and granting ratings.

1. ***Directly observed performance.*** While circulating in the environment, the instructor has the opportunity to observe learners while they are attempting to perform activities and demonstrate skills. The instructor can readily integrate direct observations when it is requested to confirm a learner-initiated rating. This is the most ideal and most frequently applied rating method.

2. ***Observation through examination of a finished product.*** The instructor may not have been able to observe performance in all stages of the development of a product, but may be able to attribute the quality of the finished product to specific levels of achievement in specific skills. It is important to realize, however, that the end product does not always clearly indicate the nature of skill performance applied in producing the product. For example, if a product demands that several skills be applied to its production, it is sometimes impossible for a rater to attribute ratings to specific skills that are not as evident in the end product.

3. ***Observation through relayed information.*** When not able to observe performance, the instructor may have information relayed by the learner or someone else who is capable of observing and assessing this performance. Being responsible for the rating assigned, the instructor must critically question the observation and assessment of performance and request further information about the performance such as nature and difficulty of the learning activity, time consumed, and amount of assistance or direction required. In this way, it is really the instructor who makes the rating, although using relayed information rather than direct observation. This is the least desirable kind of observation and should be reserved for those cases in which direct observation is not possible.

SUMMARY

In this chapter, the rating scale was introduced. The rating scale is designed to reflect the way a supervisor assesses performance in the workplace. The old saying "I can tell a good job when I see it" applies here.

The designers arrived at seven rating levels, from '0', meaning "unsatisfactory performance", to '6', meaning "able to direct the work of others". The baseline level '3' means "can perform well on their own"; the classic young journeyperson in a trade. Finally, typical distribution of skills was discussed.

REFERENCES

Adams, R. E. (1975). *DACUM: Approach to curriculum, learning, and evaluation in occupational training.* Ottawa: Dept. of Regional Economic Expansion.

EVALUATION – THE RATING PROCESS & INSTRUCTIONS

The rating process is at the heart of DACUM evaluation. Instructors and trainees must understand their role in the evaluation process for it to be successful. The intent of this chapter is to provide instructions for entry level and in-process ratings for instructors and trainees. Chapter 15 begins with an explanation of the entry rating process followed by the instructions.

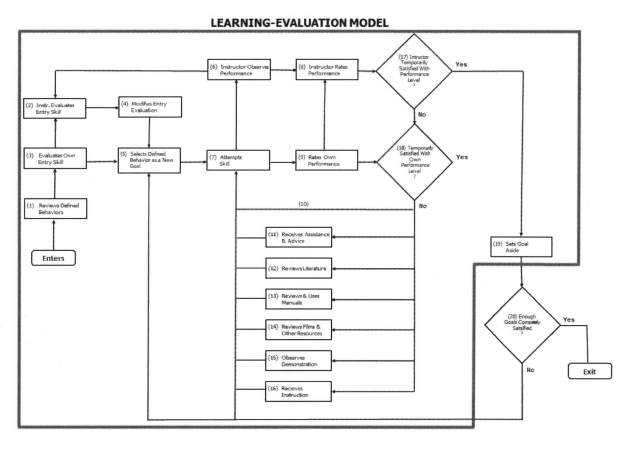

Figure 15-1. Learning-Evaluation Model

THE ENTRY RATING PROCESS

A unique feature of the DACUM rating system is the entry rating procedure, which provides the entry skill profile on which the individual program is built. Some may question the validity of assigning entry ratings by means of interview. However, experience has shown that this process is sufficiently accurate for the purposes for which it was designed. In fact, few situations have been encountered where it was necessary to modify entry ratings to any extent.

An important feature of the process is that the learner is expected to provide the initial assessment of their own ability. Without this initial assessment on the part of the learner, the initial assessment would be onerous for the instructor, for it would be necessary to interview the learner on each of the skills on the DACUM chart in order to make some judgment about that skill. By requiring the learner to make the initial assessment, the instructor can focus attention on those skills the learner feels he or she already has.

The instructor with supervisory experience in industry is capable of conducting the entry rating interview and arriving at reasonably accurate rating levels and skill profiles. If the instructor had any responsibility to share in selection of technical personnel for their own staff, they no doubt have had to perform a similar function in their former industrial environment. The questions and the nature of the questioning would be much the same. Only the level of detail skill specification would be increased.

There is also a built-in measure of control if the rating is being made for entry to a well -equipped program. Each rating can be confirmed at the first opportunity for application of the skill in the learning environment.

Advantages of conducting entry rating interviews immediately on entry to the program are:

1. It forces the learner to self-assess, and think about what must be achieved in the program.

2. It causes the learner to look at the entire program and avoid focusing attention on one specific appealing aspect or cluster of skills.

3. It forces instructor and learner to participate in face-to-face discussions about where to start and what must be done in the training program. In other words, it facilitates planning the learner's program.

4. It promotes the design of an individualized approach for each learner. Each has a different entry skill profile and must be treated individually in order to plan his or her development program.

5. It causes both learner and instructor to focus on terminal objectives right from the beginning; that is, the kind of performance required in industry. Too often final objectives are of concern only during the latter weeks of a training program.

Entry ratings found to be inaccurate can be easily modified when a need for change becomes apparent. All that is necessary in terms of recordkeeping is to eliminate the initial entry rating on the master DACUM chart and enter a new entry rating that, on the basis of more current information, is deemed more appropriate as a description of the learner's performance ability when entering the program.

Need for modification can be detected when the learner first attempts to apply the skill. If there is a change, it usually results in a reduction in the rating level. On first trying to apply the skill, it is sometimes evident that both learner and instructor were originally mistaken about the learner's ability to perform. It may have been that the learner based the decision on a more simplified application of the skill than is generally considered adequate for the specific rating level .

In other situations, learner or instructor may wish to change the rating because of information gained since the rating was made. Once the learner enters the training program, they may discover more about the skill and its requirements and wish to have that particular rating lowered in order better to reflect their ability on entry. Or in discussions with the learner the instructor may gain additional information which may cause doubt about the accuracy of one or more ratings assigned to the learner on entry. For example, the instructor may discover that the learner misinterpreted the meaning of one of the skill blocks, having another kind of skill in mind when making a self-rating and subsequently discussed it during the entry-rating interview. However, there is normally little need for modification of entry ratings. Most learners do not require any change at all. Changes required are usually limited to one or two skills.

The following rating information sheets were designed to provide guidelines for the new entrant and for the instructor making first entry ratings.

INSTRUCTIONS TO TRAINEE - ENTRY LEVEL SKILL RATINGS

You have just started a new training program. We would like to know if you already have some of the skills needed in this occupation. The instructor needs this information to help find out how much training you are going to need and the best way for you to get this training. In order to find this information, we will use the following procedure:

1. The instructor will give you a DACUM chart that shows all the skills needed in your new occupation and will go over the chart with you to explain how it will be used in the training program. The instructor will go over each block in the chart and explain what it means and be sure that you understand what all the words mean. The instructor will also explain why each block is there and how the blocks relate to each other.

2. You are asked to study the chart carefully and be sure that you understand it. If you do not understand some of the names or meanings, be sure to ask the instructor for an explanation.

3. Your chart also contains a rating scale with seven descriptions of ability to perform in occupational skills. They are numbered from *0 – 6*. These numbers are called the ratings. The instructor will describe the use of this rating scale in your training program, and will also describe the meaning of each of the levels of the scale.

4. You are asked to study these levels and be sure you know what they mean. If you have some of the skills described in the blocks on the chart, try to visualize which level best describes your ability in that skill. The instructor may help you with one or two of the skills to help you get started.

5. Study each block on the chart. If you have any skill in any of the blocks, mark in the block the number on the rating scale that best describes your ability. Leave the blocks blank if you have no ability.

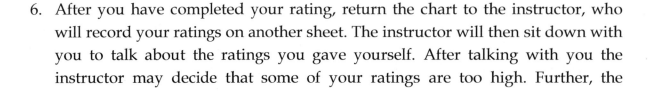

6. After you have completed your rating, return the chart to the instructor, who will record your ratings on another sheet. The instructor will then sit down with you to talk about the ratings you gave yourself. After talking with you the instructor may decide that some of your ratings are too high. Further, the instructor may also decide that some of your ratings are too low and that you

really have more ability than you thought. Together you will produce a new set of ratings that will become the starting point for your new training program.

INSTRUCTIONS TO INSTRUCTOR - ENTRY SKILL RATING

To determine how well each trainee progresses in your training program and where he or she has weaknesses that will require special attention exist, it is necessary to determine the level of skill the trainee has when entering the program. We will use the DACUM chart and performance rating scale for this purpose.

You have been involved in training sessions describing the chart and rating scale and how to use them. Proceed in the following way for making entry level skill ratings:

1. Give each trainee a copy of the chart which will become his or her record sheet while in the training program. Explain the items on the DACUM chart and the meaning of the terminology used. Be sure that the trainee understands what is meant by each. Also explain how the blocks on the chart relate to each other.

2. Explain the nature and use of the performance rating scale. Go over the categories in the scale in detail with the trainee and make sure they understand the meaning of each. Also explain how the blocks on the chart relate to each other.

3. Have the trainee rate themself to indicate what skills they already have and the level of ability they feel they have in each skill .

4. Sit down with the trainee and review their self-ratings to confirm their accuracy. It will be necessary to ask probing questions about their self-ratings and also it may be necessary to explore low ratings and blanks in the chart to determine if the trainee is really underrating their own ability. Questions might be: Where have you performed these skills? How often? How long? When? Who with? Did this person have to tell you how to do the job? Did they have to tell you how to start the job? Did they have to tell you what materials and tools to use? etc. There will be many more, and the trainee may also have questions or additional information that will help you more accurately determine their skill level .

5. When a rating is confirmed or modified through this process, mark the rating on your master chart for that trainee, hand-letter the number on the appropriate block in the DACUM chart, enclosing it in a small diamond.

6. Be sure that all ratings are made in the trainee's presence and that they have an opportunity to discuss with you any ratings on which you might disagree.

7. Have both the trainee's and your ratings transcribed on to the appropriate data-collecting forms, return the trainee's DACUM chart for use in the training program, and return your master chart to the appropriate file.

```
INSPECT &
REPLACE BRAKE
LINES
◇
```

IN-PROCESS RATINGS

In-process ratings should be recorded by the learner as soon as they feel they have increased their skill level. It is a simple matter to record these quickly together with the date, if the chart is kept near at hand.

In making a judgment about learner performance, the instructor combines observation and information provided by learners about themselves and their performance. It is important that the instructor be an approver rather than an initiator of ratings :

1. The instructor can refuse to update ratings until the learner updates their own ratings. Once the learner realizes he or she is not going to receive any new ratings until they take the first step, they will quickly begin to do this.

2. The instructor can take steps during the learner's first few skill applications to quickly reward any increase in skills. The instructor can do this by noting the achievement, bringing it to the attention of the learner, and suggesting that the learner record a new rating on their chart so they may then discuss it with the instructor.

3. The instructor can immediately reward achievement by verbal encouragement and can then suggest that the learner should consider what rating they should assign themselves.

4. The instructor can encourage self-rating by avoiding undue detailed criticism during initial in-process rating verifications, particularly for ratings at the '1' level. Undue criticism at this stage will make the learner reluctant to do further self-ratings. The instructor must realize that the '1' level often does not require extensive background knowledge and decision-making

ability. It is important to grant credit for this rating level as quickly as possible, even if only mechanical performance is observed.

5. The instructor can be alert for opportunities to assign higher ratings than the learner originally self-rated. This will have the effect of encouraging the learners to look more positively at their achievement and hopefully make more rapid progress in developing their skill profile.

The instructor must be prepared to discuss certain in-process rating issues a number of times with each learner. These are issues which must be dealt with in a flexible way and which would result in restricting the program and limiting program effectiveness if rigid rules were established.

One issue that will be much discussed will be the nature of performance required for various levels of ratings for various skills identified on the DACUM chart. Frequently, the learner will raise questions or initiate discussion about performance required for a specific level. The instructor must be able to interpret to the learner the level of decision-making ability and activity achievement required to warrant a specific rating level. More important, the instructor must be able to illustrate to the learner that these can vary considerably depending on the nature of problems or activities selected by the learner or assigned by the instructor.

Another issue raised by the learner is the number of performances required for specific ratings. The instructor must prepare a skill profile that indicates how well they feel the learner will be able to apply the skill in diverse applications once at work. The instructor must, therefore, observe enough diverse applications of the skill in the learning environment to be reasonably sure that the necessary transfer will take place. For example, the '3' rating may be granted only after the learner demonstrates they can apply the skill in several diverse applications. To confirm a '1' rating the instructor may have to observe only one or two applications of the skill in order to appreciate that, mechanically, the learner is able to repeat this performance in similar applications.

It is important to note that, in the final analysis, the instructor must be the judge. When learners become highly involved in the self-rating process, they sometimes begin to feel that they should be the final judge of their performance. Nevertheless, the position must be maintained that the instructor's decision will determine the trainee's skill profile on termination. It is important for the instructor to assure the trainee that they and the trainee will agree on most ratings by the time learners are ready to leave the program.

A recurring issue is the need for actual performance on which to base ratings. The instructor should be consistent in refusing to give ratings for skill application they have not been able to observe, unless, due to specific circumstances, this is impossible (e.g., if performance can only be exhibited in another environment). If the instructor is not firm about this, four problems may result.

1. Learners may begin to take advantage of a precedent in which they were given a rating on the basis of their description of performance which the instructor did not observe. Once the learner has successfully obtained a rating in this way, they may want to repeat this procedure for most of their ratings and fail to see why they must perform.

2. Some learners persist in declaring that they "know how to" do something even though they have never actually done it. They feel that, on the basis of their knowledge or what they have been able to observe in the training environment, they will be able to achieve should the opportunity arise. It is important that the instructor never grant a rating on the basis of such an argument.

3. Some learners assigned to a team task or project will want to acquire ratings because they were part of the team and shared in the work even though they did not actually apply the skill in question. The instructor must be prepared to differentiate performance by various members of the team so that the instructor may assign ratings only to those who have actually performed. The instructor must also observe the organization of the team carefully to determine who is making decisions and who is only applying skills in a mechanical way. This will have a bearing on ratings assigned for the same skill.

4. After completing a larger, more complex project or product, some learners will insist that they be assigned higher ratings because the finished product is satisfactory although they may not have applied the skill well, they may have taken an undue amount of time, or they may have required assistance. It is important that the instructor insist that assessments be made strictly on how well the skill was applied. If the skills will not be evident in the final product, the instructor should make it clear that it is the learner's responsibility to ensure that skill application is observed.

An important consideration in the use of rating instruments is the control of rating quality, or the control of certain biases that can creep into the rating process. It is important not to let relations between instructor and learner influence rating decisions.

The quality of ratings in the DACUM approach is effectively controlled in the following ways:

1. Assessments must normally be made on the basis of instructor-observed performance. If the instructor is occupationally competent, it is relatively easy to observe and rate individual learner performance by comparing it to performance of persons working in the occupation.

2. The rating process is applied to a large number of skills over a period of time. By isolating rating of each skill, the instructor is influenced to consider it independently of over-all factors such as attitude, apparent intelligence, or potential for growth. There is no provision for global ratings, which have a greater tendency to be subject to rater bias.

3. In-process ratings of performance observed partly by two or more instructors are established by agreement between them. They tend to keep each other objective.

4. Learner input tends to control instructor rating or confirmation. No rating is recorded on the master chart except in the presence of the learner. Learners can defend their position, criticize instructor assessments, and possibly provide information of which the instructor might not have been aware, which will make their rating more accurate.

5. Instructors are informed before they begin rating, and periodically throughout the program, that their signatures are to appear on the diploma or record of achievement. They are informed that, in effect, they are communicating with their former colleagues in industry about the quality of learner performance. They understand that their reputation will suffer if they rate extremely low an individual who quickly demonstrates that they are a competent performer in the work environment, or, conversely, if the instructor rates quite high and individual who cannot perform adequately in the work environment. Most instructors react well to this control.

The following instruction sheets were designed to provide guidelines for the trainee and for the instructor in making in-process ratings.

INSTRUCTIONS TO TRAINEE - IN-PROCESS RATINGS OF SKILL LEVEL

You have already filled out a DACUM chart for your training program to find out what skill you had when you entered the program. We would like you to continue rating your skill while you are in the training program so the instructor can see at any time how much skill you have. This will help to determine when you have enough training for some of the skills. It will also help to find out where you do not have enough skills so that the instructor may plan how to give you additional help.

The instructor is very busy and may not notice when you have increased your skill. You can help the instructor and yourself by bringing it to their attention. To keep your chart up-to-date use the following procedure:

1. If you have just received some instruction in one of the skills on the chart, wait until you have an opportunity to practice the skill. When you feel you can do it well enough to meet one of the levels in the rating scale, hand-letter the rating scale number on that block in your DACUM chart, then circle it, and mark the date nearby.

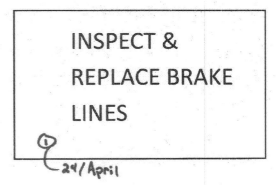

2. If you have not been instructed in the skill but have learned it from others in the training program or outside the training program and have had an opportunity to practice the skill, use the same procedure.

3. Take your DACUM chart to the instructor, show them the new rating you have given yourself, and explain why you feel you deserve this rating.

4. If the instructor agrees, they will record the new rating on the master chart.

5. If the instructor disagrees, you may be asked to complete an assignment that will show how well you can perform the skill. The instructor may then agree with your rating.

6. If the instructor still does not agree, you may have to practice the skill on your own a few times before again asking the instructor for a new rating.

7. Repeat this process each time you feel you have additional experience and enough skill to increase the rating for any of the blocks on the chart.

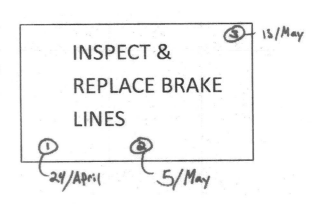

INSTRUCTIONS TO INSTRUCTOR - IN-PROCESS SKILL LEVEL RATINGS

You are requested to rate each trainee in each of the skills on the DACUM chart for your program. As the items in the DACUM chart are defined in terms of observation behavior, your ratings should be based on what you have actually seen the trainee do in the training environment. Relate this performance to performance expected of persons performing in this occupation in industry. Select the category on the rating scale that best describes the trainee's behavior as you have observed it. Focus your evaluation on behavior only, avoiding evaluation of personality, ability to present ideas, etc., which will be rated separately.

If you are not sure which category on the rating scale defines the trainee's skill level, have the trainee repeat the activity or observe their behavior closely when they repeat the activity in a normal work environment.

Please use the following procedure:

1. Be sure the trainee is present when the rating is made and that they have an opportunity to discuss this rating with you. The trainee should have their DACUM chart work sheet with them each time they discuss ratings with you.

2. Each time a new rating is established for a trainee in a specific skill, record the appropriate rating number directly on that block in the DACUM chart for the training program and note the date the rating was made nearby, circle the rating number to distinguish it from an entry level skill which would have been enclosed in a diamond.

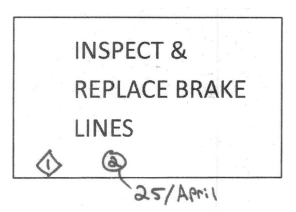

3. Ratings should be made:

    (a) When the trainee has received instruction and had an opportunity to practice a skill and has demonstrated their ability.

    (b) When the trainee has had additional opportunity to practice a skill and their performance changes significantly by at least one level as described in the rating scale.

(c) When there is no further opportunity for the trainee to participate in a skill activity in the training program (e.g., when they drop out of the program).

4. It is likely the trainee will be the first to recognize change in their performance as you are busy with other people and activities. The trainee has been directed to bring a change in their performance to your attention by self-rating and discussing this rating with you. If you agree that the level of performance has increased in the skill, record this new rating and the date on the master chart.

5. Some trainees for one reason or another may be reluctant to approach you or to request a rating. It is important that you observe trainee performance closely and encourage trainees to evaluate themselves and bring their evaluations to your attention. You should periodically review your master chart on each trainee to determine if some trainees have gone for a period of time without increasing their ratings significantly.

SUMMARY

The purpose of Chapter 15 was to explain the rating process and provide instructions for both instructor and trainee. Evaluation is unique in the DACUM system because it calls for the learner to provide an initial assessment of their own ability for each skill. This method has numerous advantages including forcing the learner to assess their ability within the occupation and forcing face-to-face interaction between learner and instructor. The trainee and the instructor meet and must agree upon the entry-level rating. After initial ratings are done, the learner will start learning activities immediately. As soon as the learner feels they have increased their skill level, they should consult their instructor. Based on the observations of the instructor, they must agree on the new rating. Although the learner has some power in self-assessment, it is key to remember that the instructor is the ultimate judge of a skill rating. Ratings prove to be of high quality because they are based on observed performance and are applied over a period of time. In addition, ratings must always be recorded with the learner present and signatures are recorded.

REFERENCES

Adams, R. E. (1975). *DACUM: Approach to curriculum, learning, and evaluation in occupational training.* Ottawa: Dept. of Regional Economic Expansion.

EVALUATION – FEEDBACK & CONTINUED DEVELOPMENT

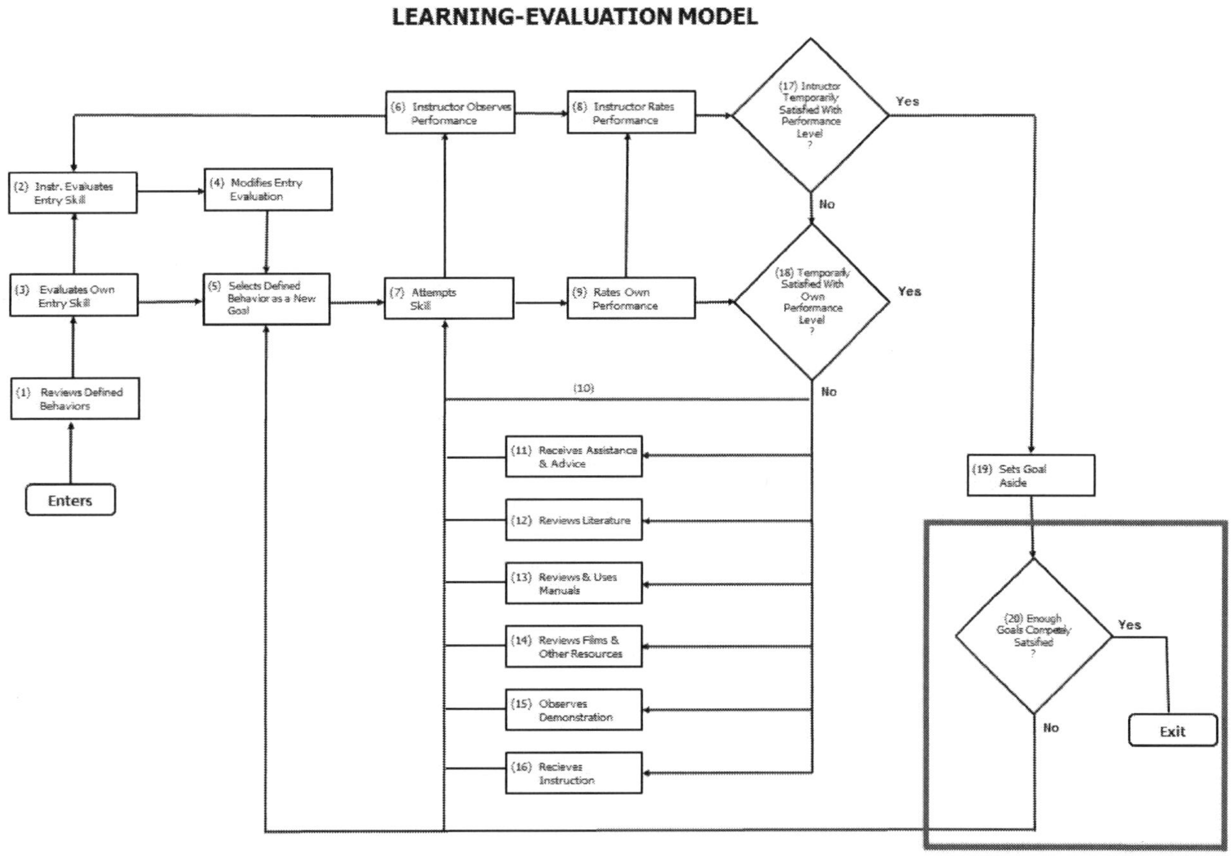

LEARNING-EVALUATION MODEL

Figure 16-1. Learning-Evaluation Model

In monitoring, reviewing, or redesigning a program, it is useful to know:

1. The degree of occupational competence that a learner has achieved.

2. The degree of occupational competence that a group has achieved.

3. The relative level the learner is capable of achieving in skills they have attempted.

4. Areas in which a learner group is achieving markedly.

5. Areas in which a learner group is not achieving.

The purpose of Chapter 16 is to show how to use progress charts which can address the previous 5 statements. Progress charts have the potential to provide feedback throughout the learning process for administrators, instructors, and learners. Further, upon successful completion of the DACUM learning process, explanation is given on how graduates could potentially be encouraged to seek additional development by continuing the ratings in the workplace.

DATA FEEDBACK

Because each learner's DACUM chart is brought up-to-date cumulatively, with ratings recorded continuously, it is possible to extract planning and progress review data at any point in time. It is necessary to collect the master chart for each learner, transfer their current skill profile to another form, summarize individual and group profiles, and determine change.

While the instructor can take responsibility for data extraction, it is suggested this activity be performed by someone in an administrative assistant capacity in the institution. The activity takes only an hour or two for each learner group for each review period, but this is valuable instructor time.

For short training programs it is suggested that data be extracted and analyzed weekly to detect lack of change and quickly respond with additional resources or attention. For longer programs, bi-weekly or monthly reviews should prove sufficient.

Review should be more frequent for programs incorporating a large proportion of skills which can be achieved quickly and less frequent for programs in which skills are more complex or require more time for development.

Figure 16-1 is a form that has been found useful for transferring summary data from DACUM charts. It is designed to match the size of the DACUM chart and line up with the General Areas of Competence. This form is for use with the chart Motor Vehicle Repair (Mechanical) contained in Appendix A.

This form is placed at the right of the learner's master chart. The skills in each band are counted and ratings recorded. All skills left blank are counted and placed in the '0' column; all skills in which the highest rating is '1' are counted and the number is placed under the '1' column, etc.

	0	1	2	3	4	5	6	Total Rating Value / No. Skills	Avg. Per Band
COMMUNICAT IN WORK								/ 8 n	
PERFORM SHOP OUT								/ 7 n	
USE AUTO SHOP EQU								/ 8 n	
USE REPAIR & EQUIPMENT								/ 10 n	
ADJUST MECHANI & CONTROL								/ 6 n	
USE MEASURE TESTING								/ 8 n	
SERVICE STEERIN & BRAKE								/ 17 n	
SERVICE COOLING SYSTEM								/ 8 n	
SERVICE FUEL SYSTEM								/ 10 n	
SERVICE ELECTRICAL								/ 9 n	
SERVICE OVERHAUL &								/ 11 n	
SERVICE ENGINES								/ 11 n	
REPAIR ENGINES								/ 14 n	
Total								/ 127 n	

Subject / Group

No. in Group

n = _____

Rating Period

(Circle)

Entry
1
2
3
4
5
6
7
8
9
10
11
12
13
14
15
16
17
18
19
20

Early
Exit

Final

Date

_____

Average per Band =

Average rating per skill attempted =

Figure 16-2. Rating Frequency Analysis form — M.V. R. (Mechanical)

When this is done, one has a visual picture of the learner's profile in each band on the chart. This is useful for quick review of progress of several learners because the DACUM charts themselves may become cluttered with notations and requires more painstaking examination to determine current progress.

The column of figures for each rating category is totaled to provide a distribution of ratings for all skills on the chart. Each of these totals is multiplied by the rating scale value for that column, the products are summed, and the total is divided by the number of skills on the chart. This can be expressed by the formula:

$$\frac{a(0) + b(1) + c(2) + d(3) + e(4) + f(5) + g(6)}{\text{Number of skills on chart}}$$

In the example (Figure 16-2)

$$41(0) + 45(1) + 23(2) + 16(3) + 2(4) + 0(5) + 0(6) = 147/127 = 1.16$$

The figure 16-2 provides a rough indication of how much of their program a trainee has completed and, assuming that their average rating will approach the '3' (or some other arbitrary) level, how much they have still to achieve before leaving the program. A measure of net change over a set period of, for example, two weeks, can be obtained by subtracting the figure for the previous period from the current figure. Little or no change indicates that an effort must be made to determine what is causing lack of achievement.

The same procedure can be used to determine net change for each band. Again a period of lack of achievement indicates need for staff to determine reasons. However, unlike the total profile achievement figure, this analysis should not cause undue concern for it may mean only that the learner is focusing attention on other bands, has not had an opportunity to work on the bands in question, or has chosen a profile that does not require skills in that band.

A further summary can be prepared for groups of learners which provide more valuable planning and review information. The same form is used but all ratings of the group are entered. The group may be a group of learners who entered a new program on the same date as an initial intake, or it may be a group who entered individually over a short time span.

This is a more valuable source of information for program review and replanning. It shows the instructor which parts of the program are not obtaining results. This will cause the instructor to examine a number of possible reasons for lack of achievement in the specific band. These may be lack of occupational resources to provide learning experiences, lack of information for learning the skills, lack of learner understanding of or identity with the skills, or lack of instructor expertise in the skill area.

	0	1	2	3	4	5	6	Total Rating Value / No. Skills	Avg. Per Band
COMMUNICAT IN WORK	3	4	1					6 / 8 n=1	0.75
PERFORM SHOP OUT	5	1	1					3 / 7 n=1	0.43
USE AUTO SHOP EQU		2	3	3				17 / 8 n=1	2.13
USE REPAIR & EQUIPMENT	4	1		4	1			17 / 10 n=1	1.70
ADJUST MECHANI & CONTROL		2	1	3				13 / 6 n=1	2.17
USE MEASURE TESTING		6	2					10 / 8 n=1	1.25
SERVICE STEERIN & BRAKE	3	11	3					17 / 17 n=1	1.00
SERVICE COOLING SYSTEM	8							0 / 8 n=1	0.00
SERVICE FUEL SYSTEM	10							0 / 10 n=1	0.00
SERVICE ELECTRICAL		9						9 / 9 n=1	1.00
SERVICE OVERHAUL &		2	3	5	1			27 / 11 n=1	2.45
SERVICE ENGINES	1	1	8	1				20 / 11 n=1	1.82
REPAIR ENGINES	7	6	1					8 / 14 n=1	0.57
Total	41	45	23	16	2	0	0	147 / 127	1.16

Chart = M.V.R (Mechanical

Subject(s): John Doe

N = 1

Total Skills = 86

Rating Period

(Circle)

Entry 1 2 3 4 5 6 7 8 ⑨ 10 11 12 13 14 15 16 17 18 19 20

Early Exit

Final

Date

March—14

Average per Band = **1.16**

Average rating per skill attempted = **1.71**

$\frac{147}{86} = 1.71$

Figure 16-3. Rating Frequency Analysis form with transferred summary data from DACUM charts

	0	1	2	3	4	5	6	Total Rating Value / No. Skills	Avg. Per Band
COMMUNICAT IN WORK	19	23	8	1				42 / 48 n = 8	0.88
PERFORM SHOP OUT	9	11	21	1				56 / 42 n = 7	1.33
USE AUTO SHOP EQU	2	11	27	8				89 / 48 n = 8	1.85
USE REPAIR & EQUIPMENT	5	10	31	12	2			116 / 60 n = 10	1.93
ADJUST MECHANI & CONTROL		6	12	18				84 / 36 n = 6	2.33
USE MEASURE TESTING	5	13	20	11				86 / 48 n = 8	1.79
SERVICE STEERIN & BRAKE	27	35	26	14				129 / 102 n = 17	1.26
SERVICE COOLING SYSTEM	17	21	10					41 / 48 n = 8	0.85
SERVICE FUEL SYSTEM	51	8	1					10 / 60 n = 10	0.17
SERVICE ELECTRICAL	28	24	2					28 / 54 n = 9	0.52
SERVICE OVERHAUL &	41	16	11	7	1			63 / 66 n = 11	0.95
SERVICE ENGINES	13	20	29	4				90 / 66 n = 11	1.36
REPAIR ENGINES	48	31	5					41 / 84 n = 14	0.49
Total	265	229	203	76	3	0	0	875 / 762	1.15

$$\frac{875}{497} = 1.76$$

Chart = M.V.R (Mechanical

Subject(s): First Entry

N = 6

Total Skills = 497

Rating Period

(Circle)

Entry
1
2
3
4
5
6
7
8
9
10
11
12
13
14
15
16
17
18
19
20

Early
Exit

Final

Date

March—14

Average per Band = **1.15**

Average rating per skill attempted = **1.76**

Figure 16-4. Rating Frequency Analysis form with first entry transferred summary data from DACUM

Because of its directness, program developers and instructors have been found to react well to this kind of information feedback. In the redesign of the Deckhand Training program, this kind of analysis pinpointed two weaknesses in a pilot run which were compensated for in the new program. First, project staff was planning to encourage proportionately more time and add learning resources for the band STEER VESSEL. The analysis showed, however, that learners had all achieved well in this area in the pilot run. Instead of expanding learning activities and resources, these were actually reduced in the redesign. On being faced with the data, the captain of the training vessel realized that he was responsible and admitted that he had required too much of the learner's time to be spent with him in the wheelhouse, to the detriment of learner exposure to other activities. Second, it was noted that most learners had low ratings in the bands RIG FISHING GEAR and MAINTAIN FISHING GEAR. This resulted in provision of more learning activities and resources for these skills in a shore training facility.

A useful indicator of each learner's achievement potential can be obtained by repeating the above analysis considering only the skills in which they have achieved. The learner's total ratings are divided by that number of skills on the chart. This, in effect, raises the average skill achievement to indicate the level they should be able to achieve in the remaining skills on the chart. This kind of analysis is useful only in earlier stages of a training program before the learner can attempt most of the skills. Two useful kinds of information may be provided. First, a high average rating would indicate that the learner probably is capable of achieving well in most of the skills, even though this achievement is based on only a portion. It indicates that the learner is capable of applying decision-making processes and reducing dependence on others to perhaps the '2' or '3' level. Second, a low average rating, e.g., '1', might indicate the learner is not capable of advancing much beyond this level and that the learner and staff may have to be satisfied with this. The learner may never achieve the '3' level (journeyman status) and must be expected to enter the industry in a junior or routine capacity.

The suggested summary sheet, Figure 16-4, is a cumulative record of learner achievement in a program or department. Only the over-all average skill rating is entered on the sheet for each learner. The first figure entered is the average entry rating for all skills while the last is the final average rating for those completing the program or the last average rating of all skills for those who exit before completion.

Displayed on a wall, this record should be useful to administrators in determining over-all program achievement as well as capacity for new intake for the program. First, it is easy to visualize how a new department is building up in terms of trainee intake and when it reaches capacity. Second, it is easy to visualize current trainee composition; the proportion of new learners with low ratings who require more instructor assistance as opposed to the proportion with higher levels who require less assistance and monitoring. Third, it is easy to predict when learning positions will become available for new entrants by scanning the time duration and pattern of rating increases to predict when each learner will complete their training. Finally, this summary provides a quick check on the progress of each learner as well as the group. It is possible to detect a non-achieving individual and initiate review of their case to determine causes. Similarly, it is possible to detect general lack of achievement in a group and to begin to investigate the reason for slowdown in skill achievement.

It should be noted that the results of these analyses are not fed back to the learner or provided to a prospective employer. They are designed only to provide information feedback to program developers and operators so they may be alerted to problems or trends and make necessary program adjustment. The learner and employer are provided with a detailed profile through which they must make decisions on the basis of each skill. Provision of summary data or a simple "average" would only encourage them to use a less meaningful single indicator.

This kind of analysis should not be allowed to replace day-to-day ratings and instructor-learner interaction. The alert instructor will not require this information for day-to-day dealing with learners. Instructors need it only to ensure that the program is working as designed.

	June		July		August		September		October		November		December	
Name	0.17	0.45	0.75	0.95	1.03	1.4	1.75	2.3	2.78	X				
Name	0.36	0.45	0.54	0.76	0.81	0.85	0.93	X inc.						
Name	0.55	0.69	0.84	1.17	1.27	1.37	1.48	1.6	1.93	2.2	2.45	X		
	Name	0.00	0.25	0.69	0.87	0.98	1.19	1.3	1.41	1.7	1.79	1.9	2.1	2
		Name	0.41	0.62	0.78	0.93	1.25	1.5	1.82	2.1	2.45	2.6	X	
				Name	1.13	1.55	1.78	2.2	2.67	2.9	3.07	X		
				Name	0.27	0.71	0.89	1	1.21	1.3	1.45	1.7	1.8	
								Name	0.34	0.4	0.71	1	1.3	
								Name	0.14	0.3	0.68	0.9	1.3	
											Name	0		

Figure 16-5. Trainee Progress Summary Chart

TERMINATION AND CERTIFICATION

Learners continue to attempt to acquire skills, assess performance, and either continue to work on the skills or set it aside because they are satisfied with their performance and rating level. Learners continue to set aside skills in this way until they have adequately recycled all or most of the skills on the chart and have reached a level where they fail to make significant rating increases or have achieved ratings that appear to be satisfactory for exit from the program and entry to work.

The learner in the DACUM environment does not "graduate" from the training program on the basis of having completed a standard amount of training time or having completed their skill profile to some predetermined standard level.

It is felt that provision of global or artificial standards which all learners must meet would cause unnecessary difficulty for some learners. It would ignore the presence in industry of entry jobs that demand less than standard performance. It would also ignore the possibility that the learner might qualify for entry to a higher level. This could not occur if the learner was required to leave the program as soon as reaching an arbitrary standard.

Learner, instructor, and a prospective employer collectively decide when the learner is ready to leave the program and enter employment. The instructor fills the role of hypothetical employer if no prospective employer is present.

Learner, instructor, and employer consider the following criteria. These same criteria are used to assist in deciding whether or not a permanent diploma or record of achievement should be issued to the learner (as opposed to merely a DACUM chart complete with recorded skill achievement ratings).

1. The learner should be deemed ready for an entry job in the occupation. It is important that entry jobs not be confused with what might be classed as helper or assisting jobs in some occupations, which do not demand much of the skill

content of the occupations, which do not demand much of the skill content of the occupation but are simply supportive. On the basis of extensive knowledge of the occupation, the instructor should readily reach a decision about the learner's adequacy for entry jobs of which the instructor is personally aware.

2. The learner should have achieved a rating of at least '1' on most skills on the chart. It is possible for an individual with only '1''s in most skills, to be considered a graduate, provided this skill level is adequate to earn entry to the occupation.

3. Because of the characteristics of the occupation, it may be necessary to meet unique entry skill requirements. For example, it may be necessary for entrants to have achieved a high level of competence in many of the skills due to concern for personal safety and the protection of valuable resources and processes. (If such conditions definitely exist, it would be useful to prepare a profile of the minimal levels of specific skills required for entry to the occupation. However, provision of such a profile for all charts should be avoided.)

4. For most learners in most occupations, ratings on most skills should approach the '3' level. The learner will then be entering the occupation with the prospect of reaching the '3' level in most skills within a short time. The learner can take advantage of exposure to diverse application of skills in more realistic situations to refine their skills to that level.

Because the instructor or employer keeps the master copy of the graduate's chart, the graduate is discouraged from attempting to modify the laminated chart on the back of their diploma to present a false skill profile. Only the highest rating achieved in each skill is recorded.

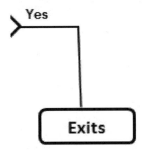

Learners exit from the training program with a completed and instructor-approved profile of their skills. This provides them with a document which can be used to describe their performance ability in job interviews and negotiations with employers. The only information provided on their profile is a rating for each rated skill on the chart. No effort is made to provide the prospective employer with more global rating assessments or global averaging of achievement. The intention is to provide a profile that the employer will have to study to detect skills that are typically overlooked in interviewing.

There will seldom be a perfect match between the trainee's exit profile and requirements of the job for which he or she is being interviewed. However, there are several possibilities for improving the chances of the learners becoming established in the most suitable entry jobs:

1. It may be apparent to the learner during the interview that they employer does not require many of the skills they have acquired in their training program. The learner may question the employer about these applications and refrain from taking the job because they feel their potential will be wasted if they cannot apply all acquired skills.

2. The employer may decide that the learner's ratings are not high enough for the entry job. It would be better for the employer to seek out other candidates with better skills who will be able to handle the specific job at the levels demanded. This decision will be in the best interest of the learner who would probably be frustrated in trying to survive in an environment in which they were not capable or prepared to function.

3. The employer may decide that the trainee's skill profile and the job requirements are reasonably close. The employer can make immediate decisions about how to orient the learner to the work environment in such a way that the learner can quickly acquire skills that appear to be missing or weak. For example, the employer might note a few skills that are rated low for their needs, but might have a well-qualified veteran on hand who should be able to help the new employee improve these skills in a short time.

4. On the basis of the applicant's skill profile, the employer may decide to alter the entry requirements for the job. Through examinations of each skill in which the applicant appears weak, the employer may have workers who can adequately handle these skills, at least until the applicant has a few months of additional experience and an opportunity to develop them. In other words, the detailed breakdown of skills causes the employer to recognize the value of the remainder of the applicant's skill profile, which the employer might have overlooked in the search for the well-rounded candidate with critical skills.

5. The employer may have to reject the candidate for a specific job. But, because of the detailed information provided, may be able to suggest alternatives. First, the employer may be able to suggest an alternate position in the organization that better fits the learner's skill profile as indicated by their DACUM chart. Second, the employer may be able to refer the recruit to another organization that can better take advantage of their skills and would have more opportunity to become more fully competent in the occupation.

CONTINUED LEARNING AND DEVELOPMENT

An important feature of the DACUM system is that it was designed to promote continued learning and development of the graduate in the work environment. The prospects for continued learning raise three main issues.

1. **Continuous Rating in Job Environment**

   A brief description on the back of the DACUM diploma or record of achievement suggests to employers that they encourage new employees to continue to rate themselves as they had in the learning environment in order to maintain a record of their achievement in acquiring new skills. This is designed to encourage learners to develop in the work environment in much the same manner as they were trained by rewarding their efforts and achievement in the same way through increased skill ratings.

   Employers are just as capable of assessing the requirements for various skill levels in the occupation as was the instructor. They should have little difficulty in using the DACUM chart and rating scale as a measuring instrument, particularly since they are not starting with a blank chart but with one on which a fairly comprehensive profile has already been established. It is relatively easy for them to make changes in the form of rating increases when the employee requests this, and, in their supervisory role, they have ample opportunity to observe the improved performance under realistic conditions.

   Employers or supervisors are requested to record their new assessment of rating on the trainee's chart and to note the date and sign their name beside each new entry. This enables other employers to judge the meaningfulness of the rating. They are as likely to respect the judgment of another employer about a worker's ability as they are to respect the judgment of the instructor in the learning environment.

2. <u>Job-Oriented Learning Behavior</u>

The learning behavior prescribed by the Learning-Evaluation Model is intended to reflect the kind of behavior required of persons who continue to develop skill competence while in a work environment.

Conditions for learning new skills or increasing skill on the job are much different from conditions one would expect in the conventional training environment. The conventional training approach can be visualized in the Learning-Evaluated Model if one reads from the bottom up through the learning resources until reaching ATTEMPTS SKILL. In the conventional training program, the learner *begins* by receiving instructions in the form of lectures or demonstrations. He or she is then exposed to videos or other audio-visual resources, shown how to use appropriate manuals, and exposed to a variety of additional literature in the form of textbooks, etc. Finally, the learner is allowed to attempt the task while performing under the direction of the instructor in the training environment. The learning behavior that is developed and reinforced in such programs is almost directly opposite to the behavior required to learn new skills when employed in a work environment. Typically, one becomes aware of the need to develop a new skill when faced with a problem that must be solved or an activity that must be completed. After identifying the skill that must be acquired, learners in the work environment do not have available to them the resources or the arrangement of resources that one finds in a conventional training model. The learner must usually begin by attempting to perform the activity, using prior experience and ingenuity. If they do not succeed, they will begin to search for and acquire specific additional resources. First, the individual might approach the boss or supervisor, a colleague, or an acquaintance in some other environment who can provide assistance and advice on how to proceed with the particular task. Someone may be able to provide the information needed to proceed. More probably, they will direct the learner to a specific manual or handbook that contains step-by-step procedures or suggest videos or other audio-visual resources that will show useful techniques. It is unlikely that the learner will be able to observe formal demonstrations and attend lectures or other kinds of information presentations unless fortunate enough to be attending a workshop or conference at the particular time when the skill development need is most felt. In effect, it is doubtful that the learner will be able to acquire the skill using the model of learning behavior in conventional training experiences. Successful graduates of conventional programs adopt a new learning behavior in the work environment.

The assumption in the DACUM system is that, if learning takes place in the work environment in the way described in the Learning-Evaluation Model, it is important that learners in the training environment be given an opportunity to develop this kind of learning behavior. Expected outcomes are: **(a)** that the learner will be more self-directive in demanding and obtaining assistance from other persons in the new work environment, **(b)** that the learner will be more alert to an opportunity to develop a new skill and will take immediate action, **(c)** that the learner will be more skilled in locating, selecting from, and applying learning resources available in the work environment.

3.   The Dichotomy of the Nonqualified Expert

One rather unfair problem that faces many highly skilled people in industry today is the fact that skills they have developed over a number of years of creative effort in a demanding work environment cannot be recognized unless they have taken courses to gain credits to prove their occupational competence. The need for formalized credentials has placed undue pressure on such persons. Some give up hope of ever becoming qualified, even for a shift to a similar job in another firm, although they have demonstrated their capability over a number of years. Others have forced themselves to leave their jobs and return to a formal institution for additional courses which provide the credits necessary to prove their capability.

The DACUM chart and rating scale would appear to offer one solution to this problem. It is conceivable that firms could take the initiative in ensuring that all persons performing in the occupation were given ratings and a record of achievement commensurate with ability, regardless of whether or not they have taken formal courses to qualify for the occupation. In this way, the final measure of performance would be the individual's ability to perform in a realistic problem-solving environment rather than their ability to complete courses.

SUMMARY

In this chapter, the feedback of ratings was discussed. Specifically, using progress charts to show average ratings, administration and instructors can easily see progress per learner. Although level 3 is deemed the base level and acceptable, the learner does not automatically "graduate" or complete the program once a rating of 3 has occurred. The prospective employer, learner, and instructor must collectively decide when the learner is adequately prepared and ready to complete the program and enter employment. Emphasis is placed on the employer because that is the basis of DACUM, satisfaction through the eyes of the employer. Upon successful completion, the graduate is to be encouraged to seek further development and continued learning. DACUM ratings were designed in this way. The learner has potential for continuous rating in the job environment and is encouraged to do so.

REFERENCES

Adams, R. E. (1975). *DACUM: Approach to curriculum, learning, and evaluation in occupational training.* Ottawa: Dept. of Regional Economic Expansion.

RELIABILITY OF THE DACUM RATING SYSTEM

The DACUM system relies heavily on procedures designed to encourage an atmosphere of free and spontaneous interaction between learners at different levels, learners and instructor, and, in those programs that are large enough, between instructors.

Although early training projects at Nova Scotia NewStart Inc. used the DACUM rating system, it was felt that the very act of isolating raters and subjects for purposes of testing reliability would inhibit the process being encouraged. In order not to affect the on-going, developing projects, it was decided to determine inter-rater reliability in a test conducted outside the projects in an actual employment situation.

The field of Auto Mechanics was selected for this test for the following reasons:

1. There was a DACUM chart for motor vehicle repair (mechanical). This chart was developed using the same procedures and control as the other charts, and it was fairly representative of current DACUM development efforts being used at the time. It was felt that an existing chart should be used rather than one developed specifically for the purpose of reliability testing as the latter might focus on development of the chart itself and on definitions rather than on the training program which the chart should be developed to facilitate.

2. A large well-organized automobile dealership and repair shop is one of the few employment situations in which one might expect to find two or more supervisors, each with a good working knowledge of the detailed abilities of 10 or more employees. This is not possible in occupations where employing firms

or departments are small and where there may be only one or two persons who can rate employees. On the other hand, the employment structure of larger organizations where larger numbers of persons in the same occupation might be employed tends to be pyramidal in nature. That is, there is normally only one supervisor who knows the performance abilities (in depth and equally well) of an adequate number of employees for the purposes of this type of testing. The field of auto mechanics is quite unique in this regard in that the well-organized dealership normally has two or more supervisors who know their work force equally well but who perform in differing roles in the work environment. One other occupation where this might apply is drafting. Consulting engineering or architectural offices normally have a pool of drafters who work interchangeably with two or more designers who might be expected to have comparable knowledge of the abilities of the drafters.

3. There are a large number of training programs for automotive mechanics. It was felt that if this field were selected for initial testing it might be feasible at some future date to continue this and similar types of testing in a number of learning environments using this set of data as the base.

It was proposed to have three supervisors employed in the same firm independently rate the mechanics employed by that firm. It was also decided to limit to 10 the number of subjects involved in the test. This is perhaps the maximum number one could expect to find in the typical employment environment that would be equally well-known to two or more supervisors (in this case, raters).

One of the suspected weaknesses of this type of testing is that the reliability evolving from the rating would be considerably lower than the unmeasurable reliability one would assume exists in the DACUM-oriented learning program. Absent in this test would be:

1. Communication between trainee and instructor regarding the trainee's progress and the instructor's evaluation of this progress.

2. The trainee's input into the rating process: Evaluations of skill achievements to date. This is normally a prime consideration on the part of the instructor in rating the trainee.

3. Group decision by two or more instructors in the same program. A team of two or more instructors normally conduct the instructors' evaluation of trainee progress as a single body. That is, they communicate with the trainee and with each other before reaching a final decision on a single rating.

4. Instructor rating in presence of learners. The instructor gets immediate feedback in the form of learner reaction and tends to modify their judgment on the basis of information added to the assessment by the learner.

An additional weakness in the test situation was that, while normally a group of instructors in a learning environment will tend to operate from the same point of view and with assumed comparability of criteria for making judgments about learners' achievement, in this case the three raters performed in different roles in the work environment, although each had opportunity to observe the subjects' performance. Nevertheless, only one, the shop foreman, served in a direct supervisory role. One of the raters served in the role of service salesman with the organization, being responsible for direct contact with the customer and for liaison between the customer and the responsible mechanic. The third rater had formerly filled the service salesman role and was currently in an administrative position and was brought into frequent contact with the mechanics.

PROCEDURE

A member of the management of the firm was contacted to solicit assistance in initiating this testing exercise. This manager was oriented to DACUM and the rating process and requested to nominate three raters and make the initial contacts. It was felt this was necessary to assure raters that the firm agreed to their participation and felt it was worthwhile. The manager was also requested to name 10 mechanics employed with the firm who, in his opinion, were equally well-known by the raters and performance was well enough known for purposes of the study. Subsequently, this manager was asked to rank the mechanics in order of their value to the firm in terms of occupational skills.

This ranked list was ordered to provide a sequence for rating. The middle mechanic in the ranking was selected as the subject for a sample rating exercise during the training session. The remaining mechanics were placed in a list that became the sequence for rating, alternating those who had been ranked low and high. This was done to avoid any tendency on the part of raters to establish a set in ratings that might have evolved if they had started with the highest ranked mechanic and worked through to the lowest or vice versa.

The raters were subsequently contacted individually at the work site by the study co-ordinator to solicit their agreement to participate in the study. Because the work involved several hours and had to be done outside normal working hours, the raters were remunerated at a rate approximately equaling overtime pay.

The first part of the rating exercise involved an orientation to what was to take place and a sample rating exercise. Approximately one and one-half hours was spent in orientation, explaining what DACUM is, what it was designed to do, how it is used in the training environment, and how the rating system would ideally be used in such an environment. In the latter case emphasis was placed on how learner and instructor would use the rating scale to establish a model for viewing the performance of typical mechanics in the community at the various levels of ability identified by the scale. Orientation was informal, and the raters freely interrupted with questions and observations that made the description more meaningful to them.

The sample rating exercise immediately following took approximately two hours. Raters were first assigned one of the bands on the DACUM chart on which they worked as a group. Each was instructed to study the skill defined in the first block and then each in turn stated verbally what rating he or she felt the sample subject deserved in that skill. Subsequently, they followed the same procedure for each of the skills in that band. All ratings were recorded on a large board. If there was any significant discrepancy, the raters stopped to discuss why they had varied in their judgments. Blocks in remaining bands on the chart were rated independently by the three raters. After a band was completed, ratings were recorded on the board for comparison purposes, and only those blocks in which there were lack of agreement were discussed. (It should be noted that raters spent a relatively short time, approximately three hours, learning and practicing the rating process. An instructor in a DACUM learning environment usually has several weeks to develop rating skills before having to make a final decision upon trainee termination.) On completing this exercise, raters stated that they found this process interesting and quite different from any way in which they had previously handled employee or trainee evaluation. They also stated at this time that they felt the instrument would be quite easy to use for their assignment.

Following the orientation session the raters worked evenings completing the independent ratings. An average of about 20 minutes was spent on each subject, rating time being reduced somewhat as the raters became more familiar with the definitions on the DACUM chart. The raters were contacted frequently during the rating period to detect any need for assistance or re-orientation and to offer assistance in redefining the skills. The raters independently responded that they were satisfied that they understood what was expected and how to use the rating scale. They continued to decline assistance in terms of further orientation.

After they had independently completed ratings, raters were assembled for a final meeting at which they collectively reviewed the individual charts for each subject, noting where they had lacked agreement and discussing causes of discrepancies in rating. At that time it was noted that one of the subjects was a newer employee of the firm who had left its employment in the weeks that had elapsed between nomination of the subjects and orientation. The raters felt that, since this mechanic had been with the firm for somewhat less than two months, during which time he had worked largely with more experienced mechanics, they were in no position to evaluate his independent performance. Because of their difficulty in rating this subject, they suggested that his ratings be disregarded. Analysis of results of the ratings indicated that the number of discrepancies for that subject was higher than for the other subjects combined. It was decided to remove his ratings from the data to be analyzed.

GENERAL RESULTS

Before making the detailed calculations necessary to estimate inter-rater reliability the individual ratings were summarized on DACUM charts in a number of ways to detect observable patterns or relationships.

Some simple criteria were used to predetermine acceptable limits of variations in ratings on the part of the three raters. These were based on the type of rating performance expected in trainee-instructor relationships and relationships between instructors evaluating the same trainee. According to these criteria independent ratings by three instructors would be within an acceptable range if the departure from the mean was not more than plus or minus one or a range not greater than two. In the first case, a score of *2, 2, 3* would be acceptable, while a score of *2, 2, 4* would not. It would be considered that the person defining the rating of *4* would be responsible for the departure. In the second case, assigned ratings of *2, 3, 4* would be acceptable while ratings of *2, 3, 5* would not be acceptable, with the person assigning the *5* rating being responsible for the discrepancy. In studying assembled ratings two significant results were noted. There are 127 skills on the automotive DACUM chart, which, multiplied by nine subjects, means 1,143 ratings conducted. A significantly high 261 of these turned out to be identical ratings, with each of the raters giving the same score to a specific subject for a specific skill. Another significant observation was that there were relatively few cases where the above rating criteria were exceeded. There was a departure from the mean greater than one in 67 instances while there was a range of three or more in only 12 in- stances out of a total of 1 ,143. Stated differently, 1,064 of the 1,143 cases fell within the acceptable range of discrepancy.

ANALYSIS OF DATA

Interrater reliability for each item was estimated using a method developed by Ebel (1951) and described by Guilford (1954) in *Psychometric Methods* pp. 395-7. This resulted in two reliability figures for each skill identified on the DACUM chart, the reliability for the three raters, and the reliability of the individual rater who caused the most variance.

Appendix I is a DACUM chart upon which are superimposed the two sets of reliability figures. In each case, the figure in the bottom of the skill block is the reliability for three raters, while the figure above the block is the reliability for one rater as indicated in the code on the right of the chart. For purposes of assessment the bands on this chart are identified with capital letters while each block in sequence is identified with numbers in brackets at the left of the block. Included on the right side of this chart are two figures which are estimates of global reliability based on the average rating per subject using the same Ebel (1951) formula. However, this tends to be rather high as an estimate of over-all reliability in using such a large number of items. Over-all (or global) reliability will be described better in Figure 17-3.

Figure 17-2 is a sequential ordering of the items by reliability for the two sets of figures. Lines drawn through each column indicate levels of significance in describing the data. For example, the first line in the column for three raters indicates that the three figures above the line are below the level of .60, while the next line indicates that the six figures above the line are below the level of .70.

It is interesting to note that the raters exhibited a reliability of less than .60 in only three items using the three-rater figure. In only six did they exhibit a reliability of less than .70. A total of 18 items fell below the level of .80 reliability for three raters. It is also interesting to note that in 71 items the three raters exhibited a reliability of .90 or greater.

SUMMARY OF RELIABILITY FOR 3 RATERS AND 9 SUBJECTS

Trainee's Name: _____

DACUM Chart: <u>MOTOR VEHICLE REPAIR</u>

Can perform this skill with more than acceptable speed and quality with initiative and adaptability and <u>can lead others</u> in performing this skill.	6
Can perform this skill with more than acceptable speed and quality and with <u>initiative</u> and <u>adaptability</u> to special problem situations.	5
Can perform this skill satisfactorily without supervision or assistance with <u>more than acceptable</u> speed and quality of work	4
Can perform this skill satisfactorily without assistance and/or supervision	3
Can perform this skill satisfactorily but requires periodic supervision and/or assistance	2
Can perform this skill, but not without constant supervision and some assistance.	1
<u>Cannot</u> perform this skill satisfactorily for participation in a work environment.	0

(Reliability for One Rater)

(Reliability for Three Raters)

Overall Reliability
Based on Average
Ratings Per Subject

0.932

0.976

Instructor's (Rater's) Name: _____

Figure 17-1. DACUM Chart with Reliability Figures Superimposed

SKILL OR ITEM	RELIABILITY FOR 3 RATERS	RELIABILITY FOR 1 RATER						
B-3	0.405	0.185	H-6	0.880	0.710	L-2	0.927	0.809
C-7	0.433	0.203	I-5	0.880	0.710	L-10	0.928	0.812
A-8	0.532	0.274	G-6	0.880	0.710	L-3	0.929	0.814
C-4	0.609	0.342	D-10	0.881	0.712	G-4	0.931	0.819
I-4	0.642	0.374	F-5	0.884	0.718	I-1	0.932	0.820
A-1	0.673	0.407	E-1	0.885	0.720	M-13	0.932	0.820
B-4	0.701	0.438	M-3	0.887	0.723	M-2	0.933	0.822
B-7	0.712	0.452	G-8	0.887	0.724	F-6	0.933	0.822
E-3	0.726	0.469	D-6	0.889	0.727	M-12	0.933	0.823
K-4	0.726	0.469	D-4	0.889	0.727	H-4	0.933	0.824
B-2	0.733	0.478	J-7	0.890	0.729	I-8	0.934	0.825
E-2	0.756	0.508	J-6	0.891	0.731	M-5	0.934	0.825
D-9	0.768	0.825	M-8	0.897	0.745	M-11	0.935	0.827
A-2	0.770	0.527	J-3	0.900	0.750	G-10	0.935	0.828
B-1	0.780	0.541	M-4	0.903	0.755	I-3	0.937	0.832
C-3	0.780	0.542	K-3	0.903	0.757	A-4	0.943	0.846
G-1	0.794	0.562	L-9	0.903	0.753	H-5	0.943	0.846
C-2	0.799	0.569	K-9	0.904	0.758	K-2	0.943	0.847
M-10	0.812	0.590	G-5	0.905	0.760	H-3	0.944	0.849
D-1	0.820	0.603	M-6	0.905	0.760	G-17	0.946	0.853
G-11	0.827	0.614	J-8	0.905	0.761	F-2	0.947	0.856
H-1	0.833	0.625	A-3	0.906	0.762	G-15	0.947	0.857
B-5	0.834	0.627	F-4	0.906	0.762	M-7	0.948	0.860
D-7	0.838	0.633	L-11	0.907	0.765	J-4	0.949	0.861
A-7	0.838	0.633	H-8	0.907	0.765	K-11	0.950	0.864
C-8	0.845	0.644	J-9	0.908	0.766	L-5	0.950	0.864
E-5	0.852	0.658	M-1	0.909	0.769	F-3	0.951	0.869
G-2	0.854	0.660	G-9	0.909	0.769	G-14	0.953	0.871
D-3	0.854	0.667	L-4	0.910	0.771	I-6	0.953	0.872
D-2	0.855	0.663	L-11	0.911	0.774	K-10	0.954	0.873
D-5	0.855	0.663	L-8	0.914	0.779	L-7	0.957	0.882
E-6	0.856	0.665	K-6	0.915	0.782	I-7	0.956	0.878
C-1	0.859	0.670	I-2	0.915	0.782	M-9	0.962	0.893
D-8	0.860	0.671	J-2	0.916	0.784	F-8	0.962	0.894
A-5	0.864	0.680	F-1	0.917	0.786	G-16	0.964	0.899
C-6	0.870	0.691	G-3	0.917	0.786	I-9	0.967	0.907
H-2	0.870	0.691	K-8	0.917	0.786	K-1	0.967	0.907
J-1	0.871	0.692	E-4	0.918	0.786	G-13	0.970	0.916
G-7	0.872	0.694	G-12	0.919	0.792	K-7	0.972	0.919
B-6	0.872	0.694	M-14	0.923	0.799	I-10	0.973	0.922
H-7	0.876	0.702	A-6	0.925	0.804	F-7	0.976	0.930
J-5	0.877	0.704	L-6	0.927	0.808	K-5	0.998	0.995

Figure 17-2. Sequential ordering of the items by reliability.

BAND	RANGE		MEDIAN (EST.)	
	3 raters	1 rater	3 raters	1 rater
A	.53 - .92	.27 -.80	0.85	0.65
B	.41 - .87	.19 - .69	0.73	0.48
C	.43 - .88	.20 - .70	0.82	0.61
D	.77 - .89	.52 - .73	0.86	0.67
E	.73 -.92	.47 -.79	0.85	0.66
F	.88 - .98	.72 - .93	0.94	0.84
G	.79 - .97	.56 - .92	0.92	0.79
H	.83 - .94	.63 - .85	0.89	0.72
I	.64 - .97	.34 - .92	0.94	0.82
J	.87 - .95	.69 - .86	0.9	0.75
K	.73 - .99	.47 - .92	0.93	0.81
L	.90 - .96	.75 - .88	0.93	0.8
M	.81 - .96	.59 - .89	0.93	0.82
GLOBAL	.41 - .99	.19 - .93	0.91	0.76

Figure 17-3 Distribution of Interrater Reliability Data by Band

Figure 17-3 summarizes by band and globally the reliabilities indicated for the 127 items. Described in each of the two columns (for the three raters and for one rater) are the reliabilities by band in terms of the range of reliabilities indicated for that band and the median reliability for the band.

Of interest in evaluating over-all reliability of this instrument is the global figure. This establishes a reliability for three raters (.91) and for one rater (.76) which is more meaningful than the previously mentioned estimate of over-all reliability (.98, .93) using the average rating per subject by each rater. (See Figure 17-1 through 17-6)

Figure 17-4 illustrates the distribution of ratings by subject for each rater. This description is particularly significant because of the high reliability estimated for individual items. These in turn indicate that the over-all distributions described on this chart are relatively accurate. It is interesting to note the marked parallel shifts in distributions for the various subjects and the high compatibility of the distributions between the raters (note the distributions for the three raters for subjects 2 and 3).

There is clearly a definite distinction between subjects who, in the eyes of the raters, perform at differing levels in the same firm.

One point of interest in the chart is that rater A has a greater tendency to cluster scores around a central point and has less range of distribution than the other two raters. This is probably not significant when one considers the high reliability per item and the closeness of rater A's distributions to those of the other two raters. This is particularly noticeable when looking at rater A's cases of least distribution as for subjects 9 and 5.

Figure 17-5 is a further summary of the DACUM ratings. Here the distributions of ratings are assembled by band rather than by subject. Again, rater A exhibits less range in distribution than do the other two raters. However, it would appear that rater A has dealt with each band more consistently.

This chart would appear to emphasize that raters have indicated acceptable variance, that is, variance generally consistent with what one might expect in assessing capability in individual skills of a representative sample of working craftsmen in a diversified skilled trade such as auto mechanics. One might expect to find that most of the scores of such a representative group would fall in the '3' or '4' categories with a somewhat smaller number falling in the '5' and '2' categories for all the individual skills identified on the chart. It is unlikely that one would ever find a single mechanic with equal ability in all the skills.

This chart also indicates, due to the rather balanced distribution by band for each rater, that there is a lack of any severe rater bias in the DACUM rating scale. The detailed definition of each category in the scale, and efforts to provide rather discrete intervals between the categories, would appear to have reduced the possibility of rater bias by focusing rater attention on specific observable skills and work behavior and away from interpersonal considerations.

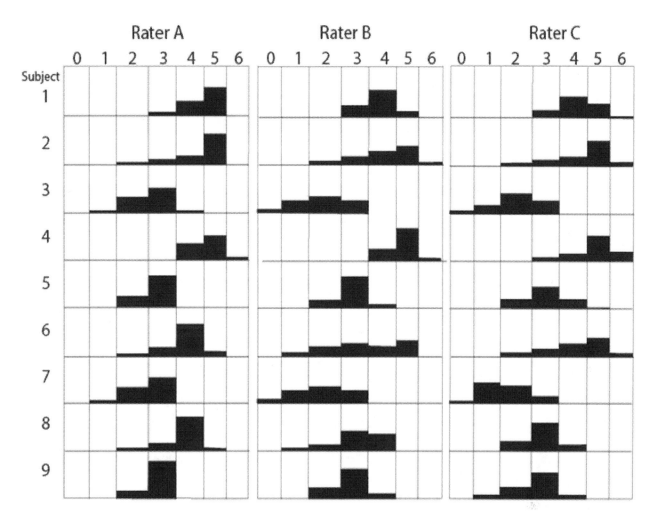

Figure 17-4. Distribution of ratings by subject for each rater.

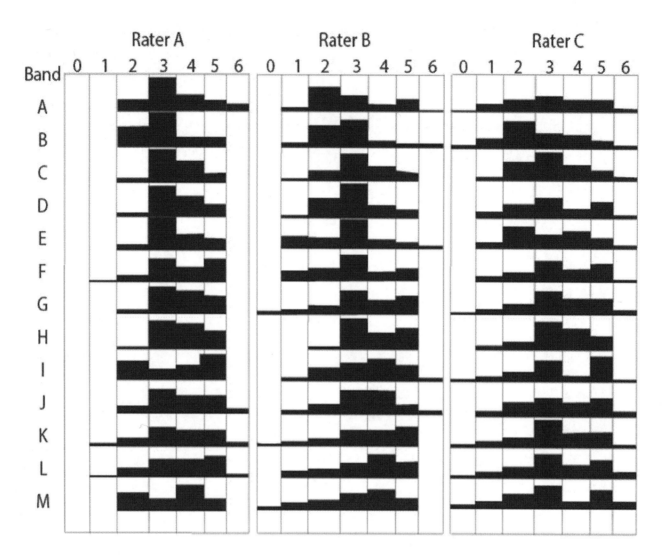

Figure 17-5. Percentage Distribution of Scores by Band for Each Rater

ASSESSMENT OF RELIABILITY DATA

As mentioned previously, six of the items had reliability at less than the .60 level, and the first three bands of the chart contained a number of the lower reliability items. It is difficult to speculate why this would be so in terms of use of DACUM in a learning environment, but easier to describe in terms of this rather artificial test situation.

Although items B-3, C-7, A-8, C-4, I-4, and A-1, in that order, have the lowest three-rater reliability, five of the six items had identical scores by the three raters for one or more subjects. It would appear then that the low reliability is not due to the instrument itself in terms of inaccurate or inadequate definition. In the final review session the raters commented that their errors of measurement were probably due to lack of knowledge of performance in specific skills by specific individuals. In both instances this could probably be attributed to the two raters with experience as service sales rep. The first three bands on the chart, which contained five of the six low-reliability items, dealt with more general shop skills. It is expected that reliability would be somewhat lower in these areas because the service sales rep is more concerned with and more closely observes direct work on vehicles and the results of this work in vehicle performance and customer satisfaction. Therefore, items B-3, PERCEIVE HAZARDS, CONDITIONS IN DAILY WORK AND TAKE NECESSARY PRECAUTIONS, and C-7, SELECT AND USE PUSHERS AND PULLERS, are both low-reliability items. Both are concerned with skills to which the service salesman might devote relatively little attention. Nevertheless, there is no consistent pattern of this sort, since other similar skills had much higher reliability, although even in these cases it was not as high as in those skills directly related to vehicle repair work.

Part of the low reliability in the first three bands may also be attributed to the manner in which this firm is organized. The DACUM chart was developed in committee and was intended to encompass the range of skills required by a typical mechanic in the variety of employment situations in the occupation in the community. Item A-1, PRACTICE GOOD CUSTOMER COURTESY AND ASSISTANCE, is typical of skills less required in this firm because, unlike the smaller garage or service station, it is highly organized, with the service sales rep handling most customer relations. The mechanic is not expected to communicate extensively with the customer, even though this does occur occasionally.

It is suspected that the low reliability in some items may be attributed to the nature of the simulated testing situation. In the final review session, the raters commented that they felt they would have achieved more accurate ratings if they could have spent time directly observing and discussing performance with the subjects. They felt that if using the instrument on a more long-term basis they would make a point of observing specific types of behavior and specific individuals. All expressed satisfaction with the review discussions which they felt helped them arrive at better decisions related to subject performance.

The foregoing indicates that reliability would be improved in a legitimate DACUM learning environment in which communication and direct observation would be encouraged rather than removed as in the test situation.

CONCLUSIONS

It was anticipated that it would be desirable to repeat the test with another firm in the same occupation, but in the light of the relatively high reliability and because the first test satisfied requirements for this study, it was decided to forego further testing of this sort. It would appear that any rerun would not show significantly less reliability and place the rating instrument outside the criteria established for acceptability of this system. Reliability could, of course, be tested in other occupations that have the necessary characteristics, but this was not considered necessary or practical for present purposes.

The high reliability achieved in this test would commend the DACUM system in terms of the quality of definition and accuracy in evaluation and would cause one to reflect on the validity of the DACUM as an instrument. Each individual item of skill defined in terms of terminal behavior and each individual category in the DACUM rating scale must therefore be well defined and have high face validity. This sort of validity would have to be present in order to facilitate interpretation by raters to result in the type of reliability indicated in this test situation.

SUMMARY

In this chapter, DACUM rating system reliability was examined using inter-rater reliability using the field of Auto Mechanics. In determining the reliability, an existing chart was used to provide a more accurate approach and gain more accurate data. The number of subjects involved in the reliability test was 10 to keep the situation as realistic as possible.

To determine the reliability, management from the firm nominated three raters to name 10 mechanics. The 10 mechanics, or subjects, were ranked in order of occupational skills to provide sequencing of rating. After orientation, where ratings were determined for each subject, the raters completed individual ratings for each.

The raters gathered to compare individual ratings given to each of the subjects to discuss disaccord and discrepancies in their ratings. Individual ratings were summarized on DACUM charts to detect observable patterns. There were a total of 1,143 ratings altogether between the three raters. Of this total number, 261 were identical – a rather high amount – and 1,064 were within the acceptable range of discrepancy. The established reliability of the three raters was .91. The reliability charts show balanced distribution for each rater and that no severe biases were involved in the rating scale.

Due to the high reliability results, it was determined that a repeated reliability test was not necessary. The high results show high quality and accuracy in using the DACUM rating system.

REFERENCES

Adams, R. E. (1975). *DACUM: Approach to curriculum, learning, and evaluation in occupational training*. Ottawa: Dept. of Regional Economic Expansion.

Ebel, R.L. (1951). Estimation of the reliability of ratings. *Psychometrika, 16,* 407-424.

Guilford, J.P. (1954). *Psychometric methods*. (2nd eds.). New York: McGraw-Hill.

STAFF ROLES & ADDITIONAL RESPONSIBILITIES

Consideration in installing the DACUM system, particularly in an institutional environment, should be given to the roles that must be filled if the system is to operate successfully. Staff roles in the DACUM system are not the same as staff roles in a conventional program.

In academic education there are two major roles, teaching and administration. The person filling the teaching role is expected to possess pedagogical skills as well as expertise in their teaching specialty. The administrator has much the same general background and, in addition, has been trained in or has developed administrative skills.

In occupational training there is a somewhat different situation. Experts in occupations are often recruited to fill instructional roles. Over time such persons are expected to gain skills in teaching and program development. The administrative role is similarly often filled by persons who were formerly occupational experts and who began instructing, developed teaching and program skill and knowledge, and, finally, administrative skills. Because the instructor is typically less well prepared pedagogically than the instructor in the academic environment, the administrator is expected to provide considerable guidance.

Because the DACUM system features an instructor role similar to the supervisory role in industry, it is suggested that a new role needs to be created (or existing roles modified) to provide *most* of the pedagogical expertise. If this role is developed, it will make possible the employment of experts in the occupation who can quickly function satisfactorily without having to add a number of new skills or a new body of knowledge.

There are two main roles in installation of the DACUM system. First, there is the instructional role which is filled by an expert in the occupation. Second, there is the co-ordinator role which would be filled by persons with a thorough knowledge of the DACUM system, who are skilled in applying techniques and decision-making processes related to setting up and operating the program, and who have skills in working with occupational experts and in drawing upon their expertise in developing and operating programs.

THE INSTRUCTOR ROLE

The DACUM chart for LEARNER EVALUATION AND ACTIVITY DEVELOPMENT in Appendix C was constructed by a team of instructors at Holland College, Charlottetown, Prince Edward Island, with technical assistance provided *by Nova Scotia NewStart Inc.* The instructors all had two years of experience in developing and operating programs based on the DACUM approach. While their programs were all two-year post-secondary programs at what might be called the technical institute level, skills defined on the chart are much the same for any level of programming. It is expected that this chart will become a most useful model for selection, orientation, and in-service training of instructors for the DACUM system. It is largely self-explanatory. It may be useful, however, to make some general observations on the instructor role and to emphasize some of the groupings on the chart.

The chart is sequenced in typical DACUM fashion. The sequencing is based on the assumption that the new instructor will be entering an operational DACUM-based training program. The skills on the left of the chart are those that the new instructor will need to use first; some must be learned, others the instructor already possesses. If this model is applied to new entrants who are expected to become program developers before filling an instructional role, the program development skills will have to be isolated and emphasized early in training.

The upper seven bands on the chart contain the core skills required to deal with the learner and provide learning opportunities and resources. The lower four bands contain supportive skills that will enable the instructor to perform the general role more competently and confidently. Counseling is an important function which has two applications in the DACUM system. First, the instructor is expected to provide a good deal of counseling related to the occupation, its employment prospects, the nature of specialties in the occupation, and demands made on new entrants. Additionally, the instructor provides counseling related to specific kinds of skill performance required to achieve occupational competence. Second, the instructor must counsel the learner in goal-setting, knowledge acquisition, and self-evaluation pursuits.

To a large extent, the DACUM instructor works directly with learners individually. They help the learner select and organize resources for occupational tasks that are used as learning activities. On the instructor DACUM, most of these skills are contained in the band ASSIST LEARNERS IN OCCUPATIONAL SKILL DEVELOPMENT. The instructor also helps the learner acquire knowledge related to task achievement. Most of the skills related to helping the learner acquire knowledge are located in the band ASSIST IN SELF-LEARNING.

Another kind of learning assistance is in the development of learning activities and supporting learning resource materials. Skills related to the development of learning activities and resources are located in the bands CREATE AND MAINTAIN LEARNING ENVIRONMENT and ASSIST LEARNERS IN OCCUPATIONAL SKILL DEVELOPMENT. Skills in developing or acquiring and installing information-based learning materials are all contained in the band DEVELOP LEARNING MATERIALS. Almost all program development activities are contained in these three bands. It should be noted that the same skills would eventually apply whether the instructor is participating in developing a new training program or in applying new resources to an existing program in which additional needs have been discovered.

Skills in monitoring are essentially contained in the band EVALUATE LEARNER PROGRESS. Most are applied in relation to the evaluation component of the Learning-Evaluation Model.

The extent to which any instructor need apply all the skills on the chart or the extent to which they need develop each skill will depend on the nature of the learning institution and the amount of co-ordinator support that will be available to them. In this model it is assumed that the instructor must gradually learn to make almost all the decisions and apply all the techniques of program development and program operation. If co-ordinator assistance is available, the instructor will have less need for high ratings in those skills located toward the right of the chart.

CO-ORDINATOR ROLE

The co-ordinator role as it relates to DACUM chart development is described in detail in Chapter 5 of this book. Two aspects of the role not described elsewhere are co-ordination of program development and co-ordination of program operation.

Although all three functions require much the same background knowledge of the DACUM system, it is possible that the program development and program operation roles might be filled by persons other than those who fill the DACUM chart development role. The latter is a technically demanding function while the other two demand more skills in stimulating and co-ordinating the work of teams of instructors.

Prospective DACUM chart co-ordinators should have the following characteristics. First, they should be technically competent in some occupation other than the occupation of educator or trainer. This provides them with background for decision-making and a wealth of concrete examples for guiding the activities of others in their occupational specialties. Second, it is helpful if they have had some previous experience as a trainer. While conventional training techniques are not applied to any extent, it is useful in working with industrial committees and program development teams to be able to explain why certain techniques are not used and how the DACUM approach differs from approaches with which they are no doubt more familiar. Finally, co-ordinators should have had an opportunity to work in some curriculum or program development capacity with a variety of occupations. This enables them to provide a variety of examples of problems and solutions, as well as giving a generalizable model for making in-process decisions while dealing with unfamiliar occupations. Persons who have worked in a single occupation tend to build features of a unique program for that occupation into others with which they begin to work.

It is not necessary that the co-ordinator be expert in the occupation with which they are dealing. In fact, the opposite is probably true. If the co-ordinator is an expert in the occupation, they may be diverted from applying certain suggested techniques or procedures by their personal knowledge of the unique characteristics of the occupation. An occupationally independent co-ordinator will not be diverted in this way and will pursue alternatives, and the development or operational team will eventually find a way to apply the techniques effectively.

The DACUM chart development co-ordinator has two additional responsibilities that are in keeping with the kinds of activities described in this chapter of this book. First, the co-ordinator should take part in the organization of development workshops. Through personal knowledge of the requirements for committees, the co-ordinator can readily advise occupational specialists on the kinds of individuals to select as committee members, the proper mix of specialties in the occupation, and other criteria for ensuring adequate coverage of the occupation. The co-ordinator should also advise on facilities and resources necessary for successful operation of workshops. Second, they should also accept responsibility for preparation of the completed charts. It has been found that these charts can be typed, mocked-up, retaining the left-right skill arrangement, and proofread in a single day immediately following the workshop. By doing this immediately, the co-ordinator can provide continuity to the activities. They can advise typists on abbreviations and expedite the printing process. It has been found that if this is not done by the co-ordinator, charts tend to remain for days mounted on the wall, creating the possibility that cards may be altered. Additionally, the longer one waits to approach the activities, the longer it takes to type, establish abbreviations, and proofread the chart.

The DACUM chart co-ordinator plays three important roles in program development activity. They normally provide more input to development (either prior to or during program operation) than to operation. The co-ordinator's role is facilitative rather than directive because they do not have the ability to make technical decisions about the occupation. The co-ordinator cannot be the final decision-maker on developing details of the program. However, they can assist project development staff by describing models, suggesting alternatives, encouraging brainstorming, and encouraging risk-taking. The co-ordinator can also affirm the adequacy of learning plans and details and stimulate re-examination of those with which they are not satisfied. As a working tool, the co-ordinator might develop a grid for the program as suggested in Chapter 8.

Co-ordinators role in the selection of learning experiences

This is the most critical stage of co-ordinator input. Development staff will not have had extensive practice in applying DACUM concepts and techniques and will need considerable assistance in selecting learning experiences that meet the criteria of the DACUM model. The co-ordinator should insist that learning experiences be considered and selected in the order suggested in Chapter 9. They should place emphasis on selection of occupational tasks that can be directly transferred to or simulated in the learning environment. Even though they may never have been instructors, persons from an occupation with a history of training will gravitate toward specification of learning experiences that are of the project or lab project variety. It is necessary for the co-ordinator to discourage this kind of thinking and initiate brainstorming to determine what kinds of occupational tasks can be readily applied in the learning environment. The co-ordinator can warn the instructors about impending difficulties in attempting to rate performance on the basis of the kinds of learning experiences they are suggesting and about difficulties the learner will encounter in attempting to transfer these learning experiences to real job problems in the work environment.

The co-ordinator can most usefully solicit a range of learning experiences from the development team (the grid is excellent for this purpose). Once they detect an extensive learning activity that encompasses a number of skills, there is a tendency for developers to designate only this activity for each of the related skills. The co-ordinator can influence them to look at each skill independently and select suitable learning activities for each in addition to those multi-skill activities that might also be suitable.

In typical curriculum fashion, developers tend to limit the number of activities for each skill to one or two they expect will be useful for all learners. The co-ordinator can influence them to identify a number of suitable activities for each skill by explaining the range of activity needs one is likely to encounter in any group of learners and the range of activities that should be on hand in order for instructors to be able to observe performance and predict success in applying the skill in diverse applications in industry.

Program developers also tend to reject useful learning activity ideas without mentioning them because they suspect they will be too expensive or resources will not be readily available. The co-ordinator can provide valuable input by encouraging the development team to take a positive approach. They must not allow anticipated problems in subsequent stages of program development to influence their judgment about what would be excellent learning experiences.

Finally, in their enthusiasm to develop an imposing learning program, developers frequently overlook some simple, easy to apply, and excellent learning experiences. By consistently stressing the need for simple, direct experiences, the co-ordinator can encourage them to suggest useful tasks generally not found in occupational training programs. While the developers have been told that there are few restrictions to the kinds of activities that can be provided in the DACUM program, they appear to be overly influenced by the more common restrictions of contemporary occupational training programs.

Co-ordinators role in the selection of occupational resources

Because the co-ordinator must rely heavily on the technical knowledge of the occupational experts, he or she has limited input into this activity. Nevertheless, the co-ordinator's input can be valuable if he or she concentrates on having the program developers explore a number of alternatives for each decision.

Much of this input can be provided by assisting the developers in selecting the learning environment(s). The co-ordinator can make sure that the developers keep in mind both the skill definition and the suggested learning activities in identifying the most suitable location for each. The co-ordinator may have to remind them that part of the training for each skill can be provided in two different environments. The co-ordinator must control two tendencies on the part of developers: First, developers tend to look at the overall chart and decide on a single environment most suitable for training in the total occupation. Typically, the choice is an institution or in-center training program. Second, they sometimes make quick decisions about each skill, specifying automatically that it should be acquired in a training center, or it should be acquired in on-the-job training, and overlooking the fact that part of the training may best be provided in each environment.

After a decision is made about location of learning environment(s), the development team selects equipment, materials, and supplies for the learning activities and the individual skills without co-ordinator assistance.

Some co-ordinator input is required when planning installation of equipment and other resources. Developers tend to be influenced by standard ways of approaching this task and need to be reminded of the flexibility of the DACUM system and the individual way in which each learner will use resources in developing skills.

Co-ordinator input is essential in selecting and assigning human resources. While developers can readily distribute responsibilities for skills and learning tasks, they tend to put aside the specification of and provision for part-time resources required for skills or learning experiences in which they do not have sufficient ability or experience. This task tends to be left incomplete if there is not immediate co-ordinator assistance and encouragement to begin specifying suitable persons and to make arrangements for their participation.

Co-ordinators role in the selection of learning resources

The co-ordinator makes two kinds of contributions to the selection and development of learning resources. First, they serve as a *stimulator of action.* The task of developing Learning Activity Batteries (LABs) can, because of the amount of work to be done, become onerous. It may also, because the approach is new, be a somewhat puzzling activity. Second, the co-ordinator *represents the interests of the learner.* Because of the intense interest of the developers in systematically organizing the resources and information of their occupation, they may stray from their prime goal of providing a program for a variety of individual learners. The co-ordinator helps them keep in mind the nature and variety of learner characteristics and needs.

1. <u>Stimulating action</u>: The following are suggested as means that might be used by the co-ordinator to stimulate action and speed up the resource development activity.

   The co-ordinator should take immediate action to ensure that the first step in developing resources is to prepare all the containers for Learning Activity Battery materials and have these organized to permit quick and easy placement of materials when they are located. While searching for materials for one skill, developers frequently run across materials suitable for other skills. With the packages prepared and well arranged, they can quickly extract the materials and deposit them in the appropriate container. This avoids the time consuming practice of noting or cross-referencing for later retrieval. Development teams to date have generally followed the latter approach unless otherwise encouraged by the co-ordinator.

   Developers sometimes encounter difficulty in retrieving materials. They appear to be reluctant to clip and discard books, magazines, manuals, handbooks, etc., even though the discarded material may have little value in the learning environment. The best technique is to remove the appropriate portions and place these in the Learning Activity Battery. The co-ordinator can frequently stimulate this kind of activity by having the developers identify useful materials and extracting them to show how easily it can be done.

   The co-ordinator should also ensure that that copiers or commercial printers are readily available. The work is needlessly slowed if developers have to wait in line for access to duplicating equipment or if they must walk some distance to this equipment. They tend then to begin noting pages, and cross-referencing, and allow a considerable amount of work to pile up which later must be resorted before it can be placed in the Learning Activity Batteries. If printing equipment is close at hand, they can quickly retrieve the specific content they desire, store it in the appropriate Learning Activity Battery, and then set that source aside and begin with another.

   Developers have to be stimulated to begin producing visual materials. They are inclined to overestimate quality of presentation required and underestimate their ability to produce it. The co-ordinator can stir developers into action by encouraging them to take risks and develop materials. Once they have done this, they are usually pleased with results. They find they can quickly produce a presentation by using a camera, arranging images, and then describing the images on video. Developers also need encouragement to produce presentations using pictures clipped from magazines and other sources. It has been found that most persons require encouragement in the use of video recording equipment. Nevertheless, they can produce satisfactory materials after only three or four hours of practice. Part of the difficulty is that commercially designed and developed programming is well planned, scripted, painstakingly prepared, and carefully edited to produce a superior product for a large market. The developer must overcome the urge to produce the same kind of resources in the same way. The co-ordinator, for example, can quickly encourage a developer to demonstrate on video a skill that they have already demonstrated many other times at work or in a training environment without extensive planning, scripting, or editing. If this does not come out satisfactorily, the developer can see their own mistakes and try again.

The co-ordinator can also help developers overcome a tendency to over-plan. Even though the obviously required materials are spread out on a table in front of them, some developers will be reluctant to proceed without first spending a half hour or so thinking about and listing all the kinds of information that might be required for a skill. The co-ordinator can illustrate how this time is wasted by encouraging them to assemble the required materials in less time than they might spend on planning.

Finally, because this is a new activity for the developers, the co-ordinator can assist them in determining when adequate information is available for each Learning Activity Battery. The co-ordinator questions them and serves as a sounding board for their decisions. In this way the developers can maintain an even balance in development work, providing the minimal amount of resources required for each Learning Activity Battery and then immediately proceeding with another to complete the task. The co-ordinator must be alert for tendencies to over-refine one or two Learning Activity Batteries to the detriment of the others in terms of the time available.

2. <u>Representing interests of the learner</u>: The co-ordinator serves as a questioner or sounding board in this kind of activity:

   a. by questioning developers on the reading level of materials they have selected, advising them if the level is too high or low and encouraging them to consider other sources that provide the same information at other levels.

b. by questioning quality or absence of illustrations and diagrams in printed materials selected, pointing out that learners have certain characteristics which demand that such illustrations be relevant to their problems and clear and meaningful to them.

    i. by stimulating consideration of varieties of resources that might be available for the same skill. It is particularly important for the co-ordinator to have the developer determine whether the skill demands opportunities to observe action or study sequences, or only an opportunity to read descriptions of techniques or conditions. Once they have developed a number of LABs using a specific resource or format, developers are likely to adopt a pattern of attempting to develop all the LAB's in the same way.

    ii. by questioning the accessibility of all resources to the learner. This will help them overcome a tendency to cross-reference bulky materials or materials that could possibly be used in a number of Learning Activity Batteries. The co-ordinator can point out that the learner will seldom follow up the suggested cross-referencing and will use only what is immediately available in the package. If necessary, materials can be duplicated for insertion in two or more LABs.

The co-ordinator can control the content of the LABs by questioning the need for each piece of material. This will cause the developers to think about whether all the information is actually needed or whether some of it may be extraneous and misleading. The co-ordinator should encourage them to remove those portions of the material that are not necessary. If it is found that this destroys continuity, they can encourage one of the developers to write brief transitional material.

Finally, the co-ordinator can control the selection of learning resources to make them relevant to the kinds of learning resources the individual will encounter on entering industry. It is easy for developers to fall into the habit of taking a format that appears to work well in some instances and attempting to apply it to other skills and at the higher levels of skill development. The co-ordinator should question the extent of use of any one resource and determine if this kind of resource will likely be found in the work environment. If it will not be, they should encourage the developers to install more materials of the sort the learner can expect to find in the work environment.

The co-ordinator as a staff resource

The co-ordinator can serve as a staff resource in three ways:

1. The co-ordinator can conduct staff training. Once an initial program is operational, any subsequent training of new recruits will have to be done on an individual basis. In fact, the co-ordinator probably will serve as a DACUM instructor in this capacity if the previously mentioned instructor DACUM chart is applied for this purpose. They will have to conduct entry ratings, monitor performance, and rate staff on the basis of their ability to grow and perform in their new roles.

2. The co-ordinator can serve as advisor when staff face operational problems in dealing with learners or begin to lose sight of DACUM concepts and objectives. Again, because the approach is new, staff will not have a history of training to which to refer in making decisions. In fact, there is a tendency for them to revert to more conventional training models for guidance. By limiting his or her contributions to review of the DACUM models the co-ordinator can assist staff to solve problems and reach decisions about how they must proceed. Lacking expertise in the technicalities of the occupation, the co-ordinator can seldom provide direct input.

3. The co-ordinator can serve as a valuable participant in program review and planning or program modification meetings. They should limit contribution to references to basic DACUM philosophy and to use of DACUM models and procedures as a framework for reaching decisions.

   The co-ordinator's input is primarily required for the initial development of a program, gradually becoming less until the first learner cycle is completed. After that, their input will be limited as instructional staff will have learned to function effectively.

   Provided that program development and start-up activities are staggered, it is possible for one co-ordinator to monitor several programs at the same time. Their input is not required on a full-time basis for any period of time for any one program. The co-ordinator's contribution should be one of stimulation and then departure from the program to allow the developers or instructors to do the work for which they are technically competent.

Plans for installation of new programs or conversion of programs should include provision for development and installation of co-ordinators. Provided some changes can be made in institutional roles this should not result in additional staff or cost. However, it does mean that the department head or supervisor role may have to change. Whereas at present, if department heads or supervisors are a technical expert in the occupation as well as a department member with the most background in training and learning theory in the DACUM system, they need not be technically competent in the occupation to fill the co-ordinating role. In fact, it is probably best that they be a trainer, have a good background in the DACUM approach to learning, and provide this expertise to departments serving occupations other than the one in which they are most expert. The supervisor can be just as susceptible to adoption of conventional practices and just as resistant to change as anyone else if dealing with their own occupation.

SUMMARY

The purpose of Chapter 18 was to explain the roles and responsibilities of staff members and institutions considering implementation of the DACUM system. This chapter suggested that new or modified roles need to be created to provide the most pedagogical expertise. Instructors are expected to work directly with learners to provide counseling, employment prospects, skill performance requirements, and real-world demands. Co-ordinators are expected to manage program development and the operation of the program with considerable assistance in selecting learning experiences as well as selecting occupational resources. Finally, co-ordinators should conduct staff training, advise staff members who face operational problems, and serves as a valuable participant in program review, planning, and modifications.

<u>REFERENCES</u>

Adams, R. E. (1975). *DACUM: Approach to curriculum, learning, and evaluation in occupational training*. Ottawa: Dept. of Regional Economic Expansion.

APPENDIX A
DACUM CHART—MOTOR VEHICLE REPAIR

Note: Appendix A through H are available FREE with the purchase of this book at:

www.edwinandassociates.com/dacumbook

APPENDIX B
DACUM CHART—ELECTRICAL TECHNOLOGY

Note: Appendix A through H are available FREE with the purchase of this book at:

www.edwinandassociates.com/dacumbook

APPENDIX C
DACUM CHART— LEARNER EVALUATION
AND
ACTIVITY DEVELOPMENT

Note: Appendix A through H are available FREE with the purchase of this book at:

www.edwinandassociates.com/dacumbook

APPENDIX D
DACUM CHART— DECKHAND TRAINING

**Note: Appendix A through H are available FREE with the purchase of this book at:

www.edwinandassociates.com/dacumbook

APPENDIX E
DACUM CHART— GENERAL NURSING

Note: Appendix A through H are available FREE with the purchase of this book at:

www.edwinandassociates.com/dacumbook

APPENDIX F
DACUM CHART— PROFESSIONAL
COUNSELING (SCHOOL)

**Note: Appendix A through H are available FREE with the purchase of this book at:

www.edwinandassociates.com/dacumbook

APPENDIX G
DACUM CHART— WELDING FABRICATION

**Note: Appendix A through H are available FREE with the purchase of this book at:

www.edwinandassociates.com/dacumbook

APPENDIX H
DACUM CHART—
PROFESSIONAL COOKING

**Note:* Appendix A through H are available FREE with the purchase of this book at:
www.edwinandassociates.com/dacumbook

APPENDIX I
DACUM CHART WITH RELIABILITY FIGURES

Note: Appendix A through H are available FREE with the purchase of this book at:
www.edwinandassociates.com/dacumbook

APPENDIX J
MINIMUM SKILLS PROFILE CHART—
PROFESSIONAL COOKING

Note: Appendix A through H are available FREE with the purchase of this book at:
www.edwinandassociates.com/dacumbook

APPENDIX K
DACUM BROCHURE

DACUM:

Develop A Curriculum

What is the role of the instructor?

To encourage the trainee in a self-directing approach to learning, the instructor functions in a supporting role. Specifically, the instructor helps the trainee find solutions to problems (which may include helping them find resources), and the instructor helps the trainee evaluate and record their progress.

Sometimes more than one instructor is involved with the trainee, and in such cases all share in the rating process and in the maintenance of the master DACUM chart.

To a remarkable degree, however, the instructor's activities are directed to respond to the trainee's initiative. The instructor resists any temptation to impose direction or to revert to a structured learning process.

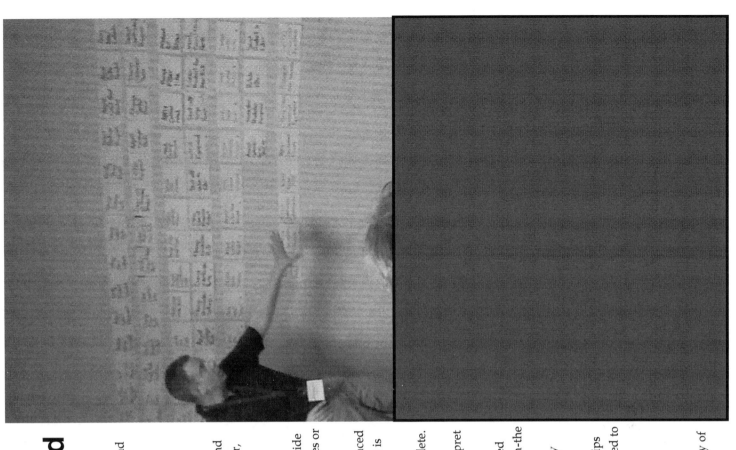

How the DACUM Chart is developed

DACUM charts are developed by committees of persons experts in the occupations for which the charts have been prepared. As an example, in developing a DACUM chart for Oil Burner Repair and Servicing, two independent servicemen, a service contractor, a fuel-company mechanic, and an employer who was formerly a mechanic participated.

Committees operate under the direction of a co-ordinator, and normally complete the task of developing a DACUM chart in three days. They begin by describing the requirements of the occupation in terms of skills required. Each contribution is lettered on a card by the co-ordinator and fixed to the wall. To ensure that the committee define requirements in terms of observable behavior, they are requested to preface the skill definition with "The individual must be able to…" followed immediately by a verb.

Step 1: Establishing General Areas of Competence. Some of these may be temporary, but they provide a framework for the skill definitions. They may be areas into which the occupation naturally divides or merely convenient way so grouping its skills.

Step 2: Identifying Skills required in each General Area of Competence. These are recorded and placed in position in the order in which they are mentioned. As much as possible, each skill band (or row) is completed before starting another.

Identification of skills continue until the committee agrees that coverage of the occupation is complete. There is much discussion before some skills are identified. The committee's agreement rests on whether or not the members feel that they and other persons in the occupation will be able to interpret the skill definitions correctly.

Step 3: Sequencing Skills, band by band, to locate them in a more desirable order. Sequence is based not on educational or learning prerequisites but on the desirability to the employer of having an on-the-jobs trained employee acquire certain skills first. Primarily the committee shifts to the left of the structure those skills an employee would want such an employee to perform early so that they may quickly get a return on investment.

Step 4: Structuring Skills into finished profile. The entire structure is examined to detect relationships among the skills. Bands or sections of bands containing skills that would be acquired first are shifted to the left while others less needed early in on-the-job training are shifted to the right.

Step 5: Final inspection for changes and additions. When the committee can suggest no further significant changes or additions, the definition task is considered complete.

The skill definitions are typed, mounted in the same structure and printed. An almost full size copy of a DACUM chart appears in later pages.

		OUTLINE SKILL PROFILE FOR SPECIALTIES IN OCCUPATION		DETECT SPECIFIC WEAKNESSES & PRESCRIBE REMEDIAL LEARNING	ADVISE LEARNING & RELATE LEARNING RESOURCE LIMITATIONS OF INSTITUTION
IDENTIFY LEARNER READINESS FOR ENTRY TO OCCUPATION	ASSIST LEARNER IN RECOGNITION OF ITERMIN OR PROGRESSIVE SKILL ACHIEVEMENT		ANALYZE INDIVIDUAL AND GROUP ACHIEVEMENT RECORDS TO ISOLATE PATTERNS & PROBLEMS		
PREDICT LEVEL OF USAGE TO SELECT QUANTITY OF EQUIPMENT & TOOLS	ANALYZE, SPECIFY & JUSTIFY SPACE REQUIREMENTS	ANALYZE COST, QUALITY, SUITABILITY, SERVICEABILITY & AVAILABILITY OF EQUIPMENT	PLAN SPACE FOR INDIVIDUAL COUNSELING OR PRIVATE DISCUSSION	PLAN FOR LEARNER ACCESS TO INSTRUCTOR(S) OR OTHER HUMAN RESOURCES	MAKE PROVISION IN PLANNING FOR FUTURE EXPANSION OR MODIFICATION
ASSIST LEARNER IN LOCATING EXTERNAL SKILL DEVELOPMENT ASSISTANCE	ASSIST LEARNER IN LOCATING EXTERNAL SKILL DEVELOPMENT ACTIVITIES	ASSIST LEARNER IN LOCATING-EXTERNAL INFORMATION OR OBSERVATION SOURCES	IDENTIFY TRAINEE LIMITATIONS & ASSIST IN ADAPTING TO DESIRED PERFORMANCE		CREATE INTER-OCCUPATION PROJECTS OR SIMULATIONS
ASSIST LEARNER IN ESTABLISHING & MAINTAINING RELEVANCE OF CONTENT OF GOAL	ASSIST LEARNER IN OUTLINING LONG TERM GOALS	COUNSEL & ASSIST LEARNER IN OUTLINING IMMEDIATE GOALS	CREATE SITUATIONS THAT FORCE LEARNER TO IDENTIFY SPECIFIC LEARNING DIFFICULTIES	CREATE SITUATIONS THAT FORCE LEARNING TO FACE REALISM OF OWN DECISIONS	
VIDEO TAPE LIVE JOB SITUATIONS	DUB IN VOICE FOR V.T.R. PRESENTATION	PREPARE TAPE, SLIDE oOR STRIP PRESENTATION		ANALYZE LACK OF PERFORMANCE TO DETERMINE NEED FOR ALTERNATE MEDIA	ANALYZE DEFINED SKILLS TO DETERMINE SUITABLE MEDIA FOR INFORMATION PRESENTATION
	DETECT LACK OF UNDERSTANDING		ASSIST TRAINEE IN PLANNING OCCUPATIONAL GROWTH		
		OFFER CONSTRUCTIVE CRITICISM		ASSISTS OTHERS IN PRESENTING IDEAS WITHIN FRAMEWORK OF BASIC MODELS	DISSEMINATE & GENERATE DISCUSSION ON ISSUES, OCCURRENCES OR TRENDS IN SYSTEM
ORGANIZE & CONDUCT EMPLOYMENT PROBLEM DEFINITION WORKSHOPS	ASSIST EMPLOYERS IN PLANNING FURTHER TRAINING	IN-EMPLOYER-LEARNER CONTACT LEADING TO POTENTIAL EMPLOYMENT	FOLLOW UP FORMER LEARNERS TO ASSESS PROGRAM EFFECTIVENESS		
				MAINTAIN PACE W/ TECHNONOLOGICAL ADVANCES IN OCCUPATIONAL SPECIALTY	KEEP ABREAST OF TECHNOLOGICAL CHANGE IN FIELD
PREPARE ESTIMATE OR BUDGET PROPOSAL	ESTIMATE OPERATING COST REQUIREMENTS	ESTIMATE CAPITAL COST REQUIREMENTS	DELEGATE RESONSIBILITY TO STAFF & COLLEAGUES	DETECT NEED FOR PROGRAM CHANGE & INITIATE REVIEW PROGRESS	PLAN & SCHEDULE STAFF LEAVES

Name _____

		OUTLINE & DESCRIBE RANGE OF EXTRA RESOURCES LEARNER CAN UTILIZE	OUTLINE EXTRA-CURRICULAR ACTIVITIES NECESSARY AS PART OF PROGRAM	ASSISTS IN DESIGN OF INDIVIDUAL LEARNING PROGRAMS
IDENTIFY LEARNER REQUIREMENT FOR TEMPORARY TERMINATION	IDENTIFY LEARNER INABILITY TO CONTINUE PROGRESS IN SKILL DEVELOPMENT		RECOGNIZE INACCURATE RATINGS & CONDUCT RE-EVALUTIONS SESSIONS	EVALUATE LEARNER PROGRESS
		INTEGRATE & PLAN TOOL, EQUIPMENT & MATERIAL STORAGE & CONTROL	ANALYZE & PLAN TRAFFIC CIRCULATION PATTERN	CREATE & LEARNING ENVIRONMENT
CREATE TEAM PROJECT OR SIMULATIONS	REP LIC STIMULATE SKILL OR PROBLEM SITUATIONS & CONDITIONS	SELECT OR DEVISE & APPLY DECISION SIMULATION GAMES	SELECT OR DEVISE SKILL DEVELOPMENT SIMULATIONS	ASSIST LEARNERS IN OCCUPATIONAL SKILL DEVELOPMENT
CAPITALIZE ON STUDENT-RELEVANT PROBLEMS TO STIMULATE SELF-DIRECTIVE ACTION	OVERCOME PERSONALITY BY TEAMING COMBINA-TIONS OF PERSONALITY TYPES	COUNSEL LEARNING IN IDENTIFYING GOAL RELATED WEAKNESSES	COUNSEL LEARNER IN IDENTIFYING SELF-LEARNING HINDERANCES	ASSIST IN SELF-LEARNING
ANALYZE DEFINED SKILLS TO DETERMINE SUITABLE MEDIA FOR INFORMATION PRESENTATION	PREPARE SHOOTING SCRIPT FOR MOVIE OR LOOP PRESENTATIONS	ASSESS COST, TIME, CONVENIENCE, URGENCY & EFFECTIVENESS IN SELECTING MEDIA	SELECT RESOURCES & MEDIA ON BASIS OF AVAILABILITY FOR COINTINUED LEARNING	DEVELOP LEARNING MATERIALS
ANTICIPATE & DETECT REACTION TO INSTITUTION & PROGRAMS			ASSESS SITUATION, DECIDE ON ACTION, & DISCIPLINE LEARNERS	COMMUNICATE WITH LEARNERS
	PRESENT & DISCUSS PREDICTIONS OF RESULTS OF TRENDS OR MODIFICATIONS IN SYSTEM	SET ASIDE PERSONAL CONFLICT OR OTHER ISSUES TO MAINTAIN PURPOSEFUL COMMUN-CATIONS	DETECT, DISCUSS & ASSESS DEVIATION FROM SYSTEM MODELS	COMMUNICATE WITH STAFF IN TRAINING ENVIRONMENT
DETECT TRAINING & TRAINEE PROBLEMS IN THE OCCUPATION			PARTICIPATE IN P.R. RELATED ACTIVITES IN THE COMMUNITY	INTERACT WITH THE COMMUNITY
	KEEP ABREAST OF LEVELS OF PERFORMANCE & PERSONAL DEMANDS OF OCCUPATION	DETERMINE PROFESSIONAL GROWTH OPPORTUNITIES	PLAN PERSONAL GROWTH	DEVELOP PERSONAL COMPETENCIES
EVALUATE & REPORT ON STAFF PERFORMANCE	INTERVIEW & MAKE RECOMMENDATIONS REGARDING PROSPECTIVE STAFF		RECOMMEND TERMINATION OF STAFF	PERFORM ADMINISTRATIVE OR RELATED FUNCATIONS

DACUM CHART *for*
LEARNER EVALUA-
AND
ACTIVITY DEVELOP-
MENT

344

Rating	Description
6	Can perform this skill with more than acceptable speed and quality, with initiative and adaptability and *can lead others* in performing the skill
5	Can perform this skill with more than acceptable speed and quality and with *initiative* and *adaptability* to special problem situations.
4	Can perform this skill satisfactorily without supervision or assistance with *more than acceptable speed* and quality of work.
3	Can perform this skill satisfactorily *without* assistance and/or supervision.
2	Can perform this skill satisfactorily but requires *periodic* supervision and/or assistance.
1	Can perform this skill, but *not* without constant supervision and some assistance.
0	*Cannot* perform this skill satisfactorily for participation in a work environment.

How skill is measured

Each skill on the DACUM chart is defined in terms of observable behavior, and it is on their observable behavior that trainees rate themselves and is rated by their instructor or employer. The DACUM rating scale attempts to evaluate performance as an employer or supervisor would evaluate it. The level "3" is the baseline, indicating performance comparable to that of a new journeyman in a trade. A "0" rating is used to indicate a level of skill which does not qualify its possessor to perform for pay.

The rating scale is attached to the right of the DACUM chart.

How the trainee uses the DACUM

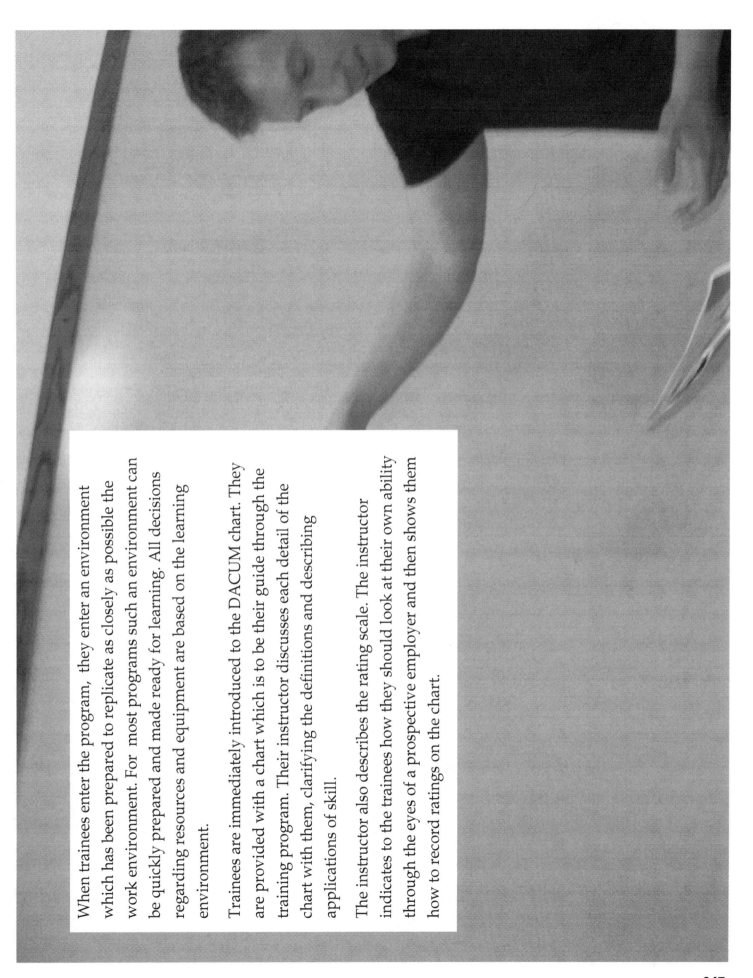

When trainees enter the program, they enter an environment which has been prepared to replicate as closely as possible the work environment. For most programs such an environment can be quickly prepared and made ready for learning. All decisions regarding resources and equipment are based on the learning environment.

Trainees are immediately introduced to the DACUM chart. They are provided with a chart which is to be their guide through the training program. Their instructor discusses each detail of the chart with them, clarifying the definitions and describing applications of skill.

The instructor also describes the rating scale. The instructor indicates to the trainees how they should look at their own ability through the eyes of a prospective employer and then shows them how to record ratings on the chart.

The trainees are faced with the new and difficult task of identifying those skills which they already possess in some measure, perhaps form experiences in other areas of work, and marking in the appropriate blocks the rating numbers that correspond to the levels of skill they feel they have. The trainees encloses rating numbers in diamond shapes to indicate that they are entry ratings.

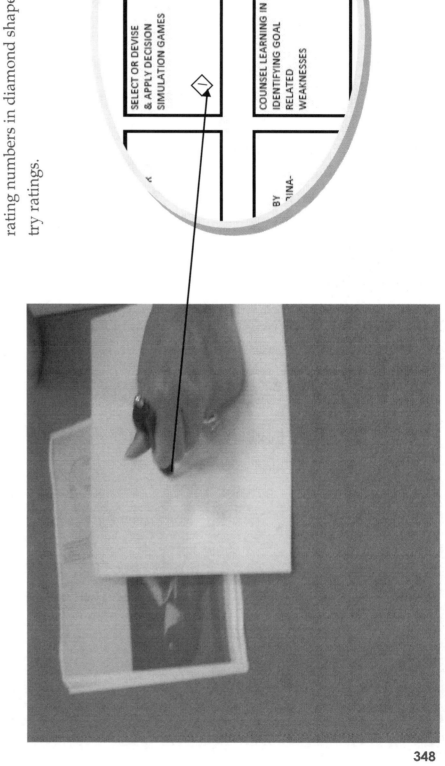

The instructor and the trainee consult each other to determine how realistic the trainee has been in self-ratings. After questioning and discussion about where, how, and when the trainee has applied the skills marked on the chart, the instructor's interpretations of the trainee's ability is recorded on the master copy of the chart. In some cases the instructor may give a lower rating, explaining to the trainee the nature of performance expected so that the trainee can see why they have overrated them self, or the instructor may give the trainee a higher rating than the trainee gave them self, explaining that the skill is not as complex as originally thought. Both the trainee and instructor now have a fairly clear picture of the trainee's entry skill and what remains to be done to obtain occupational competence.

With the instructor's help the trainee then selects the first skill they want to develop. It may be one in which the trainee already has some skill, or it may be one with which the trainee has had no previous experience but which appeals to them in some way.

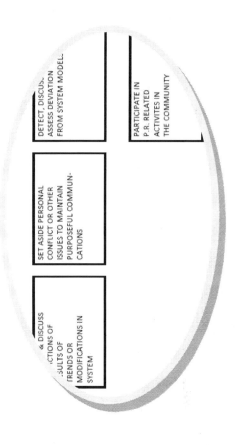

DISCUSS
ACTIONS OF
RESULTS OF
TRENDS OR
MODIFICATIONS IN
SYSTEM

SET ASIDE PERSONAL
CONFLICT OR OTHER
ISSUES TO MAINTAIN
PURPOSEFUL COMMUN-
CATIONS

DETECT, DISCUSS,
ASSESS DEVIATION
FROM SYSTEM MODEL

PARTICIPATE IN
P.R. RELATED
ACTIVITES IN
THE COMMUNITY

349

Attempting Skills

Using a discovery approach, the trainee proceeds to attempt the skill defined. For example: The trainee begins by disassembling the components and trying to determine their function.

When trainees realize they do not know how to proceed, they select materials form the appropriate Learning Activities Battery (LAB), one of which has been prepared for each unit. This is a package of learning materials which may include a manufacturer's manual, magazine articles, sections of textbooks, instructor-prepared videos/multimedia, commercially-prepared multimedia, or anything which may help the trainee in reaching this particular learning objective. At this stage a simple diagram may be enough to show them how to proceed with the skill.

If the trainee's first selection from the Learning Activities Battery does not provide all the necessary information required, the trainee may spend some time examining the total package of learning materials for this unit.

While performing the skill, the trainee is continually in view of the instructor. The instructor's role is not to teach, but to observe and assist in locating and applying appropriate learning resources. By constantly observing, the instructor is able to help the trainee detect weakness and determine skill levels.

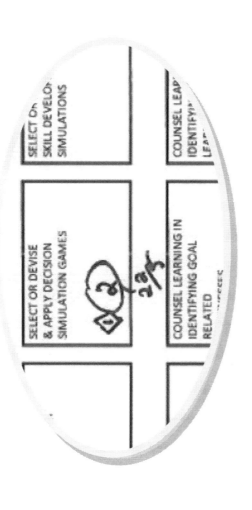

When the trainee has performed the skill often enough to assure that the skill can be performed at a higher level, the trainee records the appropriate rating on their copy of the DACUM chart, indicating the date as shown below.

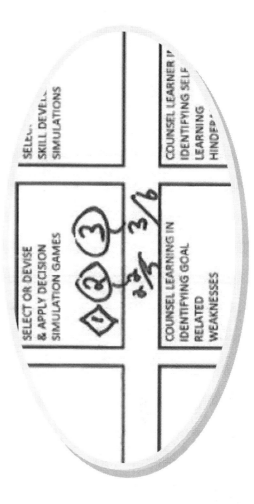

The trainee has the opportunity to raise the rating as skill performance improves.

Each time the trainee changes a rating on their chart, it is the trainee's responsibility to see that the instructor confirms the rating. The trainee shows the instructor their chart and discusses the way in which the trainee performed the skill and the results of the performance. Because the instructor has observed the performance, confirming or explaining why they disagree with trainee's rating can be readily accomplished.

They cycle of events recurs until the trainee has satisfactory ratings for most of all of the skills defined on the chart. When the ratings are satisfactory to the trainee and the instructor they are assumed to be satisfactory to the prospective or hypothetical employer, and at this point the trainee's program ends and they are awarded a diploma which contains a copy of their DACUM chart on which is recorded the highest ratings obtained in each skill.

The trainee is able to present a clear description of their ability (skill profile) to prospective employers or employment counsellors. The employer is able to take a detailed look at the trainee's strengths and weaknesses and determine, first, whether or not the trainee is qualified for the specific job available, and second, which of their skills will require immediate improvement to meet the firm's specific job requirements.

Where can the DACUM process be used?

The preceding section shows the DACUM process being used by a trainee in a program designed to train oil-burner mechanics. The process has also been tested in on-the-job, housekeeping, craft, nursing, and fishing deckhand training programs (to name a few). It has been implemented and tested on by a multitude of organizations (government, colleges, etc.) over the year. The DACUM process is each of these situations has proved to be not only beneficial in creating occupational training that is directly connected to the workplace, it has created self-directed learning environments which today's adult learners prefer.

The process has potential for most career-oriented training programs, but it will not work in the traditional environment of tests, authoritarian instruction, and rigidly-structured sequencing of activities, as these group techniques and the DACUM process will work well only in a self-directing learning environment. It requires and promotes an environment having many of the characteristics long considered by many educators to be favorable to optimum conditions for learning:

- Replication or reasonable simulation of the job situation, in which trainees encounter "real" problems and have the tools, equipment, and materials available to solve them.

- A curriculum that is a description of terminal behavior after completion of training.

- A self-determining or self-directing attitude toward learning.

- A program completely individualized to accommodate and take advantage of individual differences in adult learners.

- Trainee selection of goals and sequencing of activities.

- Evaluation based on performance rather than on retention of information for test purposes.

- Avoidance of necessity to continue program learning for skills already acquired.

What is the role of the instructor?

To encourage the trainee in a self-directing approach to learning, the instructor functions in a supporting role. Specifically, the instructor helps the trainee find solutions to problems (which may include helping them find resources), and the instructor helps the trainee evaluate and record their progress.

Sometimes more than one instructor is involved with the trainee, and in such cases all share in the rating process and in the maintenance of the master DACUM chart.

To a remarkable degree, however, the instructor's activities are directed to respond to the trainee's initiative. The instructor resists any temptation to impose direction or to revert to a structured learning process.

What is the effect on the learning process?

The DACUM process incorporates several learning principles which have long been considered desirable, particularly in occupational training programs, but which have been found difficult to incorporate in a single system:

- Immediate feedback of results to the trainee.

- Immediate analysis of program strengths and weaknesses.

- Positive communication between instructor and trainee.

- Self-evaluation by the trainee.

- Self-planning and goal-setting.

- An interesting, efficient, and practical, yet unstructured, learning environment.

- Onus for evaluation and qualification on the trainee.

- Positive relationship between training evaluation and the type of evaluation normally made by employers.

- Cumulative approach to achievement (the DACUM process will not allow negative or downward evaluation unless trainee and instructor agree that a previous evaluation was in error).

- An entry measure which takes into consideration the trainee's previous training and experience and allows them to proceed

APPENDIX L
DEVELOPMENT MODEL FOR DACUM
LEARNING PROGRAM

DEVELOPMENT MODEL FOR DACUM LEARNING PROGRAM

Learning-Evaluation Model

361

APPENDIX M
LEARNING-EVALUATION MODEL

LEARNING-EVALUATION MODEL

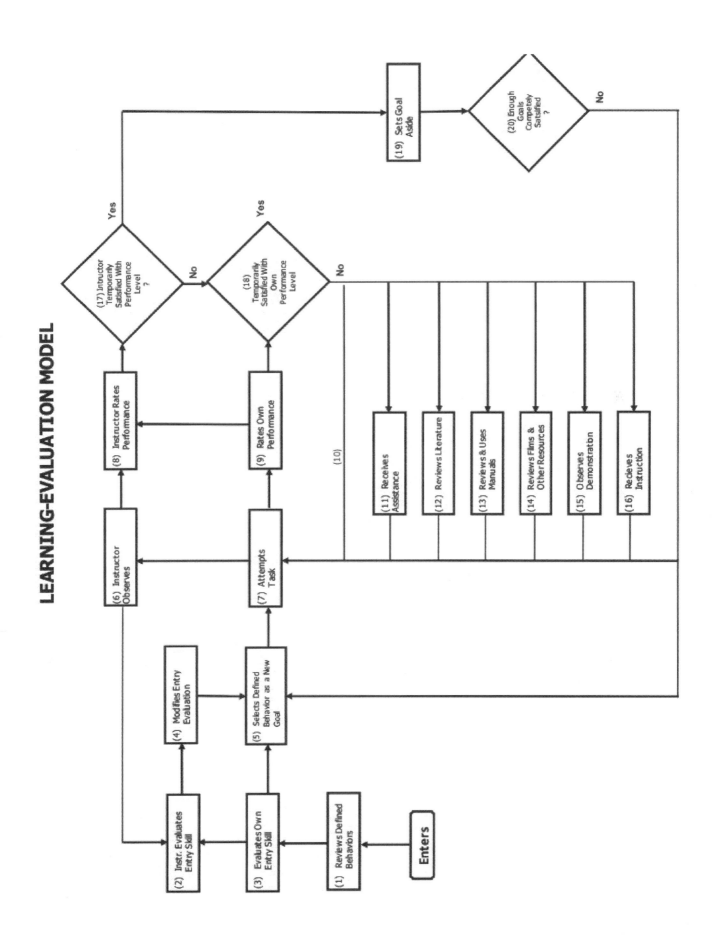

363

Index

Contents of the Website

You are invited to view and download the supplementary materials listed below.

The materials are available FREE with the purchase of this book.

To access the online materials, you will need to create user profile at:

www.edwinandassociates.com

Username: dawnwitherspoon
pass: Norquest 622

DACUM Charts

DACUM Reliability

Minimum Skill Profiles Chart

DACUM Brochure

DACUM Learning and Evaluation Models

Made in the USA
Middletown, DE
07 January 2016